# Negotiating Diversity

## Culture, Deliberation, Trust

Matthew Festenstein

polity

First published in 2005 by Polity Press

Polity Press
65 Bridge Street
Cambridge CB2 1UR, UK

Polity Press
350 Main Street
Malden, MA 02148, USA

ISBN: 0-7456-2405-7
ISBN: 0-7456-2406-5 (pb)

A catalogue record for this book is available from the British Library.

Typeset in 10 on 12 pt Monotype Times
by Servis Filmsetting Ltd, Manchester
Printed and bound in Great Britain by MPG Books Ltd, Bodmin, Cornwall

The publisher has used its best endeavours to ensure that the URLs for external websites referred to in this book are correct and active at the time of going to press. However, the publisher has no responsibility for the websites and can make no guarantee that a site will remain live or that the content is or will remain appropriate.

For further information on Polity, visit our website: www.polity.co.uk

# Negotiating Diversity

# Contents

*For Jessica*

# Acknowledgements

Paul Gilbert, John Horton, David Owen, Bhikhu Parekh, and Robert Stern generously offered invaluable comments on an earlier draft. I am also grateful to Polity's anonymous referees for their perceptive and useful suggestions. In addition, John Dunn, Cheryl Misak and Noël O'Sullivan kindly provided encouragement and help during the period of writing this book. My colleagues in the Politics Department at Sheffield University, particularly Andrew Gamble, Duncan Kelly, Michael Kenny, James Meadowcroft and Andrew Vincent, have provided a rewarding and stimulating environment. Of course, none of these individuals should be saddled with any responsibility for the end-product. A grant from the Arts and Humanities Research Council of the British Academy greatly assisted the drafting of this text, and I am very grateful to that body. Rebecca Harkin, Jean Van Altena (my copy editor) and Ellen McKinlay at Polity have been unfailingly helpful and patient. Finally, it is a particular treat for me to be able to thank Jessica Penn, and our children Sam, Natasha and Max, for their love and support. They have made not only this but everything that matters to me possible.

# Introduction

'I'll teach you differences.' This line from *King Lear*, which Ludwig Wittgenstein found 'very beautiful' and considered using as an epigraph to the *Philosophical Investigations*, could stand as a watchword for a powerful current in political thought and, more generally, in the social sciences and humanities (Rhees 1981: 171). For this way of thinking, the allegedly simplistic pictures offered by intellectual tradition and social and political practice need to be swept away, in favour of a more textured understanding of society, identity and political power, which is sensitive to the nuances of history, particularity, identity and difference. Such a textured understanding will not only provide cognitive benefits, giving us a clearer picture of the world, but has an essentially ethical and political dimension: 'the ethical watchword of the post-imperial age is always to "listen to the voices of the others" and to abide by the principle of "self-identification"' (Tully 1995: 34; and, e.g., Tully 2004b: 84–5). Behind the 'great cry for recognition', as Isaiah Berlin wrote, with the experience of both earlier European nationalisms and post-war decolonization in mind, lies a 'bitter longing for status' among peoples subject to alien rule (Berlin 1969: 157).

Yet the Earl of Kent's warning is a *threat*, accompanied by a beating, and the 'differences' that he wants the hapless servant Oswald to remember are the marks and norms of hierarchy and of the king's superior status. So we may have moral qualms about the differences whose legitimacy we are meant to recognize. In a world in which the 'differences' that Lear has taken for granted are challenged, or in which they may or should be challenged, there is a question about whether they themselves amount to a form of arbitrary tyranny. They may denote relationships that we find oppressive or harmful for those caught up in them, and societies marked by such differences may be mosaics of mistrust, in which the lines of distinction destroy bonds of solidarity, trust and cohesion. Any assertion of the significance of a given set of 'differences' may not only obscure possible areas of commonality but may itself paper over divergences of interest and identity, disagreement and dissent.

Political theory is a creature of its time and place, and the social and political world that it seeks to shed some light on also plays a role in explaining its concerns. Since the collapse of a powerful ideological competitor to capitalist democracy, struggles over identity now seem to fill much of the ideological space vacated by debates over ownership of the means of production. In the most spectacular instances, they take the form of ethnic and religious violence and civil war in former Yugoslavia, Rwanda, Sri Lanka, India, Israel, Sudan, Northern Ireland and the Basque territory. Better controlled, but apparently no less intractable, disputes about identity and power are evident in Spain, Belgium and Canada. Indigenous peoples in the Americas, Europe, Australia and New Zealand argue for greater self-determination and control over the possibility of maintaining and developing their traditional ways of life. The end of the Cold War not only shifted the lines of ideological dispute, it created the conditions for the destabilization of many state boundaries. Behind these conflicts lie the historical experiences of empire and decolonization. The states of Central Europe, for example, have emerged from the successive rule of the Ottoman, Austro-Hungarian, Nazi and Soviet empires. Other phenomena, such as mass immigration and religious fundamentalism, have also helped to put problems of identity, difference and recognition at the centre of global politics.

Both an appreciation of the more or less tense interaction of a plurality of ways of life in a shared social and political space and the sense that some fragile cultural forms are eroded in this interaction are venerable insights. It seems that there is no shortage of differences in which we need an education, including those politically salient differences that bear significantly on how we treat one another in politics – class, race, sex and gender, ethnicity, religion, region and so on (some add: species). Where does culture fit into this picture of a world of differences? In what way is cultural variety a problem for political theory? To say this is emphatically not to say that it is only a problem, or that it has to be one.

The treatment of these issues in contemporary political theory lies at the intersection of three sets of related but distinct themes, concerns and problems. The first is the development out of various strands of post-romantic thought of an ethically charged conception of identity, and of cognate concepts such as recognition, which are taken to include an important cultural ingredient. To fail to recognize or respect someone's cultural identity is to do them a wrong, according to this line of thought, and even to deny a 'vital human need', as the Canadian philosopher Charles Taylor put it in his immensely influential essay 'The Politics of Recognition' (Taylor 1995: 226). Perhaps, then, not only people *qua* members of cultures but the cultures themselves are owed respect: as Bhikhu Parekh writes, '[s]ince every culture gives stability and meaning to human life, holds its members together as a community, displays creative energy, and so on, it deserves respect' (Parekh 2000: 176–7). What such respect means, and how respect for an individual's cultural identity may relate to respect for other aspects of her identity (if we owe *those* respect), becomes grist to the mill of the political theory of cultural diversity.

The second relevant set of themes and issues is a developing concern regarding the character of liberal citizenship. How should we conceive of the fit between liberal political principles and institutions and cultural diversity? For a liberal state committed to the equal treatment (in some sense) of its citizens through a set of individual rights, such features of social and political life as a common state language, a standard working week and public holidays, presumptions about standards of dress, norms of marriage and so on, may seem to put at a disadvantage those with divergent cultural commitments and expectations. The question then arises of whether the apparent disadvantage is justifiable or not. Also at issue, as Taylor emphasized in his essay, is whether the liberal state is entitled to promote certain cultural projects or whether it is compelled to be 'difference-blind'. Finally, there is the question of the character and depth of cultural divergence that a liberal state can accommodate, while remaining identifiably liberal.

The third relevant set of themes emerges from the awareness of the multiplicity and patchwork variety of legal and political accommodations that characterize many actual liberal states. These can be drawn together under the rubric of differentiated citizenship or, more commonly, multiculturalism. The term 'multiculturalism' is sometimes used interchangeably with 'cultural diversity', but in this book multiculturalism will be considered as a new sort of theoretical language, a set of ideals and policies, or ideology. In order to gain a sense of some of the concrete issues and lay down some markers for what follows, a useful starting point is Jacob Levy's illuminating classification of cultural rights and policies. Building inductively, he distinguishes eight categories of such claims, each of which itself embodies a cluster of differing entitlements and applications (J. Levy 2000: 127). First, there are exemptions from laws which penalize particular cultural groups or practices. Some of the more celebrated examples of multicultural entitlements fall into this category. In the United Kingdom, Sikhs successfully gained an exemption from laws governing the wearing of crash helmets, in order to accommodate the turbans required by their religion, and in Canada this has famously extended to an exemption from the traditional Stetson in the uniform of the Royal Canadian Mounted Police (Parekh 2000: 244–5). Jews and Muslims in many states have won exemption from Sunday-closing legislation affecting shops and other businesses (cf. Poulter 1986: 276–7).

Where exemption rights permit members of a designated group to engage in practices that are generally not permitted, or not to fulfil requirements obligatory on others, assistance rights claimed in order to support activities on the part of a minority that the majority, or otherwise privileged group, can perform relatively easily without assistance. The most famous examples of this sort of right are embodied in affirmative action programmes and quotas that are implemented in a range of private and public organizations, particularly affecting the spheres of employment and education. But they also include language rights, such as multilingual ballot papers and legal proceedings, bilingual or minority language educational programmes, and a bi- or multilingual civil service or health service. The third category of claims is for rights to the representation of a group within the political processes of a state: for example, through consociational power sharing in the executive or through guaranteed seats in a legislature.

Some rights promote what we can broadly think of as the conditions for self-determination of groups. The fourth category is probably the most incendiary of cultural claims: that for self-government. Groups seek to establish a political unit – a roof over their heads – in which they are dominant, and demand that borders should be drawn and political powers reconfigured in order to establish this. This may take the form of a demand for a sovereign state, or for a federal or confederal relationship, or for enhanced rights within such a relationship. Fifth, there are external rules which restrict the liberties of non-members of a culture in order to preserve the identity of members. For example, laws denying the rights of non-Indians to buy or reside on American Indian tribal lands are defended in order to protect the integrity of those lands and of the community that occupies them (Kymlicka 1989: 146–7). Sixth, there is the claim for the recognition or enforcement of a traditional legal code. Cultural groups seek to have their members bound by traditional communal laws, at least with respect to some areas of life, rather than the general laws of the political community. For example, some Muslims have sought legal standing for *sharia* law in the family and civil codes of states that are not themselves governed by Muslim law, such as India. Questions of family law, and particularly divorce law, have generated some of the more controversial discussions. Seventh, there are internal rules. These do not have the status of laws, and their proponents do not attempt to endow them with that status, but they nevertheless embody a set of norms that govern members of a group. Violation of these rules may be punished by excommunication or ostracism, and their content may appear to violate liberal norms of public life. I say 'appear to', since a great deal here depends on how much illiberalism is thought permissible in the internal character of associations: for example, in the rights of religions such as Catholicism or Judaism to exclude women from office.

The final category is that of rights that take the form of symbolic recognition. Many disputes do not concern the ways in which a group's members are hampered from pursuing their lives by the lights of their culture. Rather, they concern how a group is seen, or sees itself, as part of the polity. Such various claims as the demand to rename streets and areas, redesign flags, rephrase constitutions, rewrite school history in textbooks, or for public apologies fall into this category (cf. Billig 1995).

In what follows, I offer a critical overview of important perspectives on the political theory of cultural diversity, developing and examining some of the concepts and arguments that they offer. The route is as follows. I first discuss the claim that cultural identity forms an important part of a person's identity, in the sense that something important is missing from a description of an individual's life that makes no reference to cultural membership (chapter 1). This leads into a discussion of the ways in which cultural identity has been given normative significance in political philosophy (chapter 2). The next three chapters look at conceptions of political deliberation which diverge on the question of the weight to attach to this normativity and the justification of differentiated citizenship. The shortcomings I find in so-called liberal culturalist (chapter 3) and (an ugly coinage on my part) negative universalist (chapter 4) approaches lead to a consideration of the merits of political deliberation as public dialogue (chapter 5). Analysis of the promise and difficulties of this approach leads into a discussion of an important issue for public deliberation in culturally diverse societies: namely, the problem of trust (chapter 6). In part, the aim is to provide an account of the state of play in this area of political theory, and to trace out some of the relationships among the key theoretical positions and arguments. I have tried to do this in such a way that a reader will be able to follow the arguments discussed, even if she disagrees with my responses to them or with where I take these arguments. My other purpose is to work out some arguments of my own. My intention is to develop four main points.

The first is that there are grounds for viewing culture as an important ingredient in individual identity and as possessing value or normativity. In chapter 1, I distinguish normative, semiotic and societal accounts of the importance of culture for individual and group identity, and offer a qualified defence of the claim for the importance of culture in the face of powerful sceptical arguments that appeal to the constructed and contestable character of cultural identity. Yet the constructed and contestable aspect of cultural identity – what we could call its negotiated character – should be borne in mind in considering the significance of culture for political deliberation. I further argue against collapsing the ontological question of the significance of cultural identity for selfhood into the evaluative questions about the normative pull that a cultural identity is meant to have on us, and also argue against confusing either of these with a specific case for granting a multicultural right of some sort to an individual or a group.

Second, I distinguish differing conceptions of political deliberation and argue against those that take what I call a pre-emptive stance toward the claims of cultural identity. These approaches are each developed against the common background of the liberal democratic constitutionalist state, but differ in the independent deliberative weight that they give to cultural identity in political deliberation. Pre-emption, I argue, either fails to pay attention to relevant normative features of cultural identity or does so in a way that obscures the negotiated character of these identities. For liberal culturalism, the interest in culture is so compelling that it is taken to ground a right to culture, protecting this interest from the depredations of markets and democratic majorities. By contrast, negative universalism argues for the relegation of cultural differences to the private sphere, and for the state to eschew concern with the cultural identity of citizens. In different ways, I argue, these positions fail to do justice to the claim for the deliberative weight of cultural identity.

Third, I make a case for a strategy that avoids pre-emption, and views political deliberation as a process of public dialogue. For the conception of political deliberation as public dialogue, the public or democratic character of political dialogue is crucial to allowing claims for the recognition of cultural identity to be handled in an acceptable way. Such claims must aim to withstand the test of the exchange of public reasons in processes of political discussion and argument. From this perspective, the focus of debate shifts away from justifying a pre-emptive judgement about cultural recognition and the justifiability of difference-sensitive rights toward considering what forms of public dialogue could fairly deal with the relevant array of claims and counterclaims. Public deliberation can make space for arguments for cultural recognition, and I distinguish three families of such arguments, which I call equality-based, importance and compromise arguments. At the same time, public deliberation carries with it significant costs and risks in the politicization of cultural identities and in the underdetermination of the core notion of 'public reasons'. One implication of this, I argue, is that public deliberation requires a level of mutual trust that may seem problematic in this context. Does admitting the claims of cultural minorities call into question the trust on which political dialogue rests?

Fourth, I concentrate on the frailties and contingency of such trust. I consider three accounts of the sources and character of this political trust, which are respectively grounded in the ethos of public deliberation, the identity of participants, and institutional strategies to mitigate distrust. The trust necessary for public dialogue cannot be presumed, and is not necessarily self-reinforcing. This allows consideration of a position that has been waiting patiently in the wings, the nationalist or 'positive universalist' case, that public deliberation requires or benefits from a shared national identity. Ethos, identity and institutions are at best fallible sources of deliberative political trust, I argue; furthermore, the assumptions on which they rest and the proposals that they generate may in significant ways conflict with and thwart one another.

First, however, we need to turn to another of Lear's challenges: 'Who will tell me who I am?'

# 1

# Approaches to Cultural Identification

> The inhabitant of a country has at least nine characters: an occupations charac-
> ter, a national character, a civic character, a class character, a geographic char-
> acter, a sex character, a conscious character and an unconscious character, and
> perhaps a private character as well. He combines them all in himself but he is
> nothing but a small channel washed out by these trickling streams . . . This is
> why every inhabitant of the earth has a tenth character as well, which is nothing
> more or less than the passive fantasy of unfilled space. It permits man everything
> except one thing: to take seriously what his nine or more other characters do and
> what happens to them. In other words, then, it forbids him precisely that which
> would fulfil him.
>
> Robert Müsil, *A Man Without Qualities*

Arguing for the normative significance of such a heavily theory-laden and
contested concept as culture is a precarious business. 'Culture' is an immensely
slippery term: 'the attempt to say something both general and useful about
culture might seem doomed from the very start,' Raymond Geuss depressingly
remarks at the very start of an essay on the concept (Geuss 1999: 29). There
are dozens of ways of defining the concept, some of which conflict with others,
and which refer to a wide range of different phenomena.[1] This concept is in
turn entangled with another equally obscure and multivalent notion: namely,
identity. One way to address the question 'why does culture matter to political
philosophy?' is to view it as a question about ontology, or, to put it more mod-
estly but no less vaguely, about what should properly form part of an adequate
description of a person's identity.[2] The purpose of this chapter is to try to
clarify a claim that is often gestured toward, but seldom given much precision,
at least in the political theory of cultural diversity: that a person's culture
forms an important part of her identity. This claim is sometimes assumed to

be so obviously true as to need no clarification or so problematic as not to be worth clarifying. What could be more essential to me than the language that comes out of my mouth or the way I have always lived? What could be more arbitrary and accidental than my culture, the contingent and disputable upshot of a murky history, which obscures my solid affinities with fellow human beings?

In what follows, I start by setting out in section 1 the basic claim for the socially embedded character of the self or 'practical identity' of a person. This 'social thesis' about the self is given a particular cultural specification by some writers, and I explore what is involved in this. In section 2, I compare three conceptions of culture that have been employed in explaining the significance of culture for a person's identity, which I call the normative, the societal and the semiotic, and look at some of the differing implications of each. Section 3 examines a line of criticism of this ontological claim for culture in identity. This claim, the criticism runs, is incoherent, since it requires an *essentialist* view of cultural identity. As Seyla Benhabib resonantly phrases this objection, the politics of cultural identity 'is afflicted by the paradox of wanting to preserve the purity of the impure, the immutability of the historical and fundamentalness of the contingent' (Benhabib 2002: 11). In other words, not only is generalization about the concept of culture beset by difficulties, but so is generalization about specific *cultures*. Two grounds for this objection are distinguished: that a cultural identity is so vague or contested that it has no determinate content, and that a cultural identity should be understood as constructed, the product of invented traditions, imposed narratives and strategic interactions. I argue that while these points are important for how we understand the politics of identity, they do not undermine a plausible form of the cultural thesis. In section 4, I argue that we should distinguish the ascription of a practical identity and evaluative endorsement of the reasons grounded by that ascription. I offer some general reasons not to telescope the ontological claim about the contextual character of identity with evaluative claims about the grounds for valuing or respecting social or cultural identity. Adequately distinguishing identity attributions and the evaluative claims made on behalf of identities, however, means that the cultural thesis pushes us less far toward any specific political position – support for multicultural rights and policies, negative or positive universalism – than either proponents or critics of the cultural thesis may believe.

## 1.   The Self *in situ*

A starting point for understanding the significance claimed for culture is to view this claim against the backdrop of a wider set of debates about how we should conceive of individual identity in relation to the social groups and collectivities to which individual human beings belong. One approach to the latter question holds as central the belief that we can make sense of a person's having an identity prior to the social arrangements in which she finds herself. In explaining the shape of those arrangements, then, we can appeal to the interaction of the identities of the various people involved, and, in evaluating those arrangements, we can judge to what extent they serve the interests of the different individuals involved. Critics of this abstraction argue that we can make sense of an individual person only if we understand his or her identity or self as embedded within a particular social context. This is sometimes advanced as a quasi-empirical thesis in social theory: that a range of capacities and social identities can be acquired only through exposure to the appropriate social conditions. In order to be a Samurai or a serf, or a chess grandmaster, I need to be brought up in the right kind of setting, and for that setting to sustain my identity. There is also a conceptual version: that human capacities such as language, reasoning or autonomy can in principle only be acquired in social contexts. From this point of view, collective entities such as societies should not then be understood as concatenations of pre-social atoms. Rather, it is only possible to offer an account of the individual if we refer to those social networks of which he or she is a part.[3]

This line of argument has become particularly associated with so-called communitarian political philosophers, such as Michael Sandel, Charles Taylor and Alasdair MacIntyre.[4] Yet it has its roots in the idealist criticism of the social contract tradition and affiliations with feminist, Marxist, conservative and other sceptical assessments of liberal individualism.

As such, the ontological claim has often been tangled up with another issue: whether liberal ethical individualism, which places great weight on the moral claims of individuals in evaluating the legitimacy of social and political arrangements, constitutes an acceptable political morality, as against those forms of politics that emphasize the common good. Liberals are often criticized for possessing a conception of the person as 'atomistic' or 'pre-social'. Devices such as the social contract or John Rawls's veil of ignorance at once ascribe to the individual a range of attributes and capacities that they can possess only if developed socially, commentators argue, while artificially picturing them free of any social ties, and capable of making choices about which social attachments to adopt.[5] Whether or not the critical assessment of the asocial character of some liberalism can be sustained, the view of the self as socially embedded has been an important element in the claims of political theorists for multiculturalism.

The broad commitment to culture as a significant constituent of identity is common to a variety of writers who are sympathetic to the normative claims of multiculturalism (cf. Kelly 2002b: 6). This commitment is elaborated in various ways. According to Bhikhu Parekh, human beings are 'culturally embedded', and different cultures 'define and constitute human beings and come to terms with the basic problems of human life in their own different ways' (Parekh 2000: 122). At the same time, membership allows for differing levels of attachment to a culture, for deep disagreement over what attachment entails, and for a culture's identity to be fluid and contested (Parekh 2000: 148). Iris Marion Young argues that individuals construct their own identities on the basis of their positioning within a constellation of social groups and forces: '[s]ocial processes and interactions position individual subjects in prior relations and structures, and this positioning conditions who they are' without defining or determining that identity in a way that precludes all agency or conscious self-fashioning (Young 2000: 103). Social groups are diverse in character, dynamic and interactive. While groups defined by economic class and by gender are particularly significant, she argues, culture is also a significant source of individual identity, which overlaps with, and is dynamically related to, the wider array of social relationships and structures (Young 2000: 91).[6] Will Kymlicka is less sympathetic to the tenor of the communitarian critique of liberalism than either Young or Parekh, and tends to eschew the language of 'identity'. But his central, or official, argument for the normativity of cultural identity relies on demonstrating that the possession of one's own particular cultural identity is an essential condition for the exercise of a basic and valuable human capacity, that of forming and revising a conception of the good (e.g., Kymlicka 1995a: 82–4). His claim for culture, then, has the same shape as the claim for the socially embedded character of the self: we can make sense of a basic human capacity only if we understand it as socially, and in particular as culturally, located. Kymlicka's reluctance to embrace the language of 'identity' does not mean that he is not an adherent to the cultural thesis. He argues that what he calls a societal culture has an indispensable instrumental value in sustaining the conditions for a person's individual freedom. If that is so, then he subscribes to the cultural thesis, in the terms set out here: my cultural identity is a significant part of my identity, in the sense of shaping the reasons that I have to act. Charles Taylor takes a view of the self as constituted by its orientation around goods available within the specific social matrices of which one is part. I become who I am only through 'webs of interlocution', in relating to 'those conversation partners . . . essential to my achieving self-definition' (Taylor 1989: 136). The goods made available to me distinctively through my network of cultural relationships form an important part of my identity (Taylor 1995: 136–7).[7]

Stringing together these statements misses a great deal of importance and obscures the large differences among these authors, but I want only to isolate and highlight the claim that culture is an important part of the social setting in which the self should be seen as embedded. In each case, the claim is that in some way culture plays a role in shaping someone's 'practical identity' – that is, those features of a person that ground at least some of their reasons to act. As Christine Korsgaard puts it, '[y]ou are a human being, a woman or a man, an adherent or a certain religion, a member of an ethnic group, a member of a certain profession, someone's lover or friend, and so on. And all of these identities give rise to reasons and obligations' (Korsgaard 1996b: 101).[8] For advocates of the social thesis, social roles and institutions furnish individuals with their projects and practical commitments, as well as 'shap[ing] the habits – the frames of interpretation and categorization, the primary practices, interests and motivational preoccupations – that express, actualise, and define an individual's identity' (A. O. Rorty 1994: 154). Now it is not obvious that these framing roles and institutions need to be defined primarily in cultural terms. Such other axes of identification as class, region, occupation, family, political party, leisure interests, religion, sex and age, among others, all jostle to provide significant contexts for a person's practical engagement with the world. A particular society or polity can be regarded as a palimpsest of overlapping associations, groups, affiliations, interests and identities, each making claims on the individual and shaping her conception of the world in a variety of ways. Even if one accepts the social thesis about the formation of identity, a person's *cultural* identity is not obviously a significant element in this formation; or, less sceptically, how to understand the place of culture in this complex picture is not on the face of it at all clear.

What may be called the cultural thesis, then, is the claim that a person's culture is important for her practical identity in the sense that it plays a significant role in this constitutive process, and that in describing someone's practical identity we miss something of importance if we neglect her culture. To substantiate this claim involves moving from the general 'social thesis' about the constitution of the self and its capacities, where the content of the social is yet to be filled in, to a particular specification of that content, in a claim for the significance of culture. But what makes a cultural identity, or the cultural aspect of someone's identity, important or perhaps even central for a person? In the next section, I consider three facets of culture which have been emphasized by political theorists offering accounts that seek to justify a claim for the importance of culture to practical identity.

One way of viewing culture is as an aspect or trait of an individual human being, which leads us to understand the importance of culture as importance for that person. We can distinguish a variety of ways in which a trait or aspect of a person's identity may be held to be especially significant, important or central to that person's identity (Rorty and Wong 1990: 20). A first reason for viewing an identity trait as important stems from observing the extent to which other traits are dependent on it: that is, the range of dispositions, habits, beliefs, desires, emotional responses, attitudes and so on which depend on this trait. Second, a trait may also be judged important because of the extent to which it ramifies across distinctive spheres, such as work and leisure, the public and private spheres, and across different types of relationships. One of the distinctive features of national identity, as well as the version of it that

Kymlicka calls societal culture (which will be discussed in the next section), for several liberal political philosophers is that it encompasses a wide range of social practices and relationships. Third, a trait may also be judged important by the degree to which it affects the way a person is categorized and treated by others – stigmatized, honoured, preferred, included, excluded and so on.[9] Fourth, another way of viewing an identity trait as important is by assessing the difficulty in changing the trait. Fifth, we may also think a trait important if it is dominant in situations that require coping with stress or conflict. Sixth, a trait may also be judged important according to the extent to which it is dominant when it comes into conflict with other traits. Finally, an identity trait may judged important by the degree to which a person thinks of herself as radically changed if the trait changes: that is, the extent to which she identifies with it, or, as is sometimes said, how important it is not only *for* her but *to* her. Such identification is not an all-or-nothing affair, but comes in degrees and modes. One can identify dutifully, resentfully, hypocritically or cheerfully, in a more or less stable way, with some features of an identity but not others, with a variety of identities (perhaps including incompatible ones), and so on.

In some circumstances, these different ways of assessing the significance of an aspect of an identity for an individual may be tightly correlated with one another (for example, race in apartheid South Africa would figure along most, if not all, dimensions), but they need not be: I may not think of what is relatively fixed about me as important to me, and it may not affect how the wider society treats me. An individual's cultural traits may be salient along one or more of these dimensions. For example, my language (or the way I speak) may affect how I am categorized and treated by others and may become important in stressful situations (such as during court room proceedings), but constitute a relatively easy trait to change. Many of these dimensions are affected by social and political context. For example, economic imperatives may lead to greater contact with members of other cultural and language groups, making language, which was previously an insignificant factor, an important feature of identity, which bears on how someone is treated, how she copes with stress, how easily she can occupy various social positions, and so on. This in turn may involve a person identifying with her language, coming to see it as integral to who she is. Yet it is worth preserving the distinction between subjective and objective aspects of identity, for a person may not feel this way or may actively resist a view of herself as deeply entangled with her language.

Culture may also be viewed as a feature of a group or a collectivity: it is the group which has those characteristics (for instance, certain norms governing exogamy, institutions of punishment and so on) that are taken to make up a cultural identity. For this perspective, the cultural thesis takes the form of a claim that membership of, or identification with, a group with a certain cultural character is integral to a person's identity. A group may of course be defined in non-cultural terms: as a collection of individuals with a shared set of non-cultural interests, or which acts together in some way – the red-haired, men, IBM shareholders, the international working class.[10] To say that a group is not defined culturally, however, does not mean that it lacks determinate cultural characteristics. It is therefore intelligible to think of a group as losing or changing its cultural characteristics while remaining the group that it is. This is not to say that such a change or loss is a matter of indifference to a group, or to its members. So, for example, a member of a North American indigenous tribe can regret the disappearance of a traditional way of life, but see this as not compromising her membership in the group whose way of life has changed. Alternatively, we may think of culture as (at least in part) constitutive of the identity of the group, in the sense that the group would not survive as that group if the culture changed. This is not to say that *any* change in the cultural character of a group in such a case would amount to the demise of the group. The point is that, on either of these accounts, the cultural thesis is fundamentally a claim for the importance of group membership for the individual, in which culture plays a role, rather than directly for the importance of cultural identity. I return to the significance of this distinction in chapter 2, section 2.

## 2.  Three Views of Culture in Political Theory

In this section, I will pick out three ways in which the concept of culture has been deployed in political theory, which we can call the normative, the societal and the semiotic conceptions of culture. These are not competing definitions of culture, each selecting a different set of necessary and sufficient conditions for the correct application of the predicate. Rather, each fleshes out the general 'cultural thesis' about the constitution of identity in a distinctive way, offering a different rationale for the cultural thesis. Each can admit that a culture may have the features that are emphasized by the other conceptions, or may be defined in these other ways for different purposes. But they differ in which aspects of culture they point up as central to explaining the importance of culture to identity.

The conceptions discussed here share what may be called (very loosely) an anthropological or post-Herderian conception of culture. A first feature of this conception is that culture is not viewed as the morally or historically commendable achievement of a particular people, to be contrasted with 'civilization' or 'anarchy', on the one hand, or with the second-rate ways of life of peoples who have not achieved culture.[11] It follows that there is a plurality of cultures, which may be related to the variety of social, economic, political and climatic conditions in which people live. Second, culture is underdetermined by nature: although culture is in conformity with human nature, there is no one form that specific cultural practices must take, or *telos* toward which they ought to tend. Third, culture is not simply passively received and transmitted. Rather, it must be learned and maintained intersubjectively, and can be creatively or accidentally transformed through human agency, as well as, of course, through other means.

The normative conception views the significance of culture in the constitution of practical identity as lying in a culture's containing a set of shared beliefs or norms which are distinctive of a particular group. What makes culture constitutive of a person's identity is that it is the source, or at least an important source, of a person's values and commitments. Provided that we view a person's values and commitments as central to their identity, then, we may say that we do not properly describe what is central to that person unless we take into account her culture. Ayelet Shachar's conception of an identity group as a *nomos* group falls into this category: that is, such a group possesses a 'comprehensive and distinguishable worldview that extends to creating a law for the community' (Shachar 2001: 2).[12] So, for example, Muslims who see their identity as requiring that they abide by *sharia* law constitute a *nomos* group. Parekh, who is also concerned with the normative authority that groups hold over their members, emphasizes shared belief as a central component of his conception of culture: '[t]he beliefs or views human beings form about the meaning and significance of human life and its activities and relationships shape the practices in terms of which they structure and regulate their individual and collective lives. I shall use the term culture to refer to such a system of beliefs and practices' (Parekh 2000: 142–3). Accordingly, many of the cases calling for 'intercultural evaluation' that he examines hinge on the religious or other cultural norms of members of a group, such as polygamy, Jewish and Muslim methods of animal slaughter, arranged marriages, and practices of clitoridectomy (Parekh 1999; 2000: ch. 9).[13] The relevant norms need not have any religious tincture, however. What Eric Hobsbawm calls the 'desperate French rearguard action against the ravages of *franglais*' (Hobsbawm 1992: 56) can also be viewed as an expression of the belief about the importance of a particular set of shared cultural norms for the French. For proponents of this normative conception, not only beliefs, but specific reactive attitudes and emotional responses (of disgust, celebration, disapproval and so on), form part of the normative equipment that a culture gives to an individual.

This, then, is a cultural form of a well-known communitarian claim, to the effect that, as Sandel puts it, there are 'loyalties and convictions whose moral force consists partly in the fact that living by them is inseparable from understanding ourselves as the particular persons we are' (Sandel 1982: 179). Understanding ourselves as the particular persons whom we are requires understanding ourselves as subject to certain normative commitments, which are constitutive of our identities. As I have outlined it, this normative conception does not *define* a feature of a practical identity as cultural by reference to its furnishing a person with norms. Rather, the claim is that it is the norm-providing aspect of culture that makes the latter a significant part of a person's practical identity. This allows that there may be differences and characteristics that we can plausibly call cultural (say, the difference between French- and Flemish-speaking Belgians) that are not normative, in the sense that they do not hinge on different beliefs about the meaning of life or what activities are and are not permissible. And there are normative characteristics that it would be implausible or obscurantist to dub cultural, such as the ideological differences between liberals and socialists. The point is that where culture is important for a person's identity, it is important by virtue of the role it plays is constructing that person's normative world.

The normative conception of culture used by political theorists in this way recalls the traditions within the social sciences of studying culture as a set of shared norms, social roles, and orientations, compelling for members and what renders their world meaningful. Culture is accordingly invoked in this tradition to explain, for example, why societies prove susceptible in different degrees to democracy and economic modernization, or why oppositional groups (sometimes viewed as subcultures) remained alienated from the resultant arrangements: as Adam Kuper puts it, the concept of culture was 'invoked when it became necessary to explain why people were clinging to irrational goals and self-destructive strategies. Development projects were defeated by cultural resistance. Democracy crumbled because it was alien to the traditions of a nation.' Culture was a 'fallback', deployed to explain apparent irrationality and the failure of political reforms (Kuper 1999: 10; cf. Wedeen 2002: 713). Alternatively, for instance, Francis Fukuyama explained the economic ascendancy of East Asia (in 1995) in terms of the trust fostered in cultures of 'shared moral norms or values' (Fukuyama 1995: 336). For some exponents of a normative conception, the imbrication of these norms in the social fabric of the society means that to undermine or question them is to generate an existential crisis for members of a culture, since it destroys the capacity of members of the culture to make meaningful evaluations and choices: in the absence of the *nomos*, anomie (cf. P. Gilbert 2000: 35–7, and see below chapter 2, section 5; chapter 3, section 3).

A liberal objection to taking identity to be constituted by culture in this sense is that to view my identity as constituted by norms and commitments seems to block the possibility that I may assess and potentially revise the norms and commitments that I have (Kymlicka 1995a: 92). However, I think we need to disentangle the question of our capacity to distance ourselves from our identities from the question of whether or not we take norms to be an important constitutive component of identity. (I pick up on this point in section 4 below.) To claim that norms are constitutive of the self is not to imply that we cannot critically reflect on these features of our identity. Indeed, it may be easier for someone to gain critical distance from her cultural norms than to gain distance from non-normative features of a cultural identity: for example, it may be easier to relinquish a norm of monogamy than to become fluent in a new language. The constitutive claim for the cultural norms need not include the thought that we are *wholly* constituted by cultural norms. There may be other normative constituents of our identities (family allegiances, political commitments) that pull in different directions, and often these conflicting pulls provide the occasion for troubling or agonizing choice. So there may be reasons for someone to rethink particular cultural norms, and even to call into question the person she is, without thereby rejecting the normative version of the cultural thesis (cf. Sandel 1982: 62).

There are two more pertinent reasons for cautiousness about the normative filling-in of the cultural thesis, which stem from a lack of clarity in this account about the relationship of cultural identity to norms. First, the normative account raises a particular version of a general problem about the cultural thesis. The general problem, of how to reconcile the claims for the importance of cultural identity with acknowledgement of deep and often intractable disagreement over what is involved in a particular identity, will be discussed in the following section (and in various forms this problem ripples through the chapters that follow too). But the normative conception of culture raises the problem in a particularly stark form, for cultural symbols and practices often leave their normative content underdetermined. To view norms as constitutive of identity raises the question: which norms? Even cultures that define an important element of their shared identity through the laws prescribed by a canonical text are frequently divided over the interpretation of those texts (cf. A. O. Rorty 1994: 159). For example, secular and religious groups of various sorts conflict over the politics of defining Jewish identity. Interpretations of the Torah and the Talmud are introduced in arguments over Israeli public policy, in defining who, by virtue of Jewish identity, is entitled to automatic citizenship under the law of return. Opposed positions on the public policy of membership offer differing interpretations of the texts in their support. Indeed, disagreement over quite basic normative requirements may reasonably be considered to form a part of some identities – a point I will return to in the following section (and see MacIntyre 1988).

To take another case: it is not at all clear precisely what the norms at issue in the so-called *l'affaire du foulard* in France have been. This was sparked when some Muslim schoolgirls in Creil, north of Paris, went to school wearing headscarves. When they were sent home by the school, a major public controversy developed, drawing in politicians, anti-racist and Muslim organizations, and intellectuals. Opponents of the headscarf invoked the value of *laïcité*, or the secular character of the French public school system. The difficult question of why students are permitted to wear symbols such as a crucifix in schools has been finessed by drawing a distinction between ostentatious or proselytizing and discreet religious symbols. For sceptics about this way of resolving the problem, the distinction between two sorts of symbol is contrived, masking an anti-Islamic and perhaps anti-Algerian prejudice. The point to bring out here is that, in part, the dispute has been about how to interpret the norms informing students' conduct. Did wearing the headscarf signify the expression of freedom of religion? Acquiescence in a patriarchal normative structure? Resistance to the stereotypes of French or 'Western' conceptions of femaleness? A mode of integration in a non-Muslim society, negotiating a difficult passage through symbols that do not innocently reproduce tradition but act as a demonstration of difference? Do we determine the relevant norms through consulting the students, anthropologists, educationalists or French constitutional lawyers?[14] To start from the belief that the significance of culture for a person's identity lies in its furnishing her with a particular set of norms glosses over the lack of clarity about quite what the content of the norms supplied in this way are, and how they relate to the symbols and practices of that identity.

The other reason for caution is that the normative account seems to miss out other significant ways in which the concept of culture as a part of practical identity is invoked in political argument. Consider, for example, the argument sometimes made on behalf of minority linguistic groups that children in that group should be taught at school in their own language, rather than in the majority language of the state. This argument usually makes an appeal to the effectiveness of minority language or bilingual education in helping students in the minority group have the same opportunity to do as well at school as all the rest of the population. But the argument can also appeal to the importance of identity. Particularly where the minority is geographically concentrated in significant numbers, maintaining their language through the educational system is a legitimate goal, the argument runs. For it allows and fosters for members of this group a sense of familiarity with their particular cultural heritage, a sense of continuity across generations, and a valuable sense of distinctness and cultural integrity that would be at risk in the absence of this kind of public measure. Now the significance of language in this kind of case need not be that it provides this group with values or norms, or even that the group is thought to be under some duty to preserve its traditional language (as in the case for resisting *franglais*). If this is right, then the normative account is incomplete. I want to turn now to two other ways of fleshing out the claim for the significance of culture.

Many liberal political philosophers, reluctant to identify culture with a normative identity, adopt a different conception: this takes culture to consist in what Clifford Geertz calls 'the total way of life of a people' (Geertz 1973: 4).[15] For example, Kymlicka, having noted that 'the term "culture" has been used to cover all manner of groups, from teenage gangs to global civilizations', goes on to claim that his focus is on *societal* culture – that is, a culture which provides its members with meaningful ways of life across the full range of human activities, including social, educational, religious, recreational, and economic life, encompassing both public and private spheres. These cultures tend to be territorially concentrated, and based on a shared language . . . [I]n the modern world, for a culture to be embodied in social life means that it must be institutionally embodied – in schools, media, economy, government, etc. (Kymlicka 1995a: 76, emphasis original; cf. Kymlicka 2001a: 53)

To possess a distinct culture, then, is to have (that is, to be a member of a group which has) a distinct set of social, economic and political institutions. Other writers also focus on the 'encompassing' or 'pervasive' character of culture. A common culture affects 'everything people do: cooking, architectural style, common language, literary and artistic traditions, music, customs, dress, festivals, ceremonies' (Margalit and Halbertal 1994: 497–8).[16] The political significance of this stipulation becomes clearer when we note that Kymlicka's core examples of such societal cultures include the Catalans, the Flemish, and the Quebecois, and the Indian bands and original peoples of Canada and the United States – *national* minorities which possess or can demand a 'range of rights intended to protect and reflect their status as distinct cultural communities' (Kymlicka 1995a: 12; cf. Raz 1994: 129).

For the societal conception, culture as a distinctive way of life, marked out particularly by a language, together with a more or less discrete set of institutional structures, forms a significant condition for the identities of members. It is a striking feature of the societal conception that it suggests that different cultures cannot share a political or economic system, since it seems to unify culture with political and economic systems through identifying them as part of a larger whole, a set of distinct, territorially bound and relatively self-contained institutions. Kymlicka's concern about alternative ('disembodied', 'abstract', 'ethereal') conceptions of culture as symbols, practices or beliefs lacking such a powerful institutional anchor, is that they neglect the important relationship between symbols, beliefs and practices and socio-political structures (Kymlicka 1995a: 76–7, 80). It is not the case for him that there is no permissible or intelligible sense in which there can be cultures that are not societal: indeed, societal cultures characteristically possess particular features capable of 'abstraction' from the specific institutional context, such as language, cuisine and styles of architecture. Yet only societal cultures provide the social context for the formation and revision of conceptions of the good, and hence of individual freedom. This is a momentous demarcation, since it drives a wedge between the claims of societal cultures and those of all other groups which lack a robust set of institutions to call their own, including immigrants and territorially dispersed groups. Why is societal culture the central conception for Kymlicka? One answer is that his normative case – the context of choice argument – requires it, since he believes that it is only in an institutionally bound and normally linguistically distinct unit that an individual can enjoy the conditions necessary for autonomy: 'national culture provides a meaningful context of choice for people, without limiting their ability to question and revise particular values or beliefs' (Kymlicka 1995a: 93). There are grounds, on the one hand, to strengthen existing societal cultures, and, on the other, to integrate non-societal cultural identities, which he views as principally the cultural identities of immigrant groups (with differentiated rights and policies, where necessary). I will explore the rationale for the normative claim and its political implications in the following two chapters. Here I want to explore the account offered of the properties of societal culture.

It is worth noting that Kymlicka argues that societal culture is a privileged conception not merely on account of its instrumentality for individual autonomy but also because he believes only a societal culture can preserve the 'abstract' features of a cultural identity: 'for a culture to survive and develop in the modern world, given the pressures toward the creation of a single common culture in each country, it must be a societal culture' (Kymlicka 1995a: 80; cf. Kymlicka 2001a: 53). This statement contains what we can call, following Amélie Oksenberg Rorty, an 'accordion movement, expanding and contracting . . . definitions of culture' (A. O. Rorty 1994: 156; she finds this in Taylor's essay on recognition). The first use of 'culture' cannot refer only to *societal* culture, since that is what Kymlicka is arguing a culture must be, or perhaps become, in order to survive and develop; so it must refer to culture in some 'disembodied' sense. His point is that the functional pressures on the modern state mean that a language spoken by a minority (such as Welsh in Britain) will wither unless housed under its own distinctive institutional social and political roof, including, for example, schools and broadcasting institutions that preserve the language. For states with modern industrial economies require a common language and culture diffused though a relatively highly mobile, literate and numerate population (cf. Gellner 1983; Hall 1998b). The picture that emerges of societal culture is as follows. After a great wave of modernization, colonization and nation building, in which some sub-state identities have been washed away, those that remain in possession of both a distinctive set of 'encompassing' practices and a separate institutional roof over their heads play a significant role in the constitution of their members' identities. So, for example, the Bretons have lost their distinctive societal culture – they are French *tout court* – while the Basques and Corsicans arguably still possess theirs.

We can view the self as embedded in societal culture, since societal culture is the source of the raw materials for individual deliberation and agency. In order to form and revise conceptions of the good, Kymlicka argues, people need to make decisions based on their beliefs about the value of the social practices around them. To have a belief about the value of a practice is 'in the first instance, a matter of understanding the meanings attached to it our culture' (Kymlicka 2001a: 209). A secure and largely familiar culture provides the conditions in which a person can make choices about what matters to her, providing a map of the world in which she deliberates, narratives which make it intelligible to her, and some of the skills and resources that allow her to reason and make choices. These maps, narratives and skills are in large part presented to us by the dominant surrounding institutions, such as schools, television, the workplace and so on. Since these are among the key institutions of societal culture, we can make sense of the idea that the individual self is embedded in societal culture.

The notion of societal culture requires that these resources coincide with the territorial and institutional identity of the societal culture. It is unsurprising that for critics this conception evokes 'the old logic of the nation-state . . . the view that every nation (societal culture) should have its own state, civil society, and so on' (Carens 2000: 66). For the issue at stake in the politics of cultural diversity is often that of handling the *failure* of these levels to coincide: can cultures in a narrower, less than fully institutionally 'embodied' sense share polities, and, if so, how? Canadian Francophones are not all Quebecois, and the territory occupied by the province of Quebec contains Indian and Inuit groups who also stake a claim for recognition, as well as Anglophones and immigrants. If what play the constitutive role for identity are the scripts and narratives of 'disembodied' culture, then the cultural identity of those outside the societal culture (immigrants, Francophones outside Quebec, Flemish speakers in Wallonia) is on all fours with those of members.

The alternative is to claim that only cultures with the appropriate institutional underpinnings can claim to form the context of choice for their members: only where the scripts and narratives have their own legal and educational system, schools, broadcasting media and civil service, can they hope to hold their shape against the depredations of a neighbouring cultural identity. (There is an echo in the notion of societal culture of the definition of a nation as a language with its own army and navy.) This is a point about the causal conditions for maintaining a culture – for a culture to survive and develop, as Kymlicka puts it – (in the narrow or disembodied 'scripts and narratives' sense), not about what is constitutive of that culture. The difficulty for supporting this hypothesis is, first, that it presupposes that we know what maintaining an identity consists in. Yet there are always numerous, politically contested interpretations of what it means for a cultural identity to survive, fade or develop (would the United Kingdom survive without the monarch's image on its currency?). Second, this presents a misleading account of the causal role of independent societal institutions. Quebecois or Welsh language laws, for example, unavoidably promote a particular conception or range of conceptions of the identity concerned. Autonomous or semi-autonomous educational institutions, for example, in promoting a particular language as the medium of instruction (French in Quebec, Welsh in Wales), construct a particular cultural identity for their territories. They do not do so *ex nihilo*, of course, but the point is that the institutions promote some particular vision of the identity: of Wales as bilingual rather than unilingual (Welsh- or English-speaking). More radically, of course, nascent states develop languages for their populations, such as modern Hebrew in Israel or (less successfully) Nynorsk in Norway (Hobsbawm 1992: 55). The institutions 'of' a societal culture, then, do not simply express the culture of which they are constitutive, but causally promote some particular conception of that culture. And in promoting some particular conceptions of cultural identity, these institutions erode or undermine others. As with the normative conception, then, this account glosses over the political dimension of intra-cultural (or intra-societal) disagreement over what an identity is or 'requires': whether, for example, Welsh identity is based on a single language or two, or requires the recognition of other minority languages (S. May 2001: 270). In identifying institutions as a constitutive element of a cultural identity with institutions as a part of the causal grounds for promoting that identity, this account turns the Gellnerian functional imperative on its head. For the point of the latter analysis is that the demands of a bureaucratic state and economy within a given territory require a homogeneous national culture, to be constructed as necessary from the 'shreds and patches' of existing cultural forms (cf. O'Leary 1998). It is not that any very determinate pre-existent culture requires the creation and strengthening of distinct institutions as the ground for its own preservation, for the culture (on this account) largely came into being only through creation of the institutional carapace.

Furthermore, identifying the relevant causal conditions for maintaining an identity in this sense is not solely a matter of identifying a societal culture's 'own' institutions. As an institutional entity, the paradigm cases of societal cultures form part of larger multinational polities, on this account. Belgium, for example, seems to exemplify a model of a state which houses two different societal cultures. Flemish and Walloons are linguistically divided, regionally grouped in northern and southern Belgium, possess separate institutions that deal with a range of issues intra-communally, including education, employment and transport, and negotiate bi-communal matters through a complex set of federal arrangements. Yet it is arbitrary to say that only the intra-communal institutions, which *ex hypothesi* form part of each societal culture, give rise to the context in which individuals form and revise their conceptions of the good. For they arise from, are sustained by, and interact with the federal-level institutions and processes of negotiation. This is not to suggest that *this* level should be ascribed primacy as the source of the framing context for individual identity (and both federal and regional institutions, it will quickly be pointed out, exist in a context of European political and societal institutions). The point, rather, is that the individual's 'context of choice' is not to be understood by abstracting one element of a set of relationships and ascribing to that the crucial identity-framing role. The alternative, then, is to see a societal culture as *nested*, or as the product of the interaction of different sorts and levels of institution: a person is Flemish, Belgian and European, to point at only the crudest institutional markers.[17] In practical terms, endowing the societal conception with sole or central evaluative significance seems to create an incentive for groups, on one side, to emphasize linguistic difference when a group makes a claim to political and economic self-determination, and, on the other, to give a linguistically defined group (or group possessed of some other sort of ethereal cultural feature) a reason to press for its own institutions, since only with these in hand is it valued in more than a derivative sense. If we view societal culture relationally, we are led away from the conclusion that we can identify a set of culture-defining institutions as a given, a culture's 'own'. Flemish institutions are the product of, and defined by, a set of relationships and processes which are not that identity's 'own'. Viewing institutional identity relationally makes determining the significant constituent frame for individual identity or 'context of choice' a much more complex business than simply checking to which nation or societal culture an individual can be said to belong.

I have argued that there are difficulties with making the case that societal culture plays a privileged constituent role in identity. The case for its privilege rests on the conflation of the scripts and narratives that are meant to orient deliberation and agency with a set of distinctive social, legal, economic and political institutions. However, the objections to the argument for societal culture as the privileged context for identity are not objections to the very idea of a societal culture. The appropriate conclusion to draw is not, like Benhabib, that 'there are no such "societal cultures"'. Kymlicka, she argues, conflates 'institutionalized forms of collective public identities with the concept of culture. There are British, French, and Algerian nations and societies that are organized as states; but there are no British, French or Algerian "societal cultures".' This is because in any of these societies 'there is never a single culture, one coherent system of beliefs, significations, symbolizations, and practices' (Benhabib 2002: 60). Since she holds that *all* cultural identities include competing narratives and symbolic claims, the presence of this kind of competition and dissension within a society cannot in itself be evidence for her that there is *no* culture at the societal level. As I argued earlier, the variety of different conceptions and usages in this area tends to make it a fruitless exercise to rule out a conception of culture by this kind of *fiat*.[18] In this case, ruling out the notion of societal culture obscures an important issue. If socio-political institutions serve to promote and construct particular cultural identities (Francophone Quebec, bilingual Wales), then it makes sense to speak of societal cultures, according to the definition given by Kymlicka. So the institutions of a societal culture are important, but not in the way that Kymlicka presents them: not as the privileged causal ground for the maintenance of conditions for individual autonomy, but as an important source of the *difficulties* that provoke reflection on multiculturalism. As already noted, the starting point for much current writing on the political theory of cultural diversity is the sense that states are not neutral containers for whatever homogeneity or diversity is displayed by their populations, but unevenly accommodate, tolerate and promote different cultural identities, through those institutions that Kymlicka identifies as central to societal culture.

For anthropologists such as Geertz, the difficulty in defining such notions as the whole way of life of a people led to a different way of understanding culture. For the semiotic conception, culture is understood as 'the pattern of meaning embodied in symbolic forms, including actions, utterances, and meaningful objects of various kinds, by virtue of which individuals communicate with one another and share their experiences, conceptions and beliefs' (Thompson 1990: 132), or a set of 'intersubjectively shared symbols that actors invest with meaning' (J. Johnson 2000: 409). Geertz himself variously describes culture as 'a set of symbolic devices for controlling behaviour'; 'an historically transmitted pattern of meaning embodied in symbols, a system of inherited conceptions and expressed in symbolic forms by means of which men communicate, perpetuate and develop their knowledge about and attitudes towards life'; and 'a system of symbols by which man confers significance on his own experience' (Geertz 1973; 52, 89, 250).[19] Culture in the semiotic sense cuts across societal culture; so, for example, a common language is shared by Scotland, New Zealand and India, without there existing a shared societal identity. It undercuts societal culture too, since all manner of parochial cliques, clubs and groups that do not aspire to offer their members 'a whole way of life' across a range of dimensions of social life may have distinctive practices, shared understandings, codes and symbols. As noted above, shared norms do not coincide with shared languages and symbols: a shared language can be the medium of disagreement about norms, and a shared symbol (say, a national anthem or religious practice) can be the object or occasion of disagreement about norms, as in Christian argument over the sacraments. Whereas the normative account points to a shared set of norms expressed in social practices as the crucial constitutive element in culture for the self, and the societal conception to a set of institutions and 'way of life', usually including a common language, the semiotic account points to shared symbols and meanings.

For this conception, 'the interpretation of cultures' is both the name of an epistemological account of the kind of knowledge of culture that is possible, and a name for a distinctive feature of the object of that knowledge, the acts of interpretation of the signs and symbols of a culture by its members. From a hermeneutic perspective, social inquiry involves the elucidation of meaning: it is the attempt to recover the meaning of actions from the point of view of the agents who perform them (cf. Geertz 1973: 5). The social sciences explain a realm that is constituted by the symbols and the self-understandings of the subjects of inquiry, which, like a text, requires interpretation, and is open to differing interpretations. And this domain cannot be stripped bare of the interpretations of its subjects, their self-understandings, which in turn may diverge. The picture that emerges from this conception is of culture not as a seamless and coherent web of beliefs and meanings but of a 'loose baggy monster', which is ragged, permeable, open to continual reinterpretation, and eclectic in its sources and the directions in which it is taken.[20]

This view of culture as the domain of self-interpreting animals, of course, forms part of Charles Taylor's conception of identity. If my identity is in part constituted by my self-interpretation for this account, it does not follow that it is purely subjective, in the sense that I can make up whatever identity I please for myself. For Taylor, it will be recalled, any adequate conception of the person must include reference to those frameworks of meaning that can only be acquired and maintained in a linguistic community. As self-interpreting creatures, we forge our identities only in 'webs of interlocution': 'I am a self only in relation to certain interlocutors: in one way in relation to those conversation partners who were essential to my achieving self-definition; in another in relation to those who are now crucial to my continuing grasp of languages of self-understanding' (Taylor 1989: 36). Human purposes and feelings are inseparable from the vocabulary in which we articulate them. The significance of situations for a person and range of possible reactions is conditioned by the character of the vocabulary with which one characterizes and articulates them. The full definition of a person's identity requires an account of these background conditions, which Taylor suggests that we can refer to as that person's culture 'in one possible use of this rather overworked term' (Taylor 1995: 136; compare, from various perspectives on the politics of multiculturalism, Taylor 1994: 239–40; Raz 1994: 162; Benhabib 2002: 6; J. Johnson 2000: 410; Parekh 2000: 142–3). Language and vocabulary have as their referents not only natural language – such as French, which is promoted in Quebecois legislation (Taylor 1995: 243–8) – but a broader, more socially embedded sense 'covering not only the words we speak, but also other modes of expression whereby we define ourselves, including the "languages" of art, of gesture, of love, and the like' (Taylor 1995: 230). In specifying my identity, I need to make reference to these background languages and to the webs of interlocution or 'significant others' who are essential to my self-interpretation.

This fleshes out the cultural thesis, then, by viewing culture as the background framework of meanings that provide the materials for a person's self-interpretation: my identity is formed through self-interpretation, and self-interpretation is necessarily interpretation of the resources of my culture. The importance of my culture to my identity does not derive from my happening to take the view that my culture is important to me, since my self-interpretation, no matter what its particular content, draws on the resources of my culture (cf. MacIntyre 1981: 205; Sandel 1982: 179). Further, the shared meanings that form the cultural background are not fixed, but are vulnerable to change through the process of interpretation, since it is constituted by the interpretations of its subjects. The picture that emerges is of a shared social world as an intersubjective fabric woven from shared meanings which persist and change, and whose content we assent to or dispute, as we negotiate their interpretation both internally and with others.

One may object to the significance accorded self-interpretation on this account. Is self-interpretation a universal phenomenon, or does it itself rest on a normative ideal or require a peculiar psychological disposition (cf. Flanagan 1990)? The question I want to raise, however, is more specific to the line of inquiry here, and concerns the second part of the claim: that my self-interpretation necessarily requires or draws on my culture. This is not to say that my culture is the only source that I draw on, but rather that it cannot be eliminated from any adequate self-description, in the sense of an account of what frames the concepts and categories through which I view the world, my motivations, what appears salient to me, and so on. One feature of identifying culture with this background language is that this seems to create a distinctive problem for the definition of cultural identity. For establishing what *counts* as a significant web of interlocution for a person, and the character and boundaries of that web, is in part what the activity of self-interpretation is concerned with. On the one hand, we cannot rest with the individual's assessment of what her cultural identity is, for it is meant to be an interpretation, which is sensitive to something outside her own assessment. In the previous section, I outlined (following Rorty and Wong (1990) seven ways in which we may judge an identity trait to be important, of which the last is a person's inability to view herself as being the same person without that trait. We can see now that, in spite of the significance attached to self-interpretation on this account, this semiotic conception need not hold that the importance of a trait is defined wholly by reference to how a person herself views it. For any view or interpretation is open to correction, and aims to be responsive to something outside the person's own judgement. On the other hand, what that background is, is not independent of her interpretation, and of the interpretations of others. To answer the question 'Who am I?' by saying, for example, 'I am Quebecois' is to offer a (challengeable) interpretation of a conception of identity built up from the (challengeable) intersubjective interpretations of one's interlocutors: what it means to be Quebecois, including the criteria for belonging, is a subject susceptible to reinterpretation (is it religion, a language, a shared heritage, a political identity, some combination of these?). From the hermeneutic standpoint, this difficulty is not a deficiency, since this delicate process of intersubjective negotiation is precisely its approved route to understanding meaning. Given the tendency of the normative and societal accounts to gloss over intra-cultural disagreement, the fact that this account offers a model for understanding it constitutes a particular strength.

In summary, then, I have identified three principal ways in which the concept of culture has been elaborated in order to fill out the cultural thesis:

culture as a set of normative standards, societal culture, and culture as a set of semiotic elements and practices. As noted at the outset, it is not my intention to offer an appraisal of which, if any, of these corresponds to the singular truth about culture: the notion is too riven and ambiguous for this kind of judgement to make sense. A final point about the politics of these conceptions is worth making in the light of the previous discussion, however. The societal conception identifies what is significant about culture for identity with an institutional base together with a set of semiotic practices; the semiotic conception identifies what is significant with those practices; and the normative conception identifies what is significant with the norms and values that a cultural identity gives us. While analytically distinguishable, these different conceptions can shade into one another: particular languages and vocabularies make plausible and implausible certain evaluative positions, institutions can foster languages and norms, and so on.[21] So on the ground, so to speak, a claim for 'the significance of cultural identity' may bundle together these conceptions.[22]

They offer us different accounts of what is significant about culture for the self, and pull in different political directions. Each conception of culture takes as central or paradigmatic a different kind of political claim. For the normative conception, what are central are religious claims or normative claims of a particular way of life. The societal conception takes as central the claims of well-established national minorities to strengthen their political autonomy. The semiotic conception is undoubtedly more diffuse in its implications, and does not wear its political implications on its sleeve, as do the other two accounts. Yet what it draws attention to is what, I have argued, the other two conceptions tend to neglect or repress: namely, the contestable and negotiable character of cultural identity.

## 3.   Disagreement and Construction

Emphasizing the contestable and negotiable character of cultural identity may appear to threaten the cultural thesis. If we view cultures as 'made up of negotiable, replaceable stuff, more patched together and reassembled than woven of the same cloth' (Ivison 2002: 36), we may worry that the cultural thesis requires a different and contradictory view, cultural essentialism. An essentialist view of culture is one that takes a culture to consist in a set of fixed characteristics that unchangeably inhere in particular individuals, and which parcel them out into particular groups. This undoubtedly has formed an influential, and now widely criticized, way of thinking about culture and human identity.[23] For the essentialist, the importance of culture (or some other aspect of identity) derives in part from its fixed and unchanging character, to recall one of the different dimensions along which centrality of an identity trait may be gauged. This view cuts across the three conceptions already described: we may adopt an essentialist view of culture, whether we adopt a normative, societal or semiotic account of what is important about it.[24] The cultural thesis is *compatible* with cultural essentialism, in the sense that there is no inconsistency in believing that culture is significant for selfhood and thinking of that culture as a set of fixed characteristics unchangeably inhering in a person. Cultural essentialism may also give some support to the cultural thesis in the following way. If we think of what is fixed and unchangeable about a person as being particularly important to her identity, then an essentialist view of culture gives us a reason to think of it as important. Yet the premiss that what is fixed and unchanging about a person is necessarily of particular importance seems doubtful (consider, say, shoe size). Furthermore, proponents of the cultural thesis have been keen to distance themselves from cultural essentialism (for example, Tully 1995: 10–14; 2002a: 104–5; Parekh 2000: 77–9 and ch. 5; Carens 2000: 52ff), in favour of a view of culture as a more mutable, contested and interactive entity. The issue, however, is not what proponents of the cultural thesis claim or assert, but whether in fact the cultural thesis commits them to essentialism in spite of themselves.

I want to assess the distance of the cultural thesis from essentialism by looking at a line of criticism of the latter. This is the claim that arguments for the significance of culture for identity overlook the politics of cultural identification. As Chandran Kukathas puts it, 'the most seductive and dangerous move [in the politics of identity] asserts that identity is *not* political but, somehow, natural or original. But identity is not natural, or original, or permanent, or even necessarily particularly enduring. It is fluid, ever-changing (to varying degrees) and inescapably political' (Kukathas 1997b: 150). To set this out in a different way: cultural identities have histories, and these histories are in part the histories of deliberate attempts to mould and exploit identities, and of responses to those attempts (Carrithers 1992: 8–9). This line of criticism stresses, first, that identities are subject to intra-cultural disagreement and transformation, and, second, that they may be understood as the upshot of historical processes of construction. Both these points are damaging to cultural essentialism. The first subverts the claim that culture consists in a set of fixed and incontrovertible characteristics, and the second subverts the claim that cultural identity unchangeably inheres in individuals or groups. In this section, I want to set out reasons why these objections to essentialism do not constitute objections to the cultural thesis.

The first objection rests on an observation that I have already mentioned in discussing the three different accounts of culture: namely, the empirical fact of intra-cultural disagreement about the character of a culture. It draws the conclusion from this that specific interpretations of an identity – what that identity involves or requires, its interests and demands – tend in a significant range of cases to be so contested as to be indeterminate. If cultural identity is so indeterminate, then it cannot be a significant part of an account of practical identity or selfhood. The specification of the 'needs' or 'requirements' of some identity tends to end up in the hands of the most vociferous political leaders: the cultural thesis seems to 'appeal to the poetics of idealized cultural identity without fully acknowledging the ways that characterizing the "identity" of a culture is itself a politically and ideologically charged issue', which 'disguises the powerful intracultural politics of determining the right of authoritative description' (A. O. Rorty 1994: 152, 158). In other words, proponents of multiculturalism blithely invoke, for example, Jewish or Muslim identity and discuss its distinctive features and requirements with little sense of the extent to which there exists disagreement over what that identity in fact is, and how that disagreement is the subject of political struggle within the group. Who is to say what it means to be a Serbian, Inuit, Muslim or Tamil? Do Pueblo or Hasidic women have the same interests derived from their cultural identity as their husbands, brothers or fathers? How central are certain practices (speaking Welsh, wearing the headscarf, arranged marriages) to a given identity? A further fascinating example is the dispute among the Ngarrindjeri people of South Australia over the authenticity of a belief in women's secret 'business' or 'knowledge', a dispute compounded by the reluctance of proponents of this belief to enter into the dispute on the grounds that to do so would be to flout the belief in question (Kenny 1996; Kukathas 2003: 33; Deveaux 2000b: 95–7).

Yet the empirical fact of disagreement about the content of a cultural identity, even in its most persistent and political forms, does not demonstrate that a cultural identity has no determinate character. First, disagreement does not imply that there is nothing for competing views of an identity to be views *of*, or that no view is *better* than any other. This objection adopts what pragmatists call a spectator's point of view with respect to this conflict of interpretations (H. Putnam 1995). If a cultural identity is simply indeterminate, then disputes over how to characterize an identity are literally pointless, and what appears to protagonists as this kind of dispute is not. Those Ngarrindjeri who support the authenticity of the belief in gender-segregated knowledge are simply of one opinion, while those who oppose it are of another, and each side is mistaken in imagining that its own point of view is better than that of the other side. Now some cases may be indeterminate, in the sense that there is no better or worse view. But the empirical fact of disagreement is not in itself a sufficient reason to hold this. Nor does the fact that different views of a cultural identity express different social interests, or that debates (and non-debates) express power relations, mean that the content of a cultural identity is wholly indeterminate. What we mean by a 'better' interpretation in the case of cultural identity is open to epistemological dispute, however, and our criteria for a better interpretation may well be evaluative. Consider, for example, the claim of the Croatian anti-war activist and feminist Stasja Zajovic that 'national militarists have appropriated our cultural heritage. I believe that we can redefine (it) so that we do not renounce our women's heritage, but retain a sense of belonging *based on choice, not on imposition*' (emphasis in original, cited in Jaggar 1999: 322). What would make hers a better interpretation of her cultural heritage is in part its conforming to ethical standards that are flouted by rivals. There may be other interpretations that are better by other criteria, and there may be arguments over which criteria should be given most credence.

It is worth noting that this objection undermines not only an affirmative or reformist stance toward the claims of identity, but also a more radical critical rejection of an identity on the grounds that this identity has some determinate but repugnant characteristics that merit rejection. A possible response to this is that such a radical line of criticism does not have to rely on specifying determinate features of an identity. Rather, the critic need only highlight the oppressive consequences of the identity, or the power that some have of imposing a conception of the cultural identity that has those consequences, in order to make her point. The difficulty with this response is that the critic still needs to show that those consequences are consequences of that identity, and not of something else. For example, an argument that the beliefs and practices of a religion imply the subordination of women, or have the effect of subordinating women, requires a determinate account of what those beliefs and practices are, in order to identify the religion in the source of subordination. Nevertheless, this first objection cautions us against a common pitfall of multicultural political theory, in accepting at face value any particular account of what a cultural identity is or requires.

The other objection starts from the claim that cultural identities are constructed. This claim has been pressed from rather different directions in social and political theory, including rational choice theory, Marxism, network theory and postmodernism.[25] We can tentatively suggest that what these critical standpoints share is a view of cultural identity as the upshot of the interaction of conflicting social forces. James Johnson, for example, argues that symbols and cultural practices possess 'an inescapable strategic dimension', in which actors struggle to control symbols in order to promote their political ends among those who share these symbols. Cultural identities emerge and are maintained as part of the 'struggle for power over others, a strategic contest to control the symbols and cultural practices in terms of which social and political actors envision possibilities and fashion them into viable alternatives' (J. Johnson 2000: 412). Symbols and cultural practices, then, are contested, since they are vital in establishing who is and is not 'one of us' (cf. P. Gilbert 2000: 39–40; Hardin 1995), for example. But this is not simply a matter of applying clear-cut criteria; rather, the criteria and their application at any given point are a product of the play of social forces which attempt to impose a particular vision of society, community or group (J. Johnson 2002: 215).

Constructionism emphasizes the invention of cultural traditions, and their formation through political processes. For example, one context for this is the interaction of colonial government and the colonized:

> The British wrongly believed that Tanganyikans belonged to tribes; Tanganyikans created tribes to function within the colonial framework . . . [The] new political geography would have been transient had it not coincided with similar trends among Africans. They too had to live amidst bewildering social complexity, which they ordered in kinship terms and buttressed with invented history. Moreover, Africans wanted effective units of action just as officials wanted effective units of government . . . Europeans believed Africans belonged to tribes; Africans built tribes to belong to. (Iliffe 1979: 324, cited in Ranger 1992: 252)

Further examples abound. Fijian norms governing land and chiefly authority are the product of a deal brokered between indigenous chiefs and the British colonial government (Carens 2000: 200–59; J. Johnson 2002). The pre-colonial kingdom of Burundi consisted of clans of various ethnic groups bound together in clientelist relationships. The systematic support of the Tutsi elites by the Belgian colonial administration replaced trans-ethnic clientelism with an intra-ethnic clientelism, as the Tutsis began to discriminate in their own favour and against the Hutu majority (Wimmer 2002: 94). The meaning and status of *sati*, or the immolation of widows, as purportedly central to Hindu tradition 'emerges out of negotiations between British colonial and local Indian elites' (Benhabib 2002: 6). The policy of disenfranchising Canadian native women who marry non-status Indian or non-Indian men is a product of the entrenchment of patriarchal norms in Canada's 1869 Indian Act, rather than a primordial tradition (Deveaux 2000a: 527). A second significant context, already alluded to in the discussion of societal culture, is that of nation building, as languages, festivities and religious traditions are invented or adapted in order to define a national culture – for example, with the Victorian invention of the immemorial traditions of the royal coronation in Great Britain (Cannadine 1992).

In this case too we can accept the constructionist characterization of cultural identity without drawing the sceptical conclusion about the cultural thesis. One basis for thinking that constructionism provides a reason for thinking that cultural identity cannot count as a significant element in selfhood rests on the thought that the latter claim requires cultural identity to be fixed, while constructionism shows up this idea as false. But this simply presumes that the cultural thesis must be essentialist, and this is what is at issue. To hold that it provides such a reason is to assume that the *explanandum* of a constructionist explanation cannot form a significant part of a person's identity: but to hold that identities have histories does not undermine a claim for their importance to individuals. As with the argument from disagreement, to draw a sceptical conclusion from constructionism robs the *practice* of construction of its point. For the practice of struggling over symbols and cultural practices, as Johnson puts it, relies on there being something at stake: that the outcomes of these struggles make a significant difference to the people concerned, redefining 'within limits . . . their options and identities' (J. Johnson 2000: 410). But this seems to be another way of saying that what is being struggled over is the definition of the practical identity of those involved.

Perhaps the key claim is that an identity does not have the origins that it purports to have, and which are necessary for someone to identify with it. What makes it legitimate for those who identify with it is its immemorial past, and this sense of the legitimacy of the identity cannot withstand the revelation of its constructed origins. A common thread in constructionism is the project of unmasking the historical character of cultural identities that present themselves as ahistorical or at least as the products of a far more glorious and generally older history than in fact they have. Cultural essentialists can be charged with disingenuousness by constructionists: what the former present as unchanging features of people are in reality the products of contingent historical forces. Perhaps, then, a similar disingenuousness or craftiness attaches to proponents of the cultural thesis. As Amélie Rorty and David Wong put it, '[a]ttributions of identity are standardly declarative speech acts. But even when such attributions are true, they perform numerous functions besides reporting what is true' (Rorty and Wong 1990: 33). After all, there is an indefinite number of true things that could be said about a person. What makes culture or an aspect of culture seem salient to proponents of the cultural thesis, we may think, is the specific kind of political project that they wish to promote. An apparently general argument for the significance of cultural identity is in fact an argument directed toward a specific audience which hopes to encourage them to view their cultural identity (or some aspect of it, such as language) as particularly important or integral to them. 'It is sometimes difficult to decide whether to chide the disingenuousness of philosophers detaching analyses of identity from the highly specific contexts in which they arise or to admire the rhetorical ingenuity of their masks of neutrality' (Rorty and Wong 1990: 34; cf., on Kymlicka, Markell 2003: 155).[26]

This is also an important challenge. Cultural claims may be ideological, in the pejorative sense.[27] They may mask and act as a convenient rationale for the unjustified self-assertion of some groups. Proponents of the cultural thesis should not find themselves in the position of supporting any and every claim for the significance of culture for a person's identity, still less (as I will argue) holding that every such claim imposes reasons or obligations on either members or non-members of a culture. But it is a different issue whether the discourse of cultural identity as a whole is simply an instrument of particular political projects. One response to this is a kind of generalised *tu quoque*. It is not of course only cultural forms of identity attribution that carry pragmatic force. Talk of identity in quite other terms (say, economic class, race or citizenship) or the attempt to eschew talk about identity altogether may well be yoked to various sorts of social and political project. And there is nothing in the fact that these forms of identity attribution are *not* cultural that makes them inherently less vulnerable to unmasking or to their being deployed for repugnant political goals than the cultural thesis. Finally, the importance attached to cultural identity by some writers may make sense only in context: they reflect, contribute to, and sometimes mould a consciousness of culture as a dimension of social, personal and political importance. But this is not to say that they simply create this consciousness out of nothing. Rather, they draw attention to the importance of a dimension of social life that has become politically important in particular societies at particular times.

## 4.   Distance and Endorsement

The relationship of beliefs such as these about the ontological character of identity to evaluative claims is intricate and unclear.[28] One can accept the thesis that individuality is socially constituted, while still advancing an ethical or political individualism in which individual rights outweigh the demands of the collective good. Alternatively, one can subscribe to the ontological picture of pre-societal individuality, while advancing a political theory in which the interests of particular individuals are subordinate to the requirements of society, as in, for example, some versions of utilitarianism. I want to set out some more specific reasons for not collapsing the distinction between evaluative and ontological claims in this instance. First, there is a gap, which needs bridging, between the claim about the cultural character of the embedded self and a claim about the value or respect that is owed to a cultural identity. As Parekh puts it, for example, 'since human beings are culturally embedded, respect for them entails respect for their cultures and ways of life' (Parekh 1994: 13).[29] So 'if you attack my culture, you attack me . . . in a way that goes to the heart of who I am' (Kelly 2002b: 7; cf. Tully 1995: 189–91). The temptation to pursue this line of argument is understandable. It combines a moral premiss with apparently impeccable liberal credentials with the cultural thesis, in support of the intuition that 'misrecognition' of a cultural identity in some way harms the person whose identity is not recognized.[30]

However, we need to spell out the moral premiss of the respect argument in a lot more detail before the conclusion becomes plausible. On the face of it, the requirement of respect for persons, in conjunction with a claim about cultural embeddedness of the self, does not establish that we should respect a person's culture. For it requires an explanation of why someone's having the practical identity that she has imposes reasons or obligations on others. Even if some projects and goals are important to her (her stamp collection, for instance), it does not follow that they are important for others, or should matter to them (cf. Geuss 1996). This is a broad question about normativity, but the point to hold on to is that the same issue arises when invoking culture as an aspect of practical identity. For, first, a culture may not itself display equal respect to its members, along some other significant dimension (as when a culture dictates that women are subordinate to men, or the young to elders). And, second, it is not obvious that respect for a person is necessarily displayed in deferring to whatever her cultural identity is taken to imply or require, rather than in criticizing or rejecting it: for example, in those cases where it is argued that an identity demands that the education of a particular group's children take a different and perhaps more limited form in comparison with that of the rest of the population. Of course, as I have emphasized *ad nauseam* by this point, we can *argue* about what is involved in this identity, what is compatible with it, what it requires, and so on. But we should not prejudge either way what such a process of argument will arrive at. There may be cases, in other words, in which respect for a person – including for other social aspects of her practical identity – requires rejecting the putative demands of her culture. More needs to be said, then, about what is valuable about cultural identity, before evaluative conclusions of this sort emerge: the following chapter traces some of the main lines of argument.

Another approach that may be made here is that in specifying the content of someone's identity, the cultural thesis offers an account of some of the reasons on which a person should act. This may seem more plausible than the first approach, in as much as my *having* a cultural identity may seem to offer some determinate reasons for action for me, whereas my acknowledgement of someone else's cultural identity does not. These identity-based reasons are reasons to fulfil obligations and follow practices held to be internal to the cultural identity: to eschew *franglais* for pure French, marry within the group, practise a particular religion, and so on. There may of course be dispute about how to interpret these requirements (is a Jew required by virtue of that identity to be a critic of the aberrations of the state of Israel or to refrain from criticizing them, or neither?), and to claim that there exist such reasons may be compatible with a great deal of intra-cultural criticism and dissent (cf. Parekh 2000: 159–60). In articulating these 'reasons and obligations', there may be different degrees and shades of normativity involved (some practices are required, others forbidden, others desirable, to be expected, frowned upon, held to be characteristic but foolish, etc.). But the general question is what may legitimately be inferred from the ascription of a cultural identity to someone about the reasons and obligations applying to her.

In this case too there are good grounds not to collapse the ontological and normative claims, and to treat the latter as in need of further justification, even if we establish the former to our satisfaction.[31] One reason for separating the ascription of a cultural identity to me and an account of what it is I ought to do is that there may be, and commonly is, conflict among the different interests and duties prescribed by various social roles and identities. The demands and interests of citizenship, parenthood, religion, profession and so on, along with those of some cultural identity, may pull in different directions, requiring an individual to step back from particular roles and re-evaluate the interests and demands that they present. Indeed, such conflicts are salient within the polit-ical theory of multiculturalism. For instance, the putative or prima facie demands of citizenship may clash with those of cultural identity, as in the 'headscarves' controversy, or demands of religion conflict with those of pro-fession (as in the claims of some groups to alter the working week for their members).[32] Talk of 'stepping back' seems to invoke the 'passive fantasy of unfilled space' or a 'view from nowhere'. But it is not clear that critical reflection requires unfilled space, only space that isn't filled by the particular aspect of an identity that is under consideration.

For this first objection, the tugs of a particular cultural identity may never-theless retain force as reasons. The reasons that a cultural identity furnishes may at best be of a prima facie or *pro tanto* sort, and may be outweighed by other reasons (Hurley 1989: 130–5). Prima facie reasons evaporate, so to speak, when confronted with stronger considerations; so my reason to shop for guacamole disappears when I discover that I already have some. A *pro tanto* reason has a residual force, even in the face of overriding considerations for the agent; if I promise to help you move house, the force of this reason does not evaporate even when some more compelling reason for me to act appears (say, there is something interesting to watch on television).

A stronger consideration suggests that even reasons with this more provi-sional status do not adhere to identities. Some predicates that are true of people may carry built-in 'escape interests', as Keith Graham calls them, reasons for a person to rid herself of the predicate, which eclipse any more confined interest arising from the fact that it is true of her: the interest in ceasing to be a slave, for example, eclipses interests associated with continuing to be a slave, such as staying on good terms with your owner. Such a role can legitimately be described as part of a person's practical identity, in the sense that it grounds some reasons for action for that person, but 'these limited interests, as it were, are in effect displaced by an overriding interest in shedding the characteristics in question' (Graham 2002: 114). Now we may accept that some predicates attached to a person's social identity (slave, concentration camp inmate) can carry built-in escape interests, while being chary about applying this notion to cultural identity. Clearly some kinds of social identity can be so obnoxious as to carry with them escape interests, but is this true of cultural identities? Again, I would argue that the cultural thesis, the position that culture is an important ingredient in identity, does not provide the resources to settle this. Consider a radical line of criticism of a culture. For example, if a particular cultural identity is seen as entailing a set of reasons and obligations that subordinate women to men, then there is an overriding reason for women not to have that identity (Okin 1999: 12). The reasons and obligations attaching to the identity are not then best viewed as supplying a set of reasons to act for women in that group, which just happens to be over-ridden by another sort of reason, in the way that a trivial consideration is trumped by a more important or urgent one. Rather, if the evaluation is right, then the first set of reasons has no grip at all on the women (and men) concerned. Here too it is possible to argue about the character of the culture, but that is not the core issue. The point is only that there is nothing in the cultural thesis to block the idea that sometimes cultures may be obnoxious in this way. Acknowledgement of the possible interest in escape drives a wedge between the ontological claim about the constitution of identity and the thesis that having a cultural identity means having reasons to fulfil the obligations and follow the practices claimed to be internal to that cultural identity. No less than an external attitude of respect, an internal attitude of endorsement or compliance requires evaluative justification.

One response here is that we should view practical identity as including only those features of a person that she actually endorses. For Anthony Laden, for instance, a practical identity 'consists of those things about myself that I value and regard as grounding my obligations'. Terms such as practical identity 'imply a form of endorsement on the part of the agent to whom they are ascribed' (Laden 2003: 145).[33] For the perspective developed here, these features are only a subset of a person's practical identity: a practical identity may include elements that a person does not endorse, perhaps does not even see: my consciousness may need raising about those features of an identity that ground reasons of which I am unaware or of which I am aware but do not see as grounding reasons. As I have argued in the last two sections, this does not imply an objective conception of identity wholly independent of my own interpretation, but it does suggest that my own judgement is not definitive.[34] Further, for the perspective developed here, even my endorse-ment may not in itself ground reasons: I endorse those things about myself because I take them to be valuable – and I can be wrong both about what those things are (how to characterize them, what is significant about them), and about their being valuable.

Stressing the distinctness of the constitutive argument and more specific evaluative conclusions is not to say that the former is irrelevant to the latter or (with Richard Rorty) a dispensable adornment (R. Rorty 1991: 179, 197–8). For the evaluative or political arguments make ontological claims: to argue that respecting me entails respecting my culture makes a claim about who I am; similarly, to argue that there are reasons for you to cherish and support your cultural identity suggests that you have such a thing, and that it has some significant relationship to who you are. What is needed is a clearer specification of the grounds for respecting a cultural identity, and these argu-ments are discussed in the following chapter.

## 5.   Conclusion

In this chapter I have tried to make sense of the claim that culture is an important constitutive component of an individual's identity. The dominant accounts of the significance of culture for contemporary political theory, which I called the normative, the societal and the semiotic, attach themselves to rather different sets of problems and concerns. I argued that the cultural thesis does not fall foul of the charge of cultural essentialism and become enmeshed in Benhabib's paradoxes, since it is compatible with disagreement, interpretation, challenge and negotiation over cultural identities, and is not undermined by the historical and constructed character of cultural identity.

# 2

## Culture and Normativity

The attempt to offer an account of the value of cultural identity is one of the striking and distinctive features of the recent surge of interest in issues of cultural diversity in political theory. The claim that cultural identity, or *my* cultural identity, warrants respect is now familiar. To assert that some practice is 'part of one's culture' is a well-worn step in arguments in the public defence of a practice. Behind this move is the thought that there is a reason for valuing or permitting this practice which lies in its status as an expression of the cultural identity of practitioners, and that this cultural identity should carry normative weight in political deliberation. Political philosophers have developed arguments that try to underpin this intuition about the normative status of culture. According to Joseph Raz, cultural groups have a 'moral claim to respect and to prosperity' (Raz 1994: 178). Charles Taylor proposes as a 'presumption' or 'something like an act of faith' that we owe equal respect to all cultures (Taylor 1995: 250–2). More cautiously, he argues that, although some individual rights must be applied universally, we should be 'willing to weigh up the importance of some forms of uniform treatment against cultural survival and opt sometimes in favour of the latter' (Taylor 1995: 248). Bhikhu Parekh also argues for a provisional and fallible judgement that each culture is owed respect: '[s]ince every culture gives stability and meaning to human life, holds its members together as a community, displays creative energy, and so on, it deserves respect' (Parekh 2000: 176–7). Others argue that the exercise of the liberal value of autonomy is intimately tied up with the individual's secure possession of a cultural identity, which provides a reason, within a liberal political morality, to respect that identity. What proponents of the 'respect for culture' position share is a belief that cultural identity is *normative*, in the sense that it provides a reason to act toward its possessor in a particular way.

Sceptics demur. For them, the appeal to 'culture' is decoration that adds nothing to the validity of an argument for or against some practice. There are various grounds for this scepticism. One source is, naturally enough, a critical assessment of the different positive arguments for the value of culture. This leaves the appeal to culture as nothing more than a brute appeal to things always having been done a particular way, as Barry insists: 'the appeal to "culture" establishes nothing. Some cultures are admirable, others are vile. Reasons for doing things that can be advanced within the former tend to be good, and reasons that can be advanced within the latter will tend to be bad. But in neither case is something's being part of a culture itself a reason for doing anything' (Barry 2001: 258).

In the previous chapter, I argued that we should not conflate a claim for the importance of culture for practical identity with a claim that culture should be held to be valuable. In this chapter I try to provide an overview of arguments for the value of cultural identity. In section 1, I make some points about the scope of such arguments and about the underlying conceptions of value employed. In sections 2 and 3, I consider a range of arguments based respectively on non-individualist and individualist accounts of the value of culture. In sections 4 and 5 I pay special attention to two of the most prominent lines of the individualist case: the argument that cultural recognition constitutes a vital human need and the argument that culture is an essential condition for the possession and exercise of the capacity for individual choice.

## I.   Preliminaries

An initial point is that we should be cautious about what we take a successful argument for the value of cultural identity to establish. There is a distinction between a successful argument for the normativity of cultural identity (if, *pace* the sceptic, such a thing exists) and a successful argument for some right of recognition or policy to defend or promote a cultural identity, such as the entitlements claimed for exemption, assistance, self-government, the enforcement of external or internal rules, the recognition of a traditional legal code, special representation or symbolic recognition, in the various circumstances in which these can be made.[1] For there may be strong reasons to grant rights such as these in the absence of any claim about the normativity of cultural identity. A state may grant differentiated rights purely for reasons of stability and order: for example, in order to buy off the leadership of a group or to forestall a reactionary or separatist response on the part of a group that believes itself under threat. This basis for granting differentiated rights has different implications from arguments based on respect for cultural identity. For example, the dominant strand of jurisprudential reasoning about the rationale for Canadian bilingualism views this policy as a compromise, the product of a deal struck between the two major linguistic powers, English and French (Réaume 2000: 255, 258–60, 272n). The entitlement for treatment as an official language, then, is based on the political support that each language has mustered historically. Similarly, the recognition of eleven official languages in the 1993 and 1996 South African constitutions can be understood as the upshot of political negotiations in which the African National Congress had a cautious and qualified commitment to English as a politically unifying language, whereas the Afrikaans community had an unqualified commitment to the official status of Afrikaans as a non-negotiable element in the transition of South Africa to democracy (Heugh 2002). As a normative account of the grounds for recognition, this is open to a well-known objection: that to base rights and policies solely on the product of a bargain designed to reach a stable *modus vivendi* disadvantages those with little bargaining strength. A corollary of this understanding of the rationale for legal or political recognition is that languages that have not mustered such support are cut out of this compromise, and that, when the balance of forces changes, there is no reason for the majority, or other powerful group, to refrain from asserting its will.

Furthermore, there may be reasons grounded in considerations of justice or citizenship for or against culturally sensitive policies and rights that do not themselves rest on a premiss about the normativity of culture. For example, some liberal philosophers argue that a just state ought to adopt a neutral posture with regard to specific conceptions of the good of its citizens, in the sense that an assessment of the intrinsic value of these conceptions should not form any part of the rationale for state policy. In other words, the state ought to be indifferent to the normativity of conceptions of the good, for reasons of justice. If we accept that the state ought to insulate itself from some normative considerations, or is entitled to do so, we can see that accepting the normativity of culture does not in itself pre-empt the case for the politics of universalism.[2] A second line of argument is that the state ought to promote a dominant cultural identity, in order to promote such goods as stability, justice, social trust and democracy. It is not the case that the state should eschew cultural policies; rather, these should take the form of an attempt to bolster and construct a specific national identity, and to protect it from corrosive influences. So we may acknowledge the normativity of a variety of cultural identities within a state, but still have good reason to neglect or undermine them in the interest of pursuing more fundamental civic goods: from a political point of view, we may think, the national identity is paramount.[3] There are difficulties with each of these lines of argument. But the position that each represents is intelligible: that the state should not implement policies of recognition, since the demands of justice or citizenship override the claims of cultural identity.

Finally, it is not the case that recognition or differentiated policies, if they are based on grounds other than the search for a stable *modus vivendi*, must rest on an account of the normativity of culture. The schedule of differentiated rights and policies does not in every case require either that the subject granted the right be (a member of) a culturally defined group or that the justification for granting that right rests on consideration of that subject's cultural identity. For example, affirmative action policies directed toward African Americans in the United States do not require that this group be culturally defined, and the justification for these policies typically does not rest on an account of the need to respect or promote the cultural identity of that group. Even where a group can be defined by reference to a distinctive culture, the justification of the special rights or policy need not make reference to the value of the group's cultural identity. For example, a 'just cause' argument for granting a group self-government rights may rest on the group's having been the victim of serious violations of basic human rights: if their current polity is either grossly violating this group's rights or failing to protect them against this violation, the argument runs, then this group has a well-grounded claim to secede from that polity or for some other sort of self-government right (Buchanan 1991; Norman 1998; M. Moore 2001). This is an argument that has been made, for example, with respect to the largely Albanian province of Kosovo in former Yugoslavia. Yet, for this argument to be successful, the group itself need not be culturally defined, and respect for its culture need play no part in the rationale for granting this right (cf. P. Gilbert 2000: 196). These different lines of argument for affirmative action and self-government need to be fleshed out, of course: my point here is only that the justification for a group-differentiated right or policy does not need to make the claim that there is some reason to respect the culture of the group to whom it is granted.

Two cross-cutting distinctions in the theory of value have played a significant role in treatments of culture's normativity (J. Johnson 2000: 407; Mason 2000: 42–5). The first is that between individualist and non-individualist arguments. By an individualist argument, I mean one that subscribes to the belief that only individuals and individual interests possess normative standing. Negatively, as Barry puts it, this individualist principle 'rules out appeals on behalf of God, Nature, History, Culture, the Glorious Dead, the Spirit of the Nation or any other entity unless that claim can somehow be reduced to terms in which only individual human interests appear' (Barry 1991a: 159; Tamir 1993: 84). Objects, practices, institutions, ways of life and so on may have value, but they do not have moral standing; their value derives from the ways in which they make individual lives go better (Mason 2000: 42). If cultures possess value, then, it derives from their serving the interests of their members, and perhaps of other individuals too, but not from any residual element which exists once we have subtracted this service: 'insisting that we should be fair to cultures merely as cultures is like insisting that we should be fair to paintings or to languages or to musical compositions. These things may have value, but they do not have moral standing' (Jones 1998: 36).[4] By contrast, non-individualist arguments claim that there are social entities which possess a value that is distinguishable from the value that they have for particular individuals. Entities, groups or social relationships can have a value that is not reducible to the value that they have for particular individuals. Set up this way, non-individualism is a broad category. Of course, a non-individualist is not committed to seeing as valuable *any* non-individual entity or relationship: for example, some sorts of non-individualism seek to establish the value of non-human nature, and others do not. This has bearing here, since in the previous chapter I tried to draw a sharp conceptual distinction between culture and collectivity or group. So, from a non-individualist perspective, one may view groups but not cultures as a source of value, cultures but not groups, or both as sources of value (or indeed neither).

Another distinction, which cuts across the individualist/non-individualist line, is that between instrumental and non-instrumental sources of value.[5] One line of argument aims to establish that we should value culture for its instrumental value: that is, for the value it has in helping to secure some other valued end. The value of a public transport system, for example, lies in its helping people to achieve a goal that we take to be valuable; namely, allowing them to travel reasonably cheaply and conveniently. Non-instrumental value adheres to an object that is not valued as a means to some other valued end, but is itself the end which is valued. Logically, not all value can be instrumental, since for the instrumental object to be valued requires that value adhere to what the instrumentally valued item is instrumental for. But an argument for the instrumental value of something need not seek immediately to show that this thing is tethered to something of non-instrumental value: its instrumental value may lie in its supporting something else that only has instrumental value. An understandably prominent line of argument among liberal political theorists is that cultural identity is to be valued for the sake of its contribution to the well-being or autonomy of individuals, an argument which is both individualist and instrumental. But the instrumental/non-instrumental distinction does not map on to the individual/collective distinction: there are arguments that are both instrumental and collective, and non-instrumental and individual, as well as non-instrumental and collective. Further, the notion of instrumentality here needs to be handled with some care, since it shades into a third category of value. Valuing something on the grounds that it serves as a means to something else is not the same as valuing it on the grounds that it is a necessary condition or for something else or a constitutive part of it. So (to anticipate a little) if we argue that something is valuable since it is a necessary condition for the individual capacity for choice, we do not take an instrumental view of that thing, since, logically, nothing else can ground the capacity for choice. But what we value it *for* is its being a necessary condition for this capacity. Furthermore, we can value something as a constitutive part of some other valued good: for instance, physical exercise as a part of health, not merely an instrumental means to it. Both these further conceptions of value play a role in what follows.

Focusing on the claim that a culture possesses normative significance distinguishes the arguments to be examined here from the claim that cultural *diversity* constitutes a collective good. From the latter perspective, cultures should be viewed as precious and hard-won human creations, even those which appear obnoxious to some of us, since we can all benefit from allowing a diversity of cultures to flourish: it is better to have a variety of literatures, cinematic traditions, cuisines, languages and ways of life than a cultural monopoly. This benefit principally derives from the opportunity that such diversity gives individuals to explore other ways of life, which may include enjoying aspects of them, and to reflect on one's own (Tamir 1993: 30; Kymlicka 1995a: 121; Jones 1998: 35; Deveaux 2000b: 34; Parekh 2000: 165, 168). While superficially promising, taken in isolation, this consideration has less force than appears, for four reasons.

The first is that it posits an interest in reflectiveness, or in an appreciation of the variety of the human condition. If we value cultural variety instrumentally, as a condition for individual reflection and breadth of appreciation, then it is not clear what value to attach to a person's cultural identity, when we judge that it hampers or thwarts this capacity. In this vein, Mill notoriously averred that '[n]obody can suppose that it is not more beneficial to a Breton, or a Basque of the French Navarre, to be brought into the current of the ideas and feelings of a highly civilised and cultivated people', rather than being left 'to sulk on his own rocks, the half-savage relic of past times, revolving in his own mental orbit, without participation or interest in the general movement of the world. The same remark applies to the Welshman or the Scottish Highlander as members of the British nation' (J. S. Mill [1861] 1991: 431). If the culture of the great nation provides a context in which the reflectiveness of members is exercised more fully than that of the minority cultural identity, then the value that we attach to reflection and breadth of appreciation directs us not to respect the minority identity but to encourage the assimilation of those who bear it.

The second reason why this argument falls short of providing a ground for respecting cultural identity is that what is valued is not in the first instance any particular identity, but the existence of a sufficient diversity.[6] Provided that overall the conditions of sufficient diversity for the exercise of reflectiveness continue to exist, the decline of some particular cultural identity is of negligible importance, from this point of view. There is a robust version of this in Richard Rorty's assertion that in modern Europe 'we do not miss much the culture of the Ur or of the Chaldees or of pagan Carthage', while '[p]resumably modern Indians do not much miss the cultures that were displaced and gradually extirpated as the Aryan-speaking peoples descended from the North'. This derives from the sense that there is sufficient cultural diversity, so that, given 'the rich pluralism of modern Europe nobody much cares whether the last Gaelic or Breton speakers – or the last rhyme-scheme poets or Palladian architects – die out' (R. Rorty 1998: 194). No particular culture is viewed as a repository of value for this argument: rather, what we value is a system that allows or promotes sufficient diversity for our interests in reflection and appreciation to be satisfied, and that does not require that we value, or mourn the loss of, any particular identity.

Third, emphasizing the importance of reflection and breadth of appreciation is compatible with affirming the instrumental value of cultural *insecurity*: a degree of instability and precariousness may promote reflectiveness about one's identity and engagement with global diversity better than an environment of comfortable familiarity. Finally, some degree of assimilation may serve or promote our interests in reflection and breadth of appreciation. Since very alien cultures can seem irrelevant when considering options and comparing ways of life, and since my culture's accessibility as an option or object of comparison for you relies on its 'translatability' into terms that you can grasp, an argument that rests on an interest in reflection, mutual appreciation and so on can also become a case for a modicum of cultural convergence: a lingua franca, a common code of tourist practice, and familiar fast food restaurants can all make diversity more accessible and manageable for individuals.[7] That the diversity that results has less variety than it would have in the absence of these circumstances is a consideration that needs to be held in the balance for this perspective. The upshot is that we may value cultural diversity as a collective good, then, grounded in the interests of individuals, but this does not provide us with a reason to value any particular cultural identity.

## 2. Culture as a Social Good

In developing an account of what he calls irreducibly social goods, Taylor offers an argument for the non-instrumental value of culture for groups. He does so by advancing two logically independent claims about culture: that culture is an essentially social good, and that culture is constitutive of valued goals. I will explain his argument by discussing each claim in turn. The dominant understanding of collective goods views them as public goods. On standard accounts, public goods are collective by virtue of their non-excludable character, in the sense that if clean air, street lighting or military security is provided for one citizen, this good may readily be provided for all others at no greater cost. But public goods are consumed individually: the good of my finding my way home safely after dark is consumed by me, the good of you finding your way home safely by you. Taylor seeks to distinguish goods consumed in this way from those that essentially can only be enjoyed with others, such as friendship, love, solidarity, community or participation in a culture

(Taylor 1995: 190). Part of what makes the good the particular good that it is lies in its being produced and consumed jointly with others. As Taylor puts it, '[s]ome things have value to me and to you, and some things essentially have value to us' (1995: 190). Denise Réaume calls these participatory goods, and Taylor calls them immediately common or irreducibly social goods (Réaume 1988, 1994, 2000, 2003; Taylor 1995: 137, 190–1). According to Réaume, these are activities that not only require more than one person in order to produce the good, but are valuable only by virtue of the joint involvement of many: the 'publicity of production is part of what is valued – the good *is* the participation'. Among these goods are included, as she puts it, 'core aspects of culture . . . such that each individual needs others in order to enjoy them' (Réaume 1988: 9–10). One illustration of the possibility of this form of value, which has been used by a diverse group of thinkers, is that of an orchestra, for whose members the experience of playing together constitutes the good of playing in it (cf. Marx [1867] 1976: 448–9; Rawls 1972: 523–4n; Searle 1995: 23; Graham 2002: 123–5; cf. Taylor 1995: 191). Similarly, spectators at a football match, unlike those who watch the match alone on television, 'know a good in common that [they] cannot know alone' (Sandel 1982: 183; cf. Taylor 1995: 191), since the good in part consists in their joint participation in the production and consumption of the good of watching the match with others.

The point of this line of argument is that culture, at least in some aspects, should be understood as an irreducibly social good, a good which is necessarily enjoyed only through collective production and consumption: for example, your speaking a language with fellow speakers who are as familiar with the language's nuances as you, or taking part in a ritual such as a wedding ceremony. Were the last living speaker of a disappearing language hooked to a machine which simulated the experience of speaking the language with others, for this account, we would not say that she was enjoying the good of speaking that language: the good lies in participating in the practice, and the practice is essentially social. So far, this is an argument not that cultural identity is in fact valuable, but for the possibility of a non-individualist account of its being valuable. The target is what Taylor takes to be the dominant assumption that individualism (which he calls atomism or welfarism) offers the only acceptable framework in which to mount an argument for the value of culture: but this is insensitive to the possibility of a non-individualist account, and squeezes the diversity of goods into a Procrustean bed.

In the course of describing irreducibly social goods, Taylor distinguishes them from public goods along another dimension, which lies in the relationship that a collective good of this other sort, such as culture, has to the goods that it in turn produces. In the case of public goods, 'these goods could come about by some other means, even though it may be empirically unlikely' (Taylor 1995: 137): issued with torches, each of us could find his or her way home in the absence of street lighting, perhaps. The crucial point is that if we could secure these particular goods through some other method, then this would not detract from them as goods: they would remain the same goods (unflooded crops, a fair view of the road ahead), even if arrived at by a different route. By contrast, Taylor argues, the cultural background that makes 'possible' or 'conceivable' certain goods is a constitutive part of those goods, not merely its 'contingent' causal product. A culture is not, as he puts it, 'a mere instrument of individual goods', since it cannot be 'distinguished from them as their merely contingent condition, something that they could in principle exist without. That makes no sense. It is essentially linked to what we have identified as a good' (Taylor 1995: 137).

The second claim then runs as follows. If you value a good, you have a reason to value its constitutive conditions. The culture that makes possible a good is the (or a?) constitutive condition for the creation of these goods. It follows that if you value the good, you have a reason to value the cultural background that gives rise to it. Given the constitutive relationship of a culture to the goods it makes possible, if we judge that the culture makes possible a certain good, 'it is hard to see how we could deny [the culture] the title of a good': 'If these things are goods, then other things being equal so is the culture that makes them possible. If I want to maximise these goods, then I must want to preserve and strengthen this culture' (Taylor 1995: 137).[8] One sort of case that may fit this argument is that of valuing a cultural product: if you value the movie *The Maltese Falcon*, then part of what you value are the cultural resources that produced it and made it accessible as the good that it is, such as the conventions and idioms of hard-boiled fiction and film. It is not the same good in another language (which is not to say that it may not be a different good), for example.

Taylor refers to the cultural framework as therefore 'intrinsically good', presumably by contrast to such public goods as dams, which are instrumentally good (Taylor 1995: 137).[9] But intrinsic value or goodness – in the sense in which it is contrasted with instrumental value or goodness – usually refers to the property of being 'valuable or good for its own sake', whereas instrumental value consists in being good or valuable for the sake of affairs that the instrumentally valued thing brings about. But this cannot be what Taylor means here, since his claim is that cultures should be valued *for the sake of the goods that they bring about*, as the passage cited above indicates. The crucial idea, which I have tried to capture with the term 'constitutive', is that the background culture is not a substitutable condition for the production of some good; this is distinct from the claim that a culture is a repository of value, irrespective of the value of what it brings about.

As I noted, the constitutive claim and the essentially social claim are distinct, picking out different kinds of value. Shared cultural identity is not the only essentially social good, as the examples of friendship, co-operation and solidarity suggest, while the constitutive claim for culture need not restrict

itself to those goods that are essentially social: it requires a cultural repertoire
to watch a football match (where that is taken to involve some comprehension
of what is going on) at home alone, as well as to take part in a crowd activity.
They overlap where a 'cultural good may . . . exist only to the extent that it is
commonly prized' (Taylor 1995: 140). So we may value a language, for
example, both in the sense that it discloses or makes available certain goods,
such as its distinct corpus of poetry, and itself is an essentially social good for
those who use it. For example, we may think that Catalans should value the
Catalan language 'as a presupposition of the life they value' (constitutive
claim) and as a collective good that exists and can be sought and achieved only
in common (the essentially social claim) (Taylor 1995: 140, 247).

Both these claims are suggestive, but get us less far in attaching value to cultural identity than may appear. To consider the constitutive claim first: we can
accept the claim that there is a logical tie between a good and the cultural
matrix necessary for that good's availability without accepting that valuing the
latter is a sufficient reason for valuing the former. As noted above, Taylor
qualifies this argument: 'If these things are good, then *other things being equal*
so is the culture that makes them possible' (emphasis added). Here, it may be
thought, he is helping himself to the very large assumption that other things
can ever be equal (J. Johnson 2000: 407). According to this argument, if we
value some practice, we should value the cultural matrix that makes that practice accessible as a value. But cultures, as Taylor acknowledges, contain many
elements, including reprehensible features. If some other practice, also constituted by culture C, is horrible, does it follow that this evaluation transfers on
to C? To take another example of Taylor's, this time of culture in what I called
a normative sense: in valuing classical republican conceptions of civic virtue,
we do not have reason to affirm other aspects of republicanism or of the societies in which these values flourished – slavery and the exclusion of women
from public life, for example. If C contains both admirable and vile practices,
as it seems reasonable to hold that most cultures will, then should we value C
or not? Or is it only the appropriately reformed version of the background
culture that we should value?

The other strand of this discussion, the essentially social claim, also falls
short of establishing the value of a cultural identity. While the constitutive
claim actually makes an argument for the value of culture, the essentially
social claim explicates the kind of value a culture may have. If the argument
that is based on the constitutive thesis goes through, then, where we value
some culturally constituted good, we have a reason to value the culture that
constitutes it. The essentially social claim is about the non-individualistic
character of the good which that culture may have, but it gives us no basis for
ascribing that good to the culture. By itself, something's being produced in this
participatory fashion is not sufficient to make it a good: there may be essentially social bads (such as terrifying football crowds or lousy and ill-tempered

orchestras), so we still need to specify some grounds for valuing a culture. It is worth noting that some of the paradigm cases of essentially social goods, such as solidarity, friendship and love, have a conceptual feature missing from cultures: that where they are not in fact goods, we are inclined (or at least have some reason) to say that these relationships do not in fact exist. So, when a friendship turns sour, we have reason to stop calling the relevant relationship a friendship. The concept of culture, however, does not have this feature. Even where we judge that someone's cultural attachments may thwart or limit her, this does not provide a reason not to describe it as a culture, or to think of it as somehow not hers.

The claim for the essentially social value of cultural identity locates the value of a culture in its value for a group that jointly produces and consumes it. Individualists respond that the value of a good, even if it can be produced and consumed only jointly, still rests in the contribution it makes to the lives of each individual involved (Broome 1991: 169; Hardin 1995: 68; Mason 2000: 47).[10] The character of the good may be sensitive both to the numbers and to the identity of those involved in jointly producing and consuming it, but we can only consider the good valuable for its contribution to how things go for the individuals involved. At this level of abstraction, there is very little at stake, and it is hard to settle this divergence by appeal to intuitions on either side about the location of value (cf. Taylor 1995: 127; Mason 2000: 48; Graham 2002: 95). However, it is worth underlining that accepting a non-individualist account of value does not provide an ominous and illiberal license for overriding the interests of individuals in the name of the culture. The claim is only that these are considerations that ought to have some weight in deliberation, not that these outweigh individual interests. Even if individual interests are always given greater weight in practical deliberation (are judged to be 'lexically prior' or 'trumping'), it does not follow that there is no such thing as a collective value, or that values that fall into this category can play no role in practical reasoning or political theory.[11]

Finally in this section, I want to consider a line of argument that holds culture to be instrumentally valuable for groups. By this, I mean that a group's culture contributes to properties of that group that are held to be valuable, such as stability or solidarity within the group. This view can accompany a highly unsentimental conception of culture as a manipulable social cement, and is expressed in the republican current of thought wherein civil religion and national characteristics and customs are to be promoted, since they enhance the sense of community among citizens. In *Considerations on the Government of Poland*, Rousseau argues that 'ancient practices ought to be preserved, restored and suitable new ones introduced that are distinctively the Poles' own', including the wearing of national dress and the creation of distinctive festivals and public games (Rousseau [1772] 1997: 185–6). For Mill, a state with different linguistic groups generates 'mutual antipathies', and a society in which none feel that they can rely on the others for 'fidelity' (J. S. Mill [1861] 1991: 429). He expresses a particular worry that 'soldiers, to whose feelings half or three-fourths of the subjects of the same governments are foreigners, will have no more scruple in mowing them down, and no more desire to ask the reason why, than they would have in doing the same thing against declared enemies' (J. S. Mill [1861] 1991: 429). In this vein, some recent liberal nationalists argue that a shared national culture should be valued instrumentally, since it promotes trust and common commitments in a political community (Miller 1995: 90; Barry 1991a: 178). The mutual trust fostered by nationality allows us to see beyond mere sectional advantage, so that we are prepared to bear costs on behalf of others, in the knowledge that they will reciprocate should that be necessary: bonds of national identity make redistributive obligations appear to members 'as expressions of who they are rather than arbitrary burdens' (Ripstein 1997a: 209; cf. Barry 1991a: 174–5; 2001: 79; M. Moore 2001: 3–6; 2002: 80–5). I will explore this nationalist argument and some different options in chapter 6 below. Here I want only to draw attention to some features of the general form of argument.

The normative weight to attach to culture in this case depends on the importance of the properties of the group that the culture promotes. The value that attaches to those properties may in turn be cashed out in individualist terms: so, for example, a norm of deferential queuing may be thought valuable for what it contributes to making enterprises such as getting on a bus predictable and fair for individuals. But, in the first instance, the value of culture lies in its bringing about states of affairs of the group to which value is attached. Whether a distinctive culture is valuable, or what features of it are to be valued, depends, then, on what features of the group are valued. As with Taylor's constitutive argument, the question arises of whether the particular cultural identity in question possesses reprehensible properties, as well as this instrumentally valuable feature. For example, a particular cultural identity may promote high levels of trust among members of a group, together with prejudiced and destructive hostility toward outsiders.

Furthermore, this line of argument also depends on our being able to identify the group within which solidarity, reciprocity and trust are instrumentally served. For some nationalists, the relevant group is defined by membership of the polity, and a shared public culture is held to support desirable properties of that entity. For others, this is a complacently 'statist' way of defining the character and value of the nation (cf. M. Moore 2002: 36–7). So the issue of whether or not a given public culture is valuable or not comes to turn on how we define the group for which it is meant to be instrumentally valuable. Unionists and Nationalists in Northern Ireland define in antithetical terms the 'relevant group' that the members of their territory should be seen as composing, for example. Similarly, a nationalist defender of a standard system of public education may point to the benefits of a set of common cultural

markers for the citizenry as a whole, while the defender of educational autonomy for some religious and cultural groups may appeal to the benefits of education within these particular traditions for the cohesiveness and stability of
*those* groups.

A final point is that this instrumental argument allows that assimilation is
desirable, and that the disappearance of a culture is nothing to be regretted,
provided that the group benefits from these processes. This suggests the inevitably partial character of this argument in capturing the claims made for the
normativity of culture. For it presupposes that the value or importance that a
cultural identity has for a group rests on its bringing about states of affairs for
that group that are independent of the culture itself: but what those who have
that identity may value are not these effects but features of the identity itself
– the language, practices or way of life that it embodies. The instrumental
importance of these features in securing solidarity or a sense of common
purpose is secondary for them, if it figures at all. (On a very Machiavellian or
'government house' view, the instrumental importance of phenomena such as
religious belief not only cannot form part of what those who have the identity
themselves value but must not be acknowledged by them: in order to enjoy the
benefits of belief, believers must simply believe, remaining innocent of the
relationship of their believing to the benefits.) When the language, practices or
way of life are damaged or made unavailable through exile or destruction,
what is lost is something that makes a contribution to how well the lives of
those who had that identity can now go.

## 3.   Varieties of Individualism

In the following two sections I trace out what have become the two most prominent lines of individualist argument for the value of cultural identity. Neither
of them is a fully-fledged instrumentalist or non-instrumentalist case, as we
shall see. In this section, I want to give some consideration to the latter two
positions. The instrumental account of the value of cultural identity for individuals is a natural partner to one sort of constructionist account of identity,
which takes as central the fact that 'some people do decide to assert, retain
or change their ascriptive identities quite deliberately and strategically'
(Gutmann 2003: 120). For this can explain such behaviour in terms of the
instrumental value of the identities to the individuals involved. It is open to
this account to have a broad conception of the kind of individual interests
served, from the financial to psychological self-esteem. Furthermore, this
account need not take the individuals involved to be aware that this is the case.
For instance, they may *think* that a semiotic practice like a shared language is
valuable non-instrumentally as an essentially social good, even though in
reality its value lies only in making it easier for members of the group to reap

the individual benefits of co-operation with one another. Or they may feel their norms represent the best or soundest way of life, even though the value of these norms lies elsewhere, such as in allowing them to dispense with expensive contractual and insurance mechanisms in dealing with one another.

The alternative approach finds non-instrumental value in cultural identity for the individuals who have that identity. The underlying idea is that participation in a culture is itself an important ingredient in the content of a good life for many people (Margalit and Raz 1990: 449; Buchanan 1991: 53–4; Mason 2000: 51–2; Parekh 2000: 162; Gans 2000: 446; Caney 2002: 93–4). There are two principal ways in which to interpret this idea. The first is to find a non-instrumental value in belonging to a particular culture, tradition or way of life. As Isaiah Berlin writes, setting out an idea he finds in romantic nationalists, '[h]uman customs, activities, forms of life, art, ideas, were (and must be) of value to men . . . because they were their own, expressions of their local, regional, national, life, and spoke to them as they could speak to no other human group' (Berlin 1990: 244–5). This may be associated with reactionary or chauvinist forms of nationalist, cultural, ethnic or religious sentiment, but, as Berlin is at pains to point out, it need not be. Into this category falls, I think, the argument put forward by Yael Tamir, that cultural identities are 'constitutive choices which, due to their importance to individuals, should be granted special weight' (1993: 41). The language of choice employed by Tamir here is a little misleading in its connotations: we need not picture someone as selecting a cultural identity from a menu. The key idea is not that a person *chooses*, but that this is an aspect of a person's identity which is important to her, an attachment that she affirms or embraces (cf. Raz 2001: 34).

We may object that, even if we accept that there is a human interest in belonging to some particular culturally defined group or tradition, it is not obvious that this must take the form of an interest in cultural identification, as opposed to (say) an identification with some other mode of particularity with which someone may identify – nation, region, friends, town, family, religion, occupation, economic class, gender and so on, or some more distinctive overlapping set of these. Furthermore, a person's culture may stifle or block alternative, valuable forms of belonging, as missionaries and civic nationalists find. However, the point is that culture *can* be a focus of attachment, and where it is, there is a *pro tanto* reason for respecting cultural identity. A second objection raises the question of the contingency of the interest in belonging to a distinctive culture: perhaps it is simply a product of variable psychological temperament whether one finds any value in this kind of attachment as opposed to a life of footloose eclecticism or of the sorts of cultural adaptation and negotiation that those presented with an unfamiliar environment contend with (cf. Waldron 1995: 107; Margalit and Halbertal 1994: 504; Danley 1991: 172; Gans 2000: 433; Mason 2000: 53). But the argument that belonging constitutes a good need not take the form of a claim that it is a universal good, irrespective of anything else about the psychology or social location of the people for whom it is claimed to be a good, or who claim it themselves. So the possibility that eclecticism or adaptation constitutes a valuable form of life does not undermine the claim for belonging and continuity: it does not follow from a cultural belonging's being a good that lives of either eclecticism or adaptation cannot be valuable.[12]

Another objection is that variations in these dispositions to identify with a cultural identity can be *explained* in such a way as to undermine the normative force of the identification. For example, we may explain particular identifications as the result of an underlying interest in adhering to an identity or group as a result of the material or other benefits it brings. Accordingly, we will have reasons, grounded in self-interest, both for identification with some group or practice and then for perpetuating it, acting on its behalf, etc. Speakers of a particular language have an interest in the perpetuation of the language with which they are familiar and in which communication is easy for them; if the government makes knowing that language a condition of employment in the civil service, then others have an interest in acquiring that item of cultural knowledge (Hardin 1995: ch. 3; Kukathas 1998: 693; Mason 2000: 54). In itself, this sort of causal account, even if we accept it, does not undermine the claim for non-instrumental value. This line of thought suggests that the non-instrumental argument characteristically masks what is really an *instrumental* case for the individual advantages of cultural identification. Yet description of the instrumental economic advantages of a particular identification (say) does not by itself show why that identity cannot also hold non-instrumental value for a person, including value of which that person is not aware. Even if she goes on to identify herself in some other, more instrumentally advantageous way, we can make sense of the idea that this was regrettable for her – for instance, that there were valuable attachments and options that are now gone.

The other version of this claim is that it is not attachment to some particular way of life for which non-instrumental value should be claimed, but that to which someone is attached. In other words, what is valuable for Catalans is not that they belong in the world on their particular terms but that the terms themselves – for instance, their language – are themselves valuable. *Pace* Rorty, we can make sense of responses of regret over the loss or erosion of cultural practices by appeal to the non-instrumental value of what has disappeared; as Ronald Dworkin (who writes in terms of intrinsic value) puts it, this 'explains why we think it a shame when any distinctive form of human culture, especially a complex and interesting one, dies or languishes' (Dworkin 1993: 72; cf. Musschenga 1998; Rockefeller 1994). If non-instrumental value of this sort does attach to cultural practices, then this seems to impose reasons not only on non-participants in a culture to respect that cultural identity, but also on participants to pursue it. For example, we may think that, as Daniel Weinstock puts it, 'minority languages *themselves* have rights against all others, *including their own speakers*, to have their intrinsic value affirmed' (Weinstock 2003: 255, emphases original).[13]

This may seem to be too strong a line of argument for the normativity of language, since it apparently licenses the illiberal coercion of individual speakers of language L to fulfil their duties to speak L (or make films and write poetry in L, etc.) (Weinstock 2003: 256). However, while a non-instrumental value argument for culture C may ground reasons and duties on participants in C, this is different from inferring that they license the coercion of these individuals. The intrinsic value of the culture may be a reason to accommodate or promote, but this is not to say that this licenses coercion on its behalf. The duties that the non-instrumental value of C imposes on participants may not be such that political (or social) coercion should be used to enforce them. This may be because the value of the practices derives in part from their spontaneous character. In a case where we judge that particular policies for the promotion of a language are in fact coercive, and the individual rights need to be asserted against the policies of linguistic promotion, this does not imply that a non-instrumental value argument is false, or itself has illiberal implications. As noted in considering the argument for the essentially social character of the value of cultural identity, we may think that individual rights should outweigh or 'trump' the requirements of a culture's intrinsic value, where there is some conflict between the two. But this is not to say that there is *nothing* to be outweighed. This is a good that may be promoted when there is no such conflict, and this non-instrumental value argument allows us to make sense of the thought that something valuable may be lost in the process of cultural transformation.

## 4.  Culture and Recognition

'Recognition' is an ambiguous term, and in understanding how the notion of recognition can be mobilized to shed light on the normativity of culture, we need first to draw a line between two senses of the term, each of which plays a different role in the political theory of multiculturalism. The first is recognition as a positive diplomatic, constitutional or political relationship: A endows B with a certain status, which normally comes with corresponding rights and obligations. This follows one sort of ordinary usage. When the chairperson of a meeting recognizes a speaker, she gives the speaker a status he would not otherwise have. Political claims for recognition – for example, as a nation, a state, or an official language of the state – also have this form: B or an agent of B claims from A the status (allegedly) due to B. In such situations, to achieve that status logically requires A's recognition. A certain language may be widely used, but it is not an official language until it is adopted as such by the state. The various claims on behalf of multicultural rights and policies discussed in chapter 1 can be understood as claims for recognition, in this sense: recognition consists in the wider political community's (or state system's) acknowledgement that group G qualifies for exemption, assistance, the enforcement of a traditional legal code, or some other form of exceptional support or non-interference. Recognition in this sense is a generic way of characterizing the diverse legal and political objectives which have been pursued in the name of multiculturalism.

In its second sense, the concept of recognition plays a part in an account of the social constitution of personal identity. Recognition of a person by what G. H. Mead called 'significant others' is said to be vital for his or her sense of selfhood. The core claim is that humans are constitutionally dependent on recognition by others, and that the failure to be recognized, or to be 'misrecognized', is to suffer a profound harm. It is in this sense that, as Taylor puts it, 'nonrecognition or misrecognition . . . can be a crippling form of oppression, imprisoning someone in a false, distorted, reduced mode of being. Beyond simple lack of respect, it can inflict a grievous wound, saddling people with crippling self-hatred. Due recognition is not just a courtesy but a vital human need' (Taylor 1995: 226). Or, as James Tully writes, a 'demeaning or degrading form of misrecognition tends to undermine the basic self-respect and self-esteem that are necessary to empower a person to develop the degree of autonomy and sense of self-worth that is required to participate equally in the public and private life of her society, often leading to well-known psychological and sociological pathologies' (Tully 2000b: 470). According to Axel Honneth, for individuals 'the experience of this social devaluation typically brings with it a loss of personal self-esteem, of the opportunity to regard themselves as beings whose traits and abilities are esteemed' (Honneth 1995: 134).[14] For example, a dominant racist culture projects on to stigmatized racial groups a degrading image of themselves, which itself constitutes a form of harm, additional to the other disadvantages they suffer, such as physical insecurity or restricted job opportunities. In this section, I explore the idea that the need for recognition in this second sense furnishes an argument for the normativity of cultural identity. In order to understand this claim, we need first to flesh out the relevant notion of recognition in a little more detail.[15]

The demand for recognition is a distinctively modern one, Taylor argues. It combines a belief in the equality of human beings with a commitment to their individuality. Borrowing a term from Lionel Trilling, he terms the latter ideal 'authenticity': I am 'called upon' to live my life my way, rather than moulding it to conform to external demands. Following Herder, Taylor sees this as a calling which demands not only that individuals be true to themselves, but also that whole societies or cultures express their natures, which he calls 'the seminal idea of modern nationalism, in both its benign and malignant forms' (Taylor 1995: 229).[16] The pursuit of authenticity, at least at the first of these levels, may appear to be a wholly individual affair. But the individual attempt to ignore or shrug off the social condition of selfhood is for Taylor one of the characteristic modern heresies, which he has prosecuted in a range of books and essays. Taylor locates the development of the modern conception of authenticity against the background of a 'dialogic' account of the social constitution of identity. We acquire agency and the ability to understand who we are through the acquisition of 'languages', meaning 'not only the words we speak, but also the other modes of expression whereby we define ourselves, including the "languages" of art, of gesture, of love, and the like' (Taylor 1995: 230). We acquire these languages through 'dialogue', where this concept too is used in an extended sense to encompass our interaction with 'significant others', who shape and transform our self-understandings.

There are four steps in the argument that people should have their distinctive cultural identities recognized. The first is the claim that recognition is the endowment of a certain normative status on the recognized B by the recognizer A – as an equal, a fellow member of the group, a friend. Second, this endowment occurs by virtue of the acknowledgement on the part of A of the possession of relevant attributes of B that require her recognition by A. As a cognitive act, recognition is a matter of coming to believe something about that which is recognized. In its minimal form, there is recognition as attention or noticing. This corresponds to misrecognition as neglect, which renders its object socially invisible, in what Honneth calls an 'act of non-perception' (Honneth 2001a: 112). This is the invisibility which the black narrator of Ralph Ellison's novel *Invisible Man* finds 'occurs because of a peculiar disposition of the eyes of those with whom I come in contact. A matter of the construction of their *inner* eyes, those eyes with which they look through their physical eyes upon reality' (Ellison 1965: 7).[17] This is one way in which slaves or servants, for example, may be socially dead: they are beneath the notice of their masters. This conception is distinguishable from a richer cognitive relation, recognition as comprehension. Incomprehension is not the failure to notice B, but the failure to see B for what she truly is. On a romantic conception, this recognition is of a person in all her infinite peculiarity, or perhaps of her deepest self – the recognition of authentic personal identity, in Taylor's sense. For the politics of recognition, what is usually at issue is some aspect of B's socially or publicly consequential identity: B's interests or viewpoints or needs as a Sikh or a Scot (or both). This introduces a third term to the recognition relationship: A recognizes B not as the individual that B is but *as an X*.

Each of these cognitive forms of recognition involves the acknowledgement of something about *B*: that she is *there*, and that she possesses certain attributes. This allows us to make sense of the idea of *claiming* or *struggling for* recognition: what I claim or struggle for is that others come to view me in the right way, where that may be described quite independently of how they actually view me. What is claimed, the terminus of the struggle, is acknowledgement by others of what one already really is (Appiah 1994: 149). If I really am a sensitive soul, and not the indolent buffoon you take me to be, then my struggle for recognition has as its end your comprehending my true nature.

This is not to say that the possession of normatively relevant features is in itself sufficient to endow B with the relevant normative status. The act of recognition itself is a requirement for this, as in the case of the chairperson recognizing a speaker in a debate. Nor does this imply that what *counts* as a normatively relevant feature is necessarily wholly fixed and independent of the specific judgements, interpretations and evaluations of those involved. Part of the intellectual and practical content of 'struggles for recognition' has been the effort to establish that features thought to be relevant to some recognized status are in fact not, or that the As have adhered to an unjustifiable way of specifying a relevant feature, or that features thought irrelevant are relevant. 'Recognition' in this sense is employed to refer to a form of affirmation or endorsement of the identity of those recognized. This corresponds to misrecognition as negative evaluation: A cognitively recognizes B as an X, but finds X-ness to be a degrading sort of identity.[18]

The third claim is that culture is a normatively relevant feature. Culture in its normative, societal or semiotic aspects can then enter into this account of the formation of selfhood as one of the elements of individual identity that requires comprehension and affirmation by significant others, and this is, I think, the way in which Taylor, Tully and others tether the concept of recognition to the politics of cultural diversity. As with the argument for the non-instrumental value of cultural belonging, we can, on this account, deflect the objection that there are many other aspects of identity (professional, sexual, regional, moral, etc.) that are important to individuals, the recognition of which is arguably necessary for the accomplishment of selfhood, by presenting this as only an argument about one sort of requirement, not a statement of an overriding consideration.[19]

Fourth, recognition does not only endow B with normative status, as an equal or a member of the group; it also plays a role in the formation of B's selfhood or subjectivity. What makes recognition important – a 'vital human need' for Taylor and others, it will be recalled – is that our well-being is dependent on others, or at least some significant others, affirming who we are in the right way. Recognition by others not only reflects cognitively a true image of myself, but affirms it as valuable, according it due esteem. But this filling of a gap or incompleteness in myself does not leave me as I was before: for recognition also interactively or practically shapes and enables the individual. (Perhaps, like plants that grow toward the light, we grow toward recognition, becoming more what the source of recognition pictures us as. At the same time, we cannot be pulled too far from our roots: this is misrecognition.) This mutual recognition is an ineliminable part of the individual well-being of those recognized: 'they understand me, as I understand them; and this understanding creates within me a sense of being somebody in the world' (Berlin

1969: 156).[20] In this way the recognition relationship is causal and interactive. In this case, my viewing you as an X does not constitute you as one by virtue of my seeing you that way. Rather, there is a causal chain connecting my seeing you or treating you as an X to your taking on new properties, which may or may not include becoming X. If enough people convince you of your horribleness, you may begin to act in horrible ways. Interactions of this kind may work in other ways: my seeing you as an X may lead you to become a Y, as when you respond to my contemptuous view of you as lazy by working furiously hard or by becoming depressed; or we may have only the most meagre and degrading stereotypes with which to describe your group, and this language may constitute the dominant discourse which you use to think about yourselves (Fraser 1997: 14). 'The thesis is that our identity is partly shaped by the recognition or its absence, often by the *mis*recognition of others, and so a person or a group of people can suffer real damage, real distortion, if the people or society around them mirror back to them a confining or demeaning or contemptible picture of themselves' (Taylor 1995: 225; cf. Emcke 2000; Markell 2000).

If we understand recognition like this, it becomes one of several ways in which my identity can be secured, threatened, transformed, etc. But my identity may be transformed in ways that do not involve the recognition or misrecognition of others: that is, that do not involve attention or comprehension, or their lack. For example, if demographic changes render my group a minority, this may affect how I view this identity (perhaps I will become embattled and reactionary). The interactive dimension of recognition also leaves open the possibility that misrecognition may be *beneficial* for its recipients, in that its practical effects for a group may be more advantageous than if that group or identity was viewed accurately.

This recognition argument is complex, and I do not pretend to offer a full assessment here, any more than I have offered a detailed exposition. Instead, I want to focus on just two germane elements of this account, which are linked in ways that I will explore. The first is the question of who constitutes the recognizing A group in this kind of argument. The second concerns the ethical ambiguity of any particular act of recognition on this account.

There are two prominent answers to the question of who should bestow recognition. The first is that recognition requires some form of public validation of a particular identity. As Tully puts it, 'the condition of self-respect is met only in a society in which the cultures of all the members are recognised and affirmed by others, both by those who do and those who do not share those cultures' (Tully 1995: 190). From this standpoint, I require not only recognition within my cultural group, but also public or social recognition as a condition for my self-respect. The other response is that recognition is required only among some narrower group of 'significant others'. Freedoms of thought, speech and association, perhaps especially where there is a sufficient level of economic equality, allow there to exist groups in which significant others endorse my identity and activities, and which provide a solid basis for the good of self-respect or self-esteem: 'It normally suffices that for each person there is some association (one or more) to which he belongs and within which the activities that are rational for him are publicly affirmed by others. In this way we acquire a sense that what we do in everyday life is worthwhile' (Rawls 1972: 441).[21] These conditions constitute 'the social bases of self-respect' (cf. Barry 2001: 268–9; Rawls 1999: 314, 366). There is a difference, then, between thinking that I require recognition from those who share my cultural identity as a condition of my self-respect and believing that a commitment to upholding the social bases of self-respect requires the public recognition of my culture.

The distinction between the public validation and voluntary association answers to this question does not map on to the distinction between those who support multicultural rights and policies and those who advocate difference-insensitivity. We should not conflate the notion of public recognition with the schedule of group-differentiated rights and policies: a policy such as an exemption or assistance in setting up a faith school may be justified by reference to a desire to grant a group public recognition. But they may be justified by appealing to the need to maintain the conditions for the members of a group to recognize one another. So one kind of argument for the state support of Muslim schools in Britain is that the state provides support for Jewish and Christian schools; another is that a system of instruction specifically geared for Muslim pupils will help maintain the conditions for members of this group to flourish. In other words, acceptance of recognition within the group as a ground for individual self-respect can provide a reason to revise the standard liberal conception of the institutional 'bases of self-respect' without appeal to the value of public recognition. On the other hand, public recognition may not require anything so full-blooded as entitlements to exemptions, assistance or self-government. For one thing the abolition of rules (for example, a dress code), rather than the creation of exemptions, can be taken as a form of public recognition. Furthermore, symbolic measures (such as changing the names of places or of public institutions and incorporating members of groups into public ceremonies) may suffice to give public recognition to marginalized identities.

Supporters of the voluntary association answer sometimes charge the public validation view with incoherence. Since public recognition requires 'that the cultures of different groups must be publicly affirmed as being of equal value' (Barry 2001: 267), it sets itself an impossible task. Cultures have, as Barry puts it, a 'propositional content', holding some beliefs to be true and others false, and some practices good and others bad (Barry 2001: 270). The beliefs and values embodied in different cultures are often inconsistent or contradictory. It is therefore impossible for the state (or anyone else) coherently to affirm them

as of equal value, since this entails affirming conflicting sets of beliefs and
values, with correspondingly different views of what the state should *do*: the
state cannot both tolerate and not tolerate polygamy, for example, or offer the
same degree of public validation to Christian fundamentalists and homosexu-
als (cf. Barry 2001: 270; Jones 1998: 45; 1999: 81–3; Miller 2000: 74; Waldron
2000a: 161–5). Far better, then, proponents of this position assert, for the state
to leave recognition to the narrower in-group.

   This point is most plausible when culture is viewed in its normative aspect,
in terms of the categories laid out in the last chapter: that is, as a set of beliefs
or norms. By contrast, a claim for the public recognition of a language (say,
as an official language of the state or a language of education) does not seem
to be affected by this objection. Of course, there may still be conflicts and
problems, but these are not epistemic but practical: for instance, should the
state recognize every language spoken in a territory, irrespective of numbers,
or only those spoken by geographically concentrated groups? Even within the
constraints of a normative or epistemic conception of culture, the defender of
public recognition can make some inroads into this criticism. For a defender
of public validation need not claim that this affirmation in terms of equal
value should be thought of as the assertion of the truth, and the whole truth,
of differing systems of belief and value. All that public validation has to be,
for present purposes, is affirmation of a group in such a way that the equality
of the basis of self-respect for the members of the group with those of the rest
of society is promoted. This does not have to take the form of the state's or
some other public body's endorsing that group's beliefs. A committed alcohol
drinker can make non-alcoholic drinks available at a party without her action
implying any claim about the validity of temperance. But in accommodating
teetotallers in this way, she is not just *tolerating* their presence, but trying to
make them feel just as welcome and at home as the raucous heavy drinkers. In
the case of religious schooling, for example, public authorities need not
become embroiled in affirming the truth of contradictory religious doctrines.
The 'public validation' case for support for Muslim schools is that public
support for educational institutions amounts to a sort of public affirmation of
other identities, which in turn provides an enhanced social basis for the development of self-respect on the part of members of the groups thus privileged,
and which therefore should be extended to this one, in order that members of
this group may enjoy that benefit. But none of this implies that any of these
religious beliefs is in fact correct.[22]

   In part this is a dispute about what is required to secure the conditions for
self-respect of a group, and this may be a severely contextual question (Carens
2000). Under some circumstances, the standard set of liberal rights may be
sufficient, particularly if these include egalitarian economic provisions. Under
other conditions, the standard set of liberal rights may prove inadequate, and
'[p]ublic concern for differences is necessary in order to reverse their previous

invisibility, marginality, and stigmatization' (Galeotti 2002: 194; cf. Galeotti 1999; Phillips 1999). We can consider three ways in which this is the case. First, when a group has been particularly vilified, simply allowing it formal freedoms to set up its own associations and publish its own newspapers may not be enough to create a sufficiently robust group identity: if a group is not in fact capable of setting up these institutions then its members cannot enjoy the in-group recognition that is the social condition for self-respect. Second, even where conditions for in-group recognition exist, an identity may be vilified and mocked by the wider society, and in this way the social basis for self-respect for members is eroded. In a third sort of case, some cultural identities may already be affirmed *de facto* or *de jure* by a society (there is an official language or an established church), and the case for public recognition on the part of the members of some other group rests on the claim that they be granted the status already enjoyed by members of the dominant identity.

The other point that I want to bring out is that recognition of somebody 'as an X' may be ethically ambiguous, and that this is true when the 'X' is filled in with a specific cultural identity. As I argued in the previous chapter, we need to distinguish between identification and endorsement.[23] To be recognized both by outsiders and by other members of a group as a member of that group is not a purely cognitive enterprise, as I noted above: it does not consist merely in comprehending what a person is, but plays a role in constructing her identity. But this process of construction can undermine the bases of self-respect in other aspects. Consider, first, the normative conception of culture: recognition of me as a member of C by other members of C inculcates within me the distinctive norms and outlook of C; but those norms may conflict with other aspects of my identity. Consider the Chicago sociologist W. I. Thomas's observation in *The Unadjusted Girl* that '[t]he girl as child does not know she has any particular value until she learns it from others (in the family)'. However, 'if she is regarded with adoration she correspondingly respects herself and tends to become what is expected of her. And so she has in fact a greater value', and goes on, he adds, to make a good marriage and reflect well on her family (Thomas 1928: 98, cited in Sumner 1994: 81). Recognition by members of a group in the terms of which other members approve is ambivalent for the self-respect of those members of the group whose inclinations (or other aspects of whose identity) pull them away from the form of culture recognized. Similarly, recognition of another as the possessor of some semiotic or societal cultural identity can also carry more or less overt normative nudges toward the one recognized about what views they should have, and how they should comport themselves. The causal or constructive element of recognition can be oppressive as well as liberating.[24]

In summary, then, if we accept the tie between recognition and self-respect, then there is a case for sustaining the conditions of in-group recognition and for public validation, under certain circumstances. But notions of both in-group recognition and public validation need to be handled with some care. For these arguments to hold, specific causal and contextual claims have to be made good, and there are pitfalls in the application of each. However, if these difficulties can be navigated, the recognition argument provides an account of the normativity of cultural identity in some instances.

## 5.   The Conditions for Choice

Like the recognition argument, the 'context of choice' argument is also based on a controversial premiss, about the value of individual freedom or autonomy, and views a person's cultural identity as valuable as one of the conditions for autonomy. The first step in this argument is to view individual autonomy or freedom as a foundational value for political morality: this is the value of being in charge of one's own life or the capacity to form and revise projects for one's own life.[25] Furthermore, autonomy cannot be exercised in a social vacuum. My autonomy not only requires that I not be coerced or manipulated when I make my choices. It also requires that there exists for me a menu of meaningful options among which I can choose (Raz 1994: 176; Tamir 1993: 36). The French Foreign Legion, offering the choice 'march or die', does not furnish an appropriate social setting for individual autonomy; nor, according to Raz, is a social setting adequate in which there exists an insufficient number of options that are not only meaningful but *worthwhile* (Raz 1986: 375).

The next step is to identify a secure cultural identity as one of the preconditions for the successful exercise of autonomy: what enables autonomy 'is the fact that our societal culture makes various options available to us. Freedom in the first instance, is the ability to explore and revise the ways of life which are made available by our societal culture' (Kymlicka 2001a: 53). Freedom 'involves making choices among various options, and our societal culture not only provides these options, but also makes them meaningful to us' (Kymlicka 1995a: 83; 2001a: 227).[26] By offering a person options and endowing them with meaning and familiarity, a culture forms a context in which that person is able to exercise the capacity to choose. A secure and largely familiar culture provides the conditions in which a person can make choices about what matters to her, providing a map of the world in which she deliberates, narratives which make it intelligible to her, and some of the skills and resources that allow her to make autonomous choices. If we accept that a person's autonomy is valuable, then we should value the cultural context that is a condition of it, since erosion of this cultural context weakens her autonomy. A precarious, damaged or unfamiliar cultural environment still allows a person to be an agent, but makes it more difficult for her to deliberate and reflect on the options available.

We can pick out three ways in which, it is claimed, a culture is a condition of choice. First, a culture provides options that would not otherwise exist: the

Welsh language allows speakers to speak, write and broadcast in Welsh; a social practice of polygamy permits a man multiple wives; the existence of the sonnet form allows you to write sonnets; and so on. Second, culture provides a set of interpretative and evaluative categories that allow you to understand and reflect on these options: 'only through having a rich and secure cultural structure that people can become aware, in a vivid way, of the options available to them, and intelligently examine their value' (Kymlicka 1989: 165). In order to identify and understand the practices around us, we need to understand the meanings attached to them by our culture (Kymlicka 1995a: 83). Third, the sense of identity and belonging provided by a familiar culture makes individual deliberation and choice easier: 'in the open and ever-changing modern world, life in a cultural environment that is familiar, understandable, and thus predictable is a necessary precondition for making rational choices and becoming self-governing' (Tamir 1993: 84). Culture serves as a medium for intergenerational and communal continuity and familiarity: 'cultural membership . . . instils members with a sense of collective identity and belonging and may also supply them with a social context and evaluative horizon that help to temper the emotional and psychological difficulties associated with making major life choices' (Deveaux 2000b: 132; cf. Kymlicka 1995a: 105; Margalit and Raz 1990: 447–9; Tamir 1993: 72, 85–6). My culture not only makes available a set of options and provides a vocabulary in which they are meaningful to me; it also provides me with a sense of common identity and tradition with others. This is valuable as a condition of my autonomy, as the alternative to a culturally supplied sense of identity is anomie, the lack of any stable beliefs, norms, feelings of naturalness and so on, which is held to disable the individual capacity to make reflective and autonomous choices.

A culture provides a set of options to its individual members through offering practices or social roles (polygamy, duelling, shopaholic) that shape the individuals' landscape of deliberation and choice. One response to this is that, taken in isolation, the claim for option provision runs into an objection parallel to a difficulty which afflicts the argument for the value of a diversity of cultures discussed in section 1 above. For neither the bare fact of the provision of options nor the particular number of options provided to individual members can be sufficient for grounding respect for my cultural identity. For in each case a culture's value depends on there not being some other (reasonably proximate, accessible) culture to my own which cannot either simply provide options or provide more options than this. If the respect owed to a cultural identity is meant to derive from its providing a large number of meaningful options, then Mill's claim about the desirability of assimilation for cultural minorities is compatible with it. Provided that the great nation provides more worthwhile options that make the autonomy of individuals meaningful, then the minority cultural identity is not owed the respect that this argument hopes to ground. Respect accrues to the *option-maximizing* culture, since the individual's underlying interest is in living in a cultural environment which makes her autonomy more, rather than less, meaningful. However, this objection brings out only the fact that the option-providing feature of a culture should not be taken in isolation from a culture's role in providing meaning and familiarity, although these are *distinguishable* features. For an option's salience and accessibility depend in part on that option's place in a wider network of familiar meanings and relationships.

This last argument needs to be distinguished from the claim discussed in section 3, that a person's cultural identity and the accompanying sense of community, tradition and belonging possess an intrinsic value that should be recognized. However, just as identity and community may not form part of the good life for everyone, so it seems to be a matter of contingent psychological disposition and social circumstance whether or not a sense of common cultural community is structurally necessary for the exercise of capacities of deliberation and agency. For some individuals, cultural insecurity may provide suitable conditions for the exercise of their autonomy (cf. Tomasi 1995). The *presumption* that a settled way of life is necessary for individual autonomy or well-being generally is not justified by this line of argument.[27] The appeal to familiarity also suggests that the argument requires not only that individuals have the appropriate psychological dispositions to support it, but that a particular contextual judgement holds true about the empirical sociological conditions in which a cultural practice exists. For the context of choice argument to hold, a cultural practice must be sufficiently robust and widespread that it can be meaningfully thought to provide a condition of choice for somebody. If there are only very few speakers of my language remaining, for example, it is hard to see how monolingualism for myself (or my children) is a condition of autonomy. In such a case, we may say that, even at the price of unfamiliarity, an individual's interest in choice is better served by learning another language. For a cultural practice, then, there may come a point at which it *ceases* to constitute part of an individual's context of choice – that is, when it ceases to be instrumental for the individual's interest in autonomy.

The context of choice argument is characteristically advanced in tandem with a societal conception of culture (see above chapter 1, section 2). This, it will be recalled, is the view of a culture as providing 'its members with meaningful ways of life across the full range of human activities', through an array of dominant institutions, such as schools, news and entertainment media, and economic and political institutions (Kymlicka 1995a: 76; 2001a: 25–6, 53–4; 2001b: 18–20). For Kymlicka adds to the claim that cultural identity provides options, perspective and familiarity the further claim that it is specifically membership in or access to a societal culture that is the condition of individual freedom (Kymlicka 1995a: 107; Kymlicka 2001a: 53). Advancing the context of choice argument through a societal conception of culture may appear to address the worry about the conditionality of this argument: for it is not just *any* cultural practice that is relevant, but only those that form part of the relatively institutionally robust societal cultures that are at issue here.

However, the claim that a particular societal culture makes available all (or all of the most significant) of a person's options is obscure. Does it mean that the culture is the origin of the practice, or simply that it tolerates or permits it? The first meaning seems too stringent, and the second too weak. It seems strange to say that French societal culture makes hip hop available or that Welsh societal culture makes Judaism available (cf. Carens 2000: 69–71), either in the sense that the societal cultures are the origins of the practices and norms (since they are not) or in the sense that the cultures tolerate or permit these practices. For the latter seems less a function of any special features of the cultures concerned than of the existence of liberal legal rights and exposure to the world. If we want to understand what makes an option available in the sense of providing some causal mechanism for its being available to members of a group, then the notion of societal culture has to compete with other candidates for the relevant causal ground: the state, the global economy, transnational legal traditions and institutions, sub-societal and cross-societal cultural groups, and so on. To assert that a societal culture is *the* context of choice for an individual, in the sense of the unique source of that person's options, masks this competition.[28]

Where societal culture differs from other institutional sources of options – and so where this account has an advantage over other accounts of options – is in the way that a societal culture also has a distinctive vocabulary with which to interpret and shape these options for its members. So, for example, while at one level an option such as working for a firm that manufactures cars may be available in the United States, France, South Korea and Japan, and the existence of the option cannot be traced purely to factors located in the parochial societal cultures, much of the specific shape and meaning of the option is influenced by the societal culture, since these different cultures evince different attitudes to employment, labour relations and the character of the firm.[29] This seems to me a stronger point than the blanket assertion of the priority of societal culture in making options available, but it is subject to a version of the difficulty that attached to that claim. We can accept the meaning-providing function of culture without accepting the *priority* of societal culture in providing the relevant framework of meanings. It is not obvious that societal culture provides the most influential prism through which options are made meaningful either. For societal culture is a broad and encompassing conception of culture, including economic, social and political institutions alongside a range of distinctive social practices and (usually) a shared language. Is being a Muslim or being Indonesian more important in filling out a set of options with meaning? Being a Francophone Canadian or being Quebecois? The point of these rhetorical questions is not to suggest that there is no determinate answer, but that to respond in every case that it is the societal culture, as opposed to the normative or semiotic dimensions of cultural identity, that makes available this framework of meanings expresses an over-simplified picture of the relationship between cultural identity and individual deliberation.

In sum, then, I have argued that, if we accept the premisses of the context of choice argument, there are reasons to reject its societal interpretation and to support a diversity of sources for options, meaning and familiarity in a person's life. This line of criticism is immanent, in the sense that it does not challenge the basic premisses of this account – that autonomy is a value, that it requires options, and that there are necessary conditions on these options being available and valuable to the deliberating agent. The political implications of this interpretation of the context of choice argument are much less apparent than those of the societal alternative. To anticipate a little: welding the context of choice argument to the societal conception of culture comports comfortably with support, particularly in the form of enhanced self-government rights, of whatever groups display the relevant objective features that constitute the defining criteria of societal cultures. As I have argued, the presumption that societal culture constitutes an individual's context of choice is highly problematic, and what is left is a consideration on behalf of culture's normativity the precise political implications of which need far more various and contextually arrived at specification.

## 6.    Conclusion

The main purpose of this chapter has been to spell out the principal lines of argument for the normative character of cultural identity. The matrix from which we set out organized these arguments into four boxes, depending on the argument's relationship to the distinctions between individualism and non-individualism, on the one hand, and the intrinsic and instrumental merits of culture, on the other. A case for the normativity of culture does not have to be an argument for the overriding importance of cultural identity in any particular circumstance, but one for its having deliberative weight, even if, as I suggested in section 1, there may be political grounds for blocking off this consideration. I have tried to bring out in the case of each line of argument the different kinds of conditionality that affect them, particularly the assumptions they make about the human good and about the workings of culture.

Given the prevalence of liberal approaches to political philosophy, the dominance of individualist lines of argument (and scepticism about non-instrumental arguments), in the form of the recognition and context of choice arguments, seems unsurprising. Culture is valued as a means to, or a condition of, some state of the individual in which she is taken to have a fundamental interest, such as self-respect or autonomy, no matter what her particular other goals and interests happen to be. In section 3, I considered the liberal anxiety that the non-instrumental value argument carries authoritarian implications, arguing that it does not in itself license the coercion of individual participants in a culture in order to preserve or promote it. While the non-instrumental value argument grounds reasons for an individual to respect a cultural identity, it does not follow from this that it is legitimate to coerce her in order that she fulfil those duties, or that those duties are the weightiest obligations that rest on her shoulders.

It is worth noting that a parallel worry arises for the self-respect and context of choice arguments, in spite of their individualist character. It may be thought that because this line of argument is based on the contribution of culture to the interests of individual participants, it is inoculated against the authoritarian promotion of a culture against the desires of particular participants. Yet this is not the case; at least, it is in the same position as the non-instrumental value argument in this respect. The argument is that non-participants in C need to respect C as a condition of respecting participants' autonomy or self-respect. But this condition must apply to participants in C as well, in order that they respect the autonomy or self-respect of other participants. A minority language may be eroded by the decisions of individuals to opt out of speaking it on the grounds that the state makes it difficult to continue in this language (by fostering another language, offering incentives to switch, or providing no public services in the minority language, for example). This set of circumstances embodies the kind of failure to respect a culture that is paradigmatic for these individualist arguments. Yet, if a traditional language is eroded by the relatively spontaneous decisions of individuals to opt out of speaking it, in favour of some other language, then this would seem to affect adversely the cultural conditions of self-respect or autonomy of residual speakers of the language in the same way. And if that is the case, then there is reason based on these individualist premises for curtailing the desires of individual participants to transform their culture. As with the argument for the non-instrumental value of an identity, we need not be drawn into saying that an argument of this kind necessarily implies a coercive politics. How the difficulties that this creates are dealt with in the political theory of liberal culturalism is discussed in the following chapter.

# 3

# The Limits of Liberal Culturalism

To view culture as important to identity or even as valuable is not yet to offer an argument for multicultural rights or political recognition. In this and the following two chapters I consider three major conceptions of political deliberation, each of which offers a different account of the relationship between culture and citizenship. Liberal culturalism, in the sense in which I want to treat it in this chapter, starts from the belief that cultural identities may be normatively compelling, and that this should be worked into the fabric of liberal political theory: that, as Joseph Raz puts it, 'multiculturalism requires a political society to recognise the equal standing of all the stable and viable cultural communities existing in that society' (Raz 1994: 174). This chapter proceeds as follows. I first outline a generic conception of liberal culturalism (section 1), before turning to Will Kymlicka's position (section 2). I argue (in section 3) that there are tensions between the context of choice argument that Kymlicka offers for the value of cultural identity and his conception of the multicultural rights and policies that it grounds. I then go on (in section 4) to offer an outline of alternative forms of liberal culturalism, which can be found in the work of Raz and Charles Taylor, which is non-neutralist, pluralist, and open to a broader range of arguments for the value of cultural identity than is Kymlicka's.

## I.    The Idea of Liberal Culturalism

According to Will Kymlicka, liberal culturalism is the view that 'liberal-democratic states should not only uphold the familiar set of common civil and political rights of citizenship which are protected in all liberal democracies;

they must also adopt various group-specific rights or policies which are intended to recognize and accommodate the distinctive identities and needs of ethnocultural groups' (Kymlicka 2001a: 42). In one sense, Kymlicka is right to draw attention to the way in which this formula is the focus of a theoretical consensus (*pace* Barry 2001: 6–7, but compare chapter 4, section 4 below, where I argue that even he toes this line to some extent). For example, Iris Marion Young's 'democratic cultural pluralism' requires 'a dual system of rights: a general system of rights which is the same for all, and a more specific system of group-conscious policies and rights' (Young 1990: 174). Similarly, Taylor's model of the politics of recognition combines those 'fundamental and crucial' rights 'that have been recognized as such from the very beginning of the liberal tradition: rights to life, liberty, due process, free speech, free practice of religion, and so on' with policies that promote 'strong collective goals' such as the survival of a cultural identity (Taylor 1995: 247). As I will use the term here, though, liberal culturalism includes, but refers to more than, belief in a structure of rights that includes both some difference-sensitive rights and policies together with a common core of basic rights. Building on Kymlicka's conception, we can uncover five basic commitments.

The first is the demand that the state uphold the basic legal, civil and political rights of its citizens, and that these should include those rights that protect individual freedoms of thought and choice. Second, liberal culturalists reject state policies of benign neglect and cultural *laissez-faire*. Instead, they regard the state as to some extent implicated in the construction of the cultural character of the society, and so view policies of benign neglect as incoherent. For example, public holidays in most Western countries reflect Christian traditions and do little to recognize, accommodate or support other religious or cultural identities. This way of organizing public life gives Christians, and those comfortable with the Christian way of organizing time, advantages not enjoyed by others. This disadvantage can only be addressed and rectified by a policy that in some way attends to the needs and interests of other identities – that is, by a policy that offers some political recognition to those identities.[1] Similarly, if public services happen to be conducted in a majority rather than a minority language, this disadvantages those who speak only the minority tongue, unless specific measures are taken to accommodate the minority language through ensuring that public services are offered in this language too.

The third feature of liberal culturalism is that cultural identity is viewed as possessing a normative character, in one or more of the ways explored in the previous chapter. In particular, liberal culturalists hold that there is an individual interest in cultural identity. A cultural identity may be valued as a condition for the exercise of individual choice or for the self-respect of its bearer, or it may be viewed as non-instrumentally valuable in some other way. Liberal culturalists may also argue for the irreducible instrumental or non-instrumental value of a cultural identity for a group, but the individualist form of argument tends to predominate.[2]

Fourth, what distinguishes liberal culturalism from the negative conceptions of liberalism (to be explored in the following chapter) is its taking the view that the individual interest in cultural identity is sufficiently robust to ground a right to culture, and that this right may require difference-sensitive legal rights and policies in order to be effective. By a right generally is meant a consideration or reason, usually grounded in the interests of a right-holder, which 'pre-empts' other kinds of consideration to which voters, policy-makers, legislators, judges, and so on, may appeal (Raz 1986: ch. 7); for example, that a majority would like such-and-such a measure to become law. Both particular individual choices in the marketplace and democratic decisions may be curtailed in order to protect the interest in cultural identity. The goal of the specific rights grounded usually includes the accommodation of cultural identities, including such entitlements as exemptions from dress codes for certain jobs and the right to use a familiar language in court. But they tend to go beyond this, to include rights designed to protect and promote identities, and to allow groups to determine their own cultural policies: for example, rights to self-government, internal and external rules, and specific powers over language policy and even immigration policy.

From the liberal culturalist perspective, then, multicultural rights are not grounded merely in a prudential *modus vivendi* or balance of forces. So, for example, if a liberal culturalist holds that Catalonia is entitled to pursue a language policy that promotes the use of Catalan and perhaps limits the use of Castilian/Spanish, this should not be grounded merely on a claim about the political pressure that this 'autonomous community' is able to exert on the Spanish state. Nor (as I understand liberal culturalism here) can this argument rest on a general claim about the entitlement of provinces, autonomous communities or other sub-state units to legitimate particular language policies through democratic politics.[3] Finally, this does not derive merely from the commitment to protect other, non-cultural individual rights, such as freedom of speech or even the right to life. Attacks by the state and others on the latter rights, of course, are often a route to cultural extinction or submersion. But the distinctively culturalist point is different. What marks out a liberal culturalist perspective is a concern to be just, fair or even-handed to the bearers of different cultural identities, because of the importance of their cultural identity to those individuals.[4] Why should only dominant cultures survive and flourish? Is this not unfair to those with a minority cultural identity that may have value to them? There are of course difficulties in formulating what equal treatment requires in practice in particular cases. For example, a widely dispersed linguistic minority may have a poorer case for schooling in their native language than a territorially concentrated one, by virtue of the practical difficulties that this would present. Yet the need to make practical judgements of that sort should not undermine the overall commitment to the ideal of equal treatment of different cultural identities.

Fifth, differentiated citizenship is meant 'to make it possible for members of ethnic and national groups [and presumably others too] to express and promote their culture and identity' without imposing any '*duty* on people to do so' (Kymlicka 2001a: 42, emphasis original). People are not to be compelled to maintain a cultural identity, but the state is obliged to enable them to do so, if they wish.

In one variant, liberal culturalism shares with the negative positions discussed in the next chapter the commitment to state neutrality, in the sense that an assessment of the intrinsic merits of a conception of the good is not meant to play a role in the rationale of a law or policy.[5] For the libertarian vision espoused by Chandran Kukathas, this is achieved through a minimal set of rights, centring on the individual freedoms of thought and association. Brian Barry's egalitarian conception builds on a richer notion of equal treatment, identifying a basic set of resources that it is judged to be the state's duty to equalize among citizens. For Kymlicka, cultural identity (at least in one sense to be clarified below) is understood as a part of that basic set of resources, and the state is correspondingly required to ensure its equal distribution.

Yet liberal culturalism need not take this neutralist form. The alternative strand of liberal culturalism requires that the state make judgements about the intrinsic merits of competing conceptions of the good life, which are outside the bounds of liberal justice for Kymlicka. For Raz's perfectionist point of view, 'it is the goal of all political action to enable individuals to pursue valid conceptions of the good and to discourage evil or empty ones' (Raz 1986: 133). The role of the state is to promote valuable ways of life and to curb degrading or worthless ways of life, a task that requires the assessment of the intrinsic merits of different conceptions of the good. In other words, the state's duties are not exhausted (if they are fulfilled at all) by its parcelling out equal packages of resources, regardless of what is done with those resources. A person may then be viewed as having a fundamental interest in her cultural identity as a condition of or part of a valuable way of life, which the state is then required to respect as a right. For Taylor, in a different way, liberal politics relies on the espousal of a shared social conception of the good. Accordingly, liberalism should make room, he argues, for the legitimacy of pursuing strong collective goals such as cultural '*survivance*'. For the alternative strand of liberal culturalism, liberal political deliberation may permit or require a fuller ethical appraisal of cultures and ways of life. At the same time, it emphasizes that the values at stake in such deliberation are plural, in the sense that there is no way of determining the right ordering of all the important goods involved.

## 2.   Kymlicka's Argument

The version of liberal egalitarianism endorsed by Kymlicka has three central elements. The first is a belief in the rational revisability of conceptions of the good: from a liberal perspective, 'each individual should have the capacity to rationally reflect on the ends she currently endorses and to revise these ends if they are no longer deemed worthy of her continual allegiance' (Kymlicka 2001a: 329) – deemed worthy, that is, by herself. The state should protect the conditions that allow this process of individual reflection – through supporting an appropriate form of education, for example, and through blocking the efforts of individuals and groups to suppress this capacity. Second, the state should be neutral among different conceptions of the good, in the sense, already touched upon, that it should not base its actions on an assessment of the intrinsic merits of particular conceptions of the good. The role of the state is to protect individuals' capacities to judge for themselves the merits of different conceptions of the good life. It must also provide a fair distribution of rights and resources in order to enable people to pursue their various conceptions of the good, and constrain the ways in which some conceptions of the good life are pursued by reference to the rightful claims of other people. Third, 'morally arbitrary' inequalities should be rectified. Individuals may come to have different 'holdings' as a result of the different choices that they make – the feckless grasshopper ends up less well provided for than the diligent ant. However, if people have different holdings as a result of their unchosen *circumstances*, for which they are not responsible, rather than of their own choices, then these differences are morally arbitrary and subject to egalitarian redistribution (Kymlicka 2002).

Once we add to these claims the thought that among the resources that a person ought to have equalized by the state are those necessary for the possession of her cultural identity, the bare bones of a general liberal egalitarian argument for rights and policies which are sensitive to cultural difference begin to appear. This argument requires that we show that among the basic interests that a person has according to this conception is an interest in secure possession of her cultural identity. Without that, her capacity to form, pursue and revise her conception of the good is significantly damaged, just as it is damaged if she is deprived of freedom of movement or an adequate education. It follows that one sort of morally arbitrary inequality that the state ought to rectify is the inequality in different individuals' capacities to maintain a secure possession of their cultural identities.

Here we can reintroduce two lines of thought that have already been discussed: the context of choice argument and the societal conception of culture.[6] To recall, the first is the idea that through offering a person options and endowing them with meaning and familiarity, a culture forms a context in which she is able to exercise the capacity to choose. So, if we value this capacity to choose, then we should value the cultural context that is a condition of it, since the erosion of this cultural context diminishes this capacity. A societal culture 'tends to be' territorially bound and in possession of a distinct language, and 'provides its members with meaningful ways of life across the full range of human activities, including social, educational, religious, recreational, and economic life, encompassing both public and private spheres'. For a culture to be embodied in this way means that it must be 'institutionally embodied – in schools, media, economy, government, etc.' (Kymlicka 1995a: 76).

In outline, then, the liberal culturalist argument that appears in Kymlicka's work runs as follows. First, the state is required (only) to rectify those inequalities in circumstances that impact on an individual's capacity to form, revise and pursue a conception of the good. Second, culture is one such circumstance: according to the context of choice argument, my having 'secure access' to my culture is a significant condition of my possessing and being able to exercise this capacity, since my culture provides options, meaning and familiarity that make my capacity to choose meaningful (Kymlicka 1989: 135–205; 1995a: 82–4, 89–90; 2001a: 53–5, 216, 227–9). Furthermore, cultural identity is also arguably a condition of individual self-respect, and the latter impacts significantly on my capacity to form, revise and pursue a conception of the good (Kymlicka 1995a: 89; 2001a: 228).[7] Third, these functions are performed only by a *societal* culture. Societal cultures are the possession of, or are identified with, national groups, and a state housing more than one societal culture is 'multinational'. As noted in chapter 1, for Kymlicka there are permissible or intelligible senses in which there can be cultures that are not societal: indeed, societal cultures characteristically possess particular features capable of 'abstraction' from the specific institutional context, such as language, cuisine and architectural style. Yet only societal cultures provide the social context for the formation and revision of conceptions of the good, and hence of individual freedom. Accordingly, he emphasizes the distinctness of territories that have been 'incorporated into the boundaries of the larger state, through conquest, colonization or federation' (Kymlicka 1995a: p. vii): among his core examples of such territories are those of American Indians, Puerto Ricans, the Chamorros of Guam, and native Hawaiians in the United States, Quebecois and original peoples in Canada, Maoris in New Zealand, and Aborigines in Australia, Catalans and Basques in Spain, and Scots and Welsh in the United Kingdom. In more recent work, he has tried to show how his theoretical framework can encompass such thorny cases as the various enclaves and national minorities of Eastern and Central Europe (Kymlicka and Opalski 2001). Certain kinds of group are correspondingly excluded from this core, notably immigrants, displaced populations and other sorts of non-territorial group.

Since secure access to my cultural identity is an important condition for the possession and exercise of my capacity to form and revise a conception of the good, the fourth step is to claim that it is the state's duty to rectify inequalities in the distribution of this good, where these inequalities do not flow from the choices of the individual whose cultural identity is in question. This may require differential treatment of some groups, and the particular rights or resources that need to be distributed will vary from case to case. The underlying and unifying point is that, once we have decided that cultural identity is important, then the resources necessary for maintaining it become eligible for egalitarian distribution, and failure to distribute those resources constitutes unequal treatment of citizens on the part of the state. Fifth, the state's duty lies specifically in protecting minority societal cultures, since it is secure access to the latter that constitutes the important condition for individual choice. What should be protected by the state is not any specific set of customs or practices. Rather, the state is responsible for ensuring that all societal cultures or 'national groups have the opportunity to maintain themselves as a distinct culture, if they so choose' (Kymlicka 1995a: 113). This principle forms nothing less than the basis on which 'to recognize languages, draw boundaries, and distribute powers' (Kymlicka 1995a: 13). Where a minority possesses a distinct societal culture, it deserves whatever rights permit it to preserve that culture, including rights of self-government and secession (Kymlicka 1995a: 28–30, 79–80, 103–5, 142–5, 186). Societal cultures are identified with specific groups; a group having (or being, as some formulations suggest) that culture can choose whether to change the culture, maintain it, dissolve it, and so on.[8] It is the state's responsibility to ensure that every group possessed of a societal culture has an equal capacity for effective control over its own cultural future. Once the conditions for this are furnished, the pre-emptive work of the right to culture is completed. Justice to minority cultures requires only that the conditions for the continuation of the cultural identity be put in place, but the state should keep out of the business of promoting any particular character for the cultural identity. The 'cultural marketplace' can then take over in determining the character of the culture. Decisions about which particular aspects of a culture are worth maintaining, revising, developing or abandoning 'should . . . be left to the individual members. For the state to intervene at this point to support particular options or customs . . . would run the risk of unfairly subsidizing some people's choices' (Kymlicka 1995a: 113).

This way of setting up the claims of societal culture puts at the centre of its political theory self-government rights and those 'external rules' that limit the freedom of outsiders to influence a group's identity.[9] The paradigmatic case of a circumstantial inequality that should be set right is the position of a minority group in a democratic state, which will tend to lose out in decisions over the cultural character of the state; for example, if it has a different language from the majority, the minority tongue will probably not be the principal language of state business: 'in a democratic society the majority nation will always have its language and societal culture supported, and will have the legislative power to protect its interests in culture-affecting decisions' (Kymlicka 1995a: 113). Where a minority possesses a distinct societal culture, it deserves those rights of territorial and linguistic autonomy necessary to protect its cultural identity. So the Quebecois provincial government, for example, is justified in tailoring its own language policy in order to protect and promote the French language – for example, by ruling that the children of all immigrants to the province be educated in French. Similarly, the government of the autonomous community of Catalonia is entitled to promote Catalan as the principal language of education and public affairs.

Consider another of the central examples of a remediable disadvantage for the theory. Preservation of hunting and trapping traditions plays an important part in maintaining the societal cultures of some aboriginal Canadians. This requires that ecological habitats and patterns of animal migration remain undisturbed. However, activities that the majority community may be content to endorse or permit, such as logging and mining, threaten these conditions. The minority is disadvantaged in the sense that it may always be outbid or outvoted on issues such as this – that is, by the vulnerability inherent in its minority status. Members of minority cultures in this position ought, then, to be granted rights that allow them to limit or ban such activities (or allow them, if they decide to do so). This involves the foregoing of opportunities on the part of some of the majority community, but 'the sacrifice required of non-members by the existence of these rights is far less than the sacrifice members would face in the absence of these rights' (Kymlicka 1995a: 109) – *viz.* damage to their societal culture. Such rights are justified only when there is a disadvantage to be corrected, and when the rights in fact do so. Where these conditions are met, failure to assign these rights would violate the state's neutrality, in Kymlicka's sense: for members of the minority would be disadvantaged in the pursuit of their chosen ways of life.

The point is that the interest in cultural identity is such that egalitarian distribution is justified in order to protect the identity of the minority. It is worth noting that on this view cultural identity is not assimilated to a 'handicap' that is the appropriate object of rectification or compensation. Rather, what are to be remedied are disadvantages flowing from the relationship to a more numerous or powerful alternative cultural identity with which one shares the state. If we understand the argument this way, we can see that the remedy is envisaged not for costs flowing from cultural identity but for the structural disadvantage of being in a minority when voting over resources essential for cultural identity. It is my being in a minority in votes over the distribution of resources or forced to pay a high price for the maintenance of my societal culture that generates a claim for remedy. If my tastes (say, for opera) are expensive or not widely shared, then that is just bad luck. But if my preferences reflect the needs of my societal culture, then this is a different matter. No one can reasonably ask me to sacrifice my cultural identity in order to satisfy others' preferences.

While groups possessed of societal cultures are owed self-government rights in order to secure equality of control over the character of their cultural identity, Kymlicka identifies another sort of minority group, which is owed another kind of entitlement. The other sort of minority group is constituted principally by voluntary immigration. Immigrant groups do not seek national self-rule or claim a homeland territory in their new state. Their cultural distinctness manifests itself in the private sphere of family life and voluntary associations, and is consistent with the groups' integration into the public institutions of the societal dominant culture, such as that culture's language: in Australia and the United States, immigrants are required to learn English as a condition of citizenship (Kymlicka 1995a: 14). These groups do not characteristically claim entitlements to self-government, but a different cluster of rights, which Kymlicka calls 'polyethnic rights' or 'accommodation rights' (Kymlicka 2001a: 51; 1996b; 1998a; 1998b). While the rights of self-government to which societal cultures are entitled are granted in order to maintain distinctness, polyethnic rights are granted in order to promote integration into the 'common culture' rather than to establish a separate public or institutional life (Kymlicka 1995a: 66–8, 171–81; Spinner 1994: 76–8). Polyethnic rights allow immigrants to feel a sense of continuity with their original cultures while at the same time living in a new societal culture. These are rights that allow a group to maintain some distinctive practices while simultaneously integrating them into a society's mainstream institutions – that is, into its societal culture. For example, decisions about the timing of public holidays or about dress codes for certain sorts of employment (construction work, the army) can be made with reference to groups with different norms and practices – that is, where there are significant differences along what I have called the normative or semiotic dimensions. These tend to be measures to counteract discrimination and to preserve some features of their original cultures while permitting them to participate in the social, economic and political activities of their host country. However, since immigrants have no interest in preserving their ancestral culture in their new society grounded in the need to preserve a meaningful context of choice, these rights characteristically fall far short of the self-determination rights allowed to national minorities.

### 3. Tensions in the Right to Culture

Kymlicka's line of argument offers a particular way of fleshing out the link between a neutralist form of liberal egalitarianism and the claim that there is an individual interest in cultural identity sufficiently robust to ground difference-sensitive rights. Having outlined this argument and some of its main implications, I now want to draw out the tensions between three key components of his account: the view of the value of cultural identity as resting on the individual interest in autonomy, the idea that cultural identity should be protected by self-government rights and external rules, and the claim that the state ought neutrally to protect with such cultural rights the underlying right to maintain and develop a culture but not the duty to do so, or the duty to do so in any particular way. My discussion is structured in the following way. I first pick up some of the threads from the previous chapter, and recall the difficulties in tethering the context of choice argument to the societal conception of culture. This leads, second, to an objection to the hard and fast distinction between immigrants and national minorities, and the normative implications derived, which Kymlicka draws. Third, I go on to focus on a tension between ascribing rights of self-government and external protections to national minorities and the individualist tenor of the context of choice argument. Considering this relationship leads, fourth, to an objection to the way in which the link between equality and culture is forged in Kymlicka's argument. Fifth, I argue that there are difficulties facing this attempt to fold the right to culture into the model of liberal neutrality and the priority of the right on which the argument is based. This objection has three parts: I suggest that there is an obscurity in the notion of equalizing the conditions under which a group can develop and maintain its culture; I argue that it is difficult to justify neutralist agnosticism about the use made of cultural resources; and I question whether Kymlicka's premises lead to the conclusion that he suggests that they do: namely, grounding the entitlement of members of a group to maintain and develop their culture, but not a duty to do so, or to do so in any specific way.

The arguments that an individual's culture may be valued as a context of choice and that it is an important condition for individual self-respect were discussed in the previous chapter. In essence, I argued there that the idea that a given culture makes options available to its members needs to be handled with some care, but that we can make sense of the idea that cultural identity is a condition of choice. In the case of the self-respect argument too, there is no general conceptual link between recognition of a cultural identity (and *a fortiori* legal or political recognition in the particular sense of granting differentiated rights) and the maintenance of self-respect. If we view culture as valuable to individuals, it is possible to combine the moral individualism of liberalism with a belief in cultural identity as a ground for group rights and recognition. At the same time, it is important to recognize that there are circumstances in which cultural insecurity or precariousness may constitute a fruitful context of choice for an individual. Furthermore, there is only a contingent relationship between the meaning- and option-providing functions of a cultural identity and that identity's being tied to a bounded and identifiable societal culture.

The important differences between accommodation rights, owed to immigrants, and self-government rights, owed to societal cultures, rest on the significance attached to the latter by Kymlicka's interpretation of the context of choice argument.[10] But we have seen that he is not persuasive in linking these two elements. Kymlicka views immigrants as in a very different situation from members of societal cultures. There is an 'expectation of integration' on the former that is 'not unjust' provided that they have 'the option to stay in their original culture' (Kymlicka 1995a: 96; Ripstein 1997b: 611). One objection to this distinction between cultural minorities is that we may view membership of a national minority as voluntary. A member of a national minority (say, a Scot, Quebecois or Catalan) may have the option of embracing the multinational state identity without severe costs, but chooses not to. If we can view minority identity in this way, why are those who opt for it not in the same position as voluntary immigrants (cf. Kukathas 1997c: 413)? The wider society would be under no obligation to support their choice of identity except by way of 'polyethnic' rights to aid integration. This objection breaks down, however, when the terms of what Kymlicka counts as voluntary are recalled: this requires that I am only understood to be choosing a cultural identity when I have the option to stay in my original culture. If, in the absence of provision for self-government, this culture will be eroded, then the expectation that I integrate is unjust. It follows that we can view assimilation into a new cultural identity as voluntary only if the original culture remains in existence and is furnished with what it needs in order to exist. This response creates a new problem, however, since this condition presumably holds in the case of immigrants from outside the multinational state as well. So, for example, if Spain fails to offer sufficient protection for the national identity of Catalonia, Catalan immigrants to (say) Canada would seem to be entitled to protection of their societal culture.

A second objection to Kymlicka's distinction between national minorities and immigrants is that the class of dispersed cultural minorities is by no means co-extensive with the class of voluntary minorities, on any plausible interpretation of the latter. Kymlicka offers a fourfold typology of 'ethnocultural groups' (Kymlicka 1995a, 2001c; Kymlicka and Norman 2000). National minorities are characterized as possessing territorial concentration, a shared history, a shared language or culture, a history of treaty or federal arrangements with the state. National minorities often seek to maintain or enhance their autonomy with respect to the state of which they form part, sometimes through secession but often through other means such as federal or consociational arrangements. The Quebecois, the Catalans, the Scots and the Slovenians fall into this category. This also includes the 'indigenous peoples', 'whose traditional lands have been overrun by settlers, and who have then been forcibly, or through treaties, incorporated into states run by people they regard as foreigners' (Kymlicka 2001b: 23), such as the Sami in Scandinavia, the Inuit in Canada and the Maori in New Zealand. These groups usually seek the capacity to maintain certain aspects of a traditional way of life, and often control over a portion of territory, rather than a fully-fledged provincial status or statehood. This is frequently allied to a demand for recognition of their distinctive history of oppression. The second key group is that of immigrant minorities within a state with a different dominant, majority culture. This group may be subdivided again according to the kinds of difference that members exhibit with respect to the society into which they emigrate (linguistic, religious, cultural), and according to their legal status (legal, illegal, refugee). Third, there are religious groups: these may be more isolationist (for example, the Amish or Hutterites in North America, or the Haredim in Israel) or less (for example, Catholics and Muslims in predominantly Protestant countries).[11] Finally, there are non-territorial and non-immigrant groups: this class covers a range of very different identities, including Russians in the Baltic states and other scattered East European populations, Crimean Tartars, the Roma, Indians scattered through the colonial system of indentured labour, and African Americans.

While this classification gives us a flavour of the sociological variety of groups (as it is undoubtedly principally intended to do), the principles behind it are unclear. Immigrants are identified by the route by which they came into a state or society, while religious groups are identified by their traditional beliefs, and, in the case of some isolationists, by occupation of a specific territory. National minorities are variously and multiply defined by constitutional status, numbers and territorial concentration, political behaviour, cultural and linguistic traits, and ethnic origins – in other words, by the many conflicting ways in which nationality is identified. And the final category, of course, tries to sweep up residual anomalies. In this connection, Kymlicka glumly refers to 'hard cases and grey areas', noting for example that African Americans do not fit his scheme very well (Kymlicka 1995a: 101). Furthermore, there are groups that 'have' their own nation-state but through forced resettlement or flight have resettled elsewhere, sometimes in enclaves that pose political problems. Examples include Germans in Slovakia, Hungary, the Czech Republic and Romania; Poles in Lithuania; Albanians, Serbians and Croatians in the Balkans; and Hungarians in Slovakia and Romania (cf. Festenstein 1998; Kymlicka 2001b, 2001c). And there are groups that have been forcibly resettled or concentrated with no 'home' nation, such as the Chechens. The communities of Northern Ireland constitute another case in which the opposition of a national or indigenous group and voluntary minority has no grip. Similarly, it is not clear that refugees persecuted on political, religious or ethnic grounds, or (as Kymlicka concedes) the victims of severe economic need, are immigrants by virtue of free choice (Kymlicka 1995a: 99).[12] Finally, some further argument is required to establish that dependants who accompany even voluntary immigrants themselves count as voluntary immigrants.

The contingency of this relationship between the context of choice argument and societal culture is even clearer when we consider the link between the context of choice argument and the case for self-government rights for groups, or for external rules limiting the ability of outsiders to have an impact on the character of a culture. By identifying the cultural framework necessary for successful individual choice (according to the context of choice argument) with a societal culture, Kymlicka runs together an argument for an individual right to a secure cultural framework with an argument for a nation's right to political self-determination. One way of bringing out the puzzling and contentious nature of this conflation is as follows. The value of a societal culture which grounds the claim for political protection lies in its providing a secure context from which an individual can deliberate and make choices. The context of choice argument posits no particular value for the individual chooser in self-rule by the group that possesses such a culture; what is valuable for the individual is the cultural framework itself. But of course granting political power to a group that represents the societal culture is not the same as protecting the framework itself. If what is valuable in culture C from the point of view of the context of choice argument is that it provides options x, y, z, then the obligation of the multinational state is to protect x, y, z, rather than to devolve power to a group that possesses C (or is dominated by those that possess C, or is on a territory claimed as historically important to C). Self-government is valuable only in an instrumental or pragmatic way, for the context of choice argument, for the protection it affords to the cultural framework of the individuals so ruled; so where self-government does not in fact serve this purpose, it is not clear why it should be granted. For example, if a tradition of coal mining forms a crucial part of a region's cultural framework, in the sense of supplying the options, scripts and familiar landmarks that the context of choice argument draws our attention to, then the multinational state's duty is to preserve this tradition, rather than to devolve powers to the sub-unit. After all, depending on how boundaries are drawn and on the vagaries of politics in the region, the sub-unit may not use its devolved powers to support coal mining.

On the context of choice argument, however, the state's duty is owed not to the politically organized sub-unit but to the individuals and their threatened cultural framework. Nor does assuming that the relevant context must be a societal culture make self-government rights the natural expression of the individuals' interest in secure access to this context. If the regional government fails to secure the context of choice of members, then the context of choice argument provides a reason for the multinational state to *intervene* in the internal government of that region in order to protect the context of choice of (some) citizens. Consider language policy in Wales, which since 1998 is set by the devolved Welsh Assembly. Compulsory education in Welsh in state schools and the promotion of the language through its being made a requirement for some public sector jobs secures the 'context of choice' of those (relatively few) monoglot Welsh speakers in Wales. For the rest (the fluently bilingual, English speakers and others), this sort of language policy transforms their contexts of choice, and, by Kymlicka's reasoning, may be viewed as creating the conditions of disorientation and unfamiliarity which *ex hypothesi* unfairly impact on their capacity to form and revise their conceptions of the good on equal terms with the monoglot Welsh. In this case, the duty of the multinational state, the United Kingdom, would seem to be (in Kymlicka's view) to intervene to constrain this sort of language policy, since the cultural resources distributed to citizens in this case are unequal. This would be the case even if the numbers were different and the solely Welsh speakers constituted a very large majority. The individualist character of the context of choice argument that is inserted into the structure of liberal egalitarian theory means that the duty of the state is primarily to the particular contexts of choice of individual citizens.

One way of understanding this link is in terms of the greater degree of trust that a minority group may feel for governing institutions staffed by people who share their identity, particularly when it comes to protecting valued aspects of that identity. For instance, a territorially concentrated linguistic minority may distrust exposure to the superior voting strength of a state-wide legislature, and instead wish to control language policy within the territory. Perhaps sharing an identity itself gives members of the minority greater reason to trust a government of their own than that of the majority. I pick up on these considerations in chapter 6. Here, however, let us assume that in some instances the state's duty to protect the context of choice of its members is sometimes most effectively discharged through the devolution of political powers over language and other culturally relevant policies. This is where different cultural populations are so neatly divided that there are no enclaves or overlap, and where, in addition, the provincial sub-states do in fact reflect the cultural choices of their members. But the world in fact, and certainly the parts of the world that exercise multicultural political theory, is not neatly divided in this way, and the distinctive problems for this theory arise in part from that fact. In *Nations and Nationalism*, Ernest Gellner draws a vivid distinction between two conceptions of the relationship between culture and territory by contrasting the artistic styles of Kokoschka and Modigliani. In the paintings of the former shreds and patches of colour and shade predominate, and in the latter sharply delineated blocs of colour. The landscapes of nationally and culturally homogenized industrial societies resemble the clearly separated areas of colour in Modigliani paintings, he suggests, in contrast to the Kokoschka world of intersecting, overlapping and diffused colours (Gellner 1983: 139–40; Van Parijs 2000: 239). In effect, Kymlicka's moral theory requires a Kokoschka-like sensitivity to particular skeins and splashes of cultural identity across political space, while his political theory rests on a Modigliani world of clear demarcation, for which '[t]he freedom which liberals demand for individuals is not primarily the freedom to go beyond one's language and history, but rather the freedom to move around one's societal culture' (Kymlicka 1995a: 90).

One response to this is that it is an absurdity to think that, in the case of Welsh language policy (or Quebecois or Catalan language policies), the English (or Castilian) speakers in fact enjoy unequal access to their societal culture. For their context of choice is preserved in the majority language and culture of the multinational state. Even if an English-speaking child in Wales foregoes some opportunities as a result of the region's language policy, such as being able to study French, the range of societal options available to her remains robust. While communities are entitled to revise a range of practices and beliefs, they need some secure cultural moorings in order to do so (if we follow the context of choice argument). While English or Spanish/Castilian speakers have these moorings elsewhere in the multinational polity, Welsh-speakers or Catalan-speakers can have this cultural context only in their particular province. Furthermore, self-government for a group is typically the best way in which this security can be achieved. For example, if government and other public institutions, such as education, are dominated by the language and other cultural traits of the majority in this territory, this domination will usually provide a secure foundation on top of which individuals and the society more generally can maintain some practices and ditch or revise others. Yet it is not clear what weight to attach to the presence *somewhere else* of a flourishing societal culture. For members of the majority language or cultural community stranded in the zone in which the minority enjoys hegemony must then pay a cost in uprooting themselves and travelling in order to enjoy access to this societal culture. But Kymlicka's argument started from the unfairness of some having to pay a price to maintain their culture that others do not. Stranded members of the majority seem then to be in the unequal position that Kymlicka sets out to correct.

Finally, the right to equalization of access to societal culture takes its place within an overall account of the character of the liberal state in relation to particular conceptions of value. The liberal state, to recall, should be neutral among these different conceptions, and concerned only with providing an equal set of conditions under which people can form, pursue and revise the particular conceptions of the good that they possess. The goal of Kymlicka's form of liberal multiculturalism is to permit practitioners of a minority culture the right to preserve, maintain and develop that culture, but without imposing on them a duty to do so in any particular way. However, the arguments laid out do not reach this conclusion. The state is meant to put in place rights which protect the ability of a group to control its own cultural development, and thereafter to let the group do as it pleases. Decisions about the course that this development should take should be left to individual members of the group. For the state to intervene to promote some cultural options at the expense of others is for it to breach its commitment to neutrality

(Kymlicka 1995a: 113). The argument in practice is meant to have something like the following effect. A national minority is entitled to operate (say) a language policy in its schools and public services, which limits the use of the majority language of the multinational state and promotes the minority language. It is entitled to do so, since such measures support the conditions of autonomy enjoyed by members of the group, and they would lack an important resource affecting autonomy without such a right. This entails no assessment of the value of this cultural identity or language on the part of the multinational state beyond a judgement about its value for an individual's capacity to form, pursue and revise particular conceptions of the good.

However, invoking a vision of a cultural marketplace that is allowed to flourish in the wake of an initial equalization of cultural resources is obscure in several ways. An initial point is that the notion of the decision or will of the group about how to develop its culture papers over important issues. For example, Kymlicka writes that 'we should aim at ensuring that all national groups have opportunity to maintain themselves as a distinct culture, if they so choose' (Kymlicka 1995a: 113). A preliminary objection to this is that we should resist the identification of *cultures* with *groups*. Once a group is picked out, however, what it means to give it the opportunity to maintain a distinct cultural identity, if its members so choose, is unclear. Groups tend to be characterized by disagreements over what in the cultural heritage is central, worth preserving, or should be rejected, as well as disagreements over who is entitled to take part in this debate. They do not speak with a single voice. Moreover, it is not the contingent fact of empirical disagreement but the interpretative contestability of cultural phenomena that makes it implausible to ascribe a monolithic cultural identity to a group. A second problem, following from the first, is that any particular way of assigning the right to a group to maintain and develop its cultural heritage will advantage some conceptions of how the culture should develop and disadvantage others. The general right of access to a secure societal culture requires specification in particular contexts, and this specification does not remain above the fray; rather, it will unevenly impact on different conceptions of what an identity is or requires. Consider language rights once again. For example, the state may grant a territorially concentrated linguistic minority the right to maintain its language through giving the province in which that group is a majority the right to set its own language policy. If the procedure that generates this policy is majoritarian democracy, then this way of granting the right to maintain and develop a linguistic identity advantages whatever policy is supported by the majority in that territory. So, for example, if a majority of the Welsh Assembly supports making knowledge of the Welsh language a requirement for service in the public sector in Wales, this advantages those in this province with this particular conception of Welsh culture and identity. If the policy issue is dealt with in some other fashion – through official bilingualism, votes among stakeholders in particular segments of the public services, or in some other way – the particular way in which the right is specified and implemented will advantage some conceptions of identity and disadvantage others.

To this objection Kymlicka could reply that language and culture survive only if they are defended and promoted, that this can happen only in particular ways, and that this process will inevitably have an unequal impact on people with different conceptions of the relevant identity. ('There is evidence that language communities can only survive intergenerationally if they are numerically dominant within a particular territory, and if their language is the language of opportunity in that territory' (Kymlicka 2001a: 79).) This is a price worth paying, however, if the alternative to granting cultural rights with an uneven impact on different conceptions of the identity is the disappearance or erosion of the linguistic or cultural identity. This response, however, either relaxes the assumption of neutrality or suggests that uneven impact on different cultural identities is not relevant to the assessment of the neutrality of the liberal state. The latter position, as we shall see, is adopted by writers such as Barry and Kukathas, who seek to show that the unevenness of impact of a law or policy on different groups and identities does not compromise the neutrality of the law or policy. Yet it is hard to see how Kymlicka can make it his own. For the attack on the strategy of benign neglect is based on the claim that uneven impact on different cultural identities affects an interest of fundamental importance to liberal justice.

Nevertheless, there are independent reasons for thinking that the assumption of neutrality should be relaxed. It is an important part of Kymlicka's liberal egalitarianism that no evaluation of the *use* made of resources enters into the assessment of the entitlement to difference-sensitive rights. Whatever we make of this claim in general, it is difficult to sustain in this context. For cultural policies may impact on the equality of opportunity of individuals along different dimensions. This may be to promote equality: for example, the Quebecois language laws governing business have arguably played a role in narrowing the gap between Francophone and Anglophone incomes (Keating 2001: 105). However, laws such as these may also promote inequalities, for example, in limiting individuals' employability across North America as a whole. Further, the interest of a group in its cultural identity needs to be weighed alongside other interests in political deliberation, and it is not plausible to set it aside as a prior and overriding consideration. The interests of aboriginal communities for which fishing has been part of a traditional way of life need to be weighed against environmental considerations, for example. In sum, it is hard to see how a posture of benign neglect on the part of the state, which was criticized as a profoundly incoherent conception of the state's role in cultural construction, is appropriate when considering the specification and use made of a right to culture.

The right of access to a secure cultural identity is meant to protect members of a cultural minority from the unfettered marketplace or process of majoritarian decision making, in which their weakness in terms of numbers or resources may lead to the erosion of the culture. A third difficulty afflicts the notion that this takes the form of a right to perpetuate a culture but no duty to do so. For if disruption to context of choice is a bad experienced individually, then members of the minority owe it to one another to preserve the conditions for their autonomy, which they all enjoy. Preservation of the ancestral culture as a public good, in this sense, is a condition for the autonomy of each that can be maintained only by collectively imposed constraints. The proposed analogy is with the regulation of pollution, for example: we all have an interest in a clean environment, but each of us may have an interest in not acting in such a way as to preserve that environment. The state can then legitimately intervene with legislation to ensure that the natural environment that we all enjoy is protected from our own individual short-sightedness. Critics of the public good argument believe that it pits a spurious conception of the 'authentic' interests of individuals against their actual cultural preferences (J. Levy 2000: 118–21; Weinstock 2003: 264). When individuals in aggregate prefer to leave their culture or to transform it radically, then (unlike in the case of pollution) they are not acting against an interest that they identifiably have. Yet, if we accept the context of choice argument, then there is an interest that all have and which may legitimately be weighed against the preferences of particular individuals. If that is the case, then we have an argument for the duty to preserve a culture, rather than just for the right to maintain and develop a cultural identity – a far stronger conclusion than Kymlicka and some other liberal culturalists are inclined to accept (cf. Weinstock 2003: 255–6).

Pulling together the threads of this last part of the discussion, we can see that what makes this too strong a conclusion is not that what is arrived at is a duty imposed by the fact of sharing a cultural identity, but the kind of duty that it becomes when placed in the framework of Kymlicka's conception of liberalism. For there are various reasons, as I suggested in the previous chapter, why we may think that cultural identities exercise a normative pull on us. The distinctive problem that this argument presents is twofold. The right to a stable or secure context of choice is located by this strand of liberal culturalism among those core human interests that require political protection from the inequalities in power allowed by majoritarian political decision making and by the market. In respecting these interests through a system of rights, we respect the capacities of others (and of ourselves) to form, pursue and revise the various specific views of what is valuable in life. However, if so, we seem to be under a duty not to disrupt the culture *qua* context of choice of fellow citizens, since to do so is to interfere with this capacity. This empties the capacity of forming, pursuing and revising a conception of the good of much of its point. In the previous chapter, we considered the possibility that, *contra* the context of choice argument, cultural instability may be a condition for autonomy for some people. Perhaps cultural instability is also a sign of the widespread exercise of autonomy. For as we pursue and revise our conceptions of what is valuable, and quite generally as we go about living our lives, we impact on our own and others' cultural identities, in both intended and unintended ways.

## 4.   Culture, Pluralism and the Good

I want to turn now to consider an alternative version of liberal culturalism, which breaks with some of the key premisses of Kymlicka's form of liberal egalitarianism. Each is sketchier than Kymlicka's comprehensive and lucid attempt to derive quite specific political conclusions from premisses about the place of culture in political morality, however. They do not offer a clear alternative line on specific policy questions – how to draw boundaries, assign powers, offer political recognition, and so on.[13] These accounts take the general form of a liberal culturalist position outlined in the first section, arguing that there exists a legitimate interest in cultural identity that grounds the promotion or affirmation of that identity by the state, and that this interest can be knitted into liberal political theory. First, they break with the neutralist account of the legitimate use of political power, holding that the political community not only is entitled to evaluate and promote conceptions of the good life, but to some degree is required to endorse a conception of the good. Second, they espouse pluralist conceptions of ethical and political value. Third, they make room for a wider range of conceptions of the value of cultural identity.

First, from different directions, Raz and Taylor endorse the claim that liberal political theory cannot duck the assessment of different conceptions of the good, but requires substantive judgements about what is valuable in life. Raz's version of liberal multiculturalism insists that substantive judgement of the character of different communities and practices is an essential part of liberal political morality. According to Raz, liberalism's core value is autonomy, 'the value of being in charge of one's own life, charting its course by one's successive choices' (Raz 1994: 70; 1986: 369). It is the role of political society to support and promote autonomy, as an essential element of human well-being. This requires substantive judgement of the particular ways in which people live their lives. For 'a person's well-being depends on the value of his goals and pursuits' (Raz 1986: 298), not merely on pursuing a conception of the good that he happens to believe is valuable. The liberal state fails to respect a person's fundamental interest in well-being if it suspends judgement on the validity of conceptions of the good.

Taylor offers a different line of argument against the neutralist priority of the right. For Taylor, this form of liberalism deprives itself of the concepts and categories necessary for making sense of the conditions of a liberal society. This is so in two linked ways. The first is that in order to understand the *desirability* of a liberal system of rights, we need to invoke a conception of the good. For in reflecting on this desirability, he argues, we unavoidably engage in substantive judgement about whether the social forms it makes possible and fosters are valuable. For someone reasoning about what makes liberalism a credible political morality, there must exist a language of 'qualitative distinctions' about the good in which to articulate a position on this: so, 'in a sense, the good is always primary to the right . . . the good is what, in its articulation, gives the point of the rules which define the right' (Taylor 1989: 89). Second, Taylor also argues that a liberal polity requires 'a socially endorsed common end' in the form of a 'common allegiance to a particular historical community' (Taylor 1995: 198). The liberal state requires for its sustenance a patriotic commitment on the part of its citizens to its institutions, without which citizens will lack the motivation to bear the burdens of life in a political society. This is a commitment about which the liberal state cannot be neutral. Yet, Taylor argues, it is a commitment always to a particular polity, tradition or set of customs, not merely to an abstract set of liberal principles. What connects this second, functional claim to the first point about the need for a substantive evaluative language in order to reflect on liberalism's desirability is that for Taylor this republican patriotic discourse must form part of the qualitative language which liberals need in order to understand their own position fully. In failing to acknowledge the need for a substantive evaluative language, liberal 'proceduralists', as Taylor calls them, cut themselves off from the patriotic concepts needed to sustain their own position.

Now these are different ways of uprooting the neutralist position embraced by liberals such as Kymlicka, and it is not my aim here to dwell on all the distinctive issues that each account raises. What they have in common, and what is important here, is that they readmit the struggle among competing conceptions of what is valuable that the latter position seeks to exclude from liberal political theory. Admitting specific conceptions of what is valuable allows entry to the second and third defining commitments of this strand of liberal culturalism: value pluralism and non-instrumental as well as instrumental conceptions of the value of culture. The second feature of the alternative strand of liberal culturalism is an appeal to the importance of an irreducible diversity of human goods. Value pluralism, Raz writes, is an idea which 'lies at the heart of multiculturalism' (Raz 1994: 67). For value pluralism, 'there is, in historical reality, an irreducible diversity of worthwhile ways of life, each with its own virtues and excellences, and to any of which a reasonable and specific allegiance may be owed' (Gray 1995a: 118). Raz, following the immensely influential model of Isaiah Berlin, allows that there are incompatible and valuable forms of life, each with its own distinctive virtues, and that any person who cultivates to the greatest degree the virtues constitutive of one form of life will not be able to attain the virtues of others. One cannot be both a (successful) sprinter and a long-distance runner, for each discipline requires the development of distinct capacities; the active life and the contemplative life cannot both be lived to the fullest by one person; and so on. This conflict can take the form of disagreements over fundamental ethical or other evaluative commitments, so that, for example, one can find value in abstract terms in both a life of religious devotion and one of passionate disbelief, while in practical terms it is impossible to reconcile oneself to both sorts of life. To adopt value pluralism, then, is to allow the existence of a real tension between one's own practical commitments and other acceptable forms of life, and to reject the monistic assumption that there is only one acceptable form of life.[14]

The plurality of ultimately valuable ends does not imply that a 'reasonable settlement' is impossible for particular agents confronted by particular choices (Larmore 1996: 157; cf. Berlin and Williams 1994: 306; Crowder 2002: 49–54). Pluralists sometimes reach straight for the language of arbitrariness or tragedy, but the pluralist may hold that one consideration clearly carries more weight in rational assessment than another. While the heterogeneity of values may preclude commensurability, it does not rule out comparison or ranking of alternatives. This is not *ex hypothesi* the ranking of the values in their most ultimate forms, so to speak, but the legitimate comparison of the recommendations, the particular requirements on action, of alternative values.[15] For example, we can hold that neither the values of filial love nor those of justice ultimately trump one another, yet still condemn nepotism in our public officials, with no remorseful sense that a tragic choice has been made. In particular, the moderate pluralist claims that once one begins to describe some conflict in more detail and with respect to the problem confronting a particular agent, reasoned comparisons and rankings become far more plausible. There are strong arguments against a general scepticism which attacks comparability of any sort, and this moderate pluralism raises the sticky issue of how to conceive of comparison in the absence of a general priority rule, or cardinal scale (cf. Chang 1997). But let us (for our purposes here) accept that this is what a moderate pluralist asserts, and that we can make some sense of reasoned comparison against a background of value pluralism. Of course this does not rule out the abstract possibility of a situation calling for radical choice, where our reasons for and against options run out, or offer nothing determinate to an agent.

Value pluralism should not be conflated either with a doctrine about cultural diversity or with an argument for respect for cultural identities (cf. J. Levy 2000: 98–105; but compare Crowder 2002: 236–46). The plurality of values or diversity of goods identified by value pluralism is distinct from cultural diversity. This is apparent, first, in that we can draw distinctions among ways of life in ways unrelated to different values or to competing assessments of the value of different ways of life. French and Flemish speakers in Belgium may agree about most evaluative issues, and share a lot in terms of other customs and practices, while nevertheless constituting distinct language groups. Second, it is the case, as Raz puts it, that 'in our day and age, pluralism exists within every society, indeed within every culture' (Raz 1994: 72). The internal plurality of cultural identities militates against the thought that a culture can be taken to embody a particular value. Value pluralism also needs to be distinguished from an argument for respecting particular cultural identities. The acknowledgement of different values need not translate into respect for particular cultures; nor need respecting a variety of cultures suggest a subscription to value pluralism. A conservative may value the conservative aspects of various cultures, for example, without any pluralist appreciation of alternative, non-conservative values.

The third feature of this alternative version of liberal culturalism is that it allows a wider range of arguments for the value of cultural identity than does the neutral brand of culturalism. For the latter, the value of cultural identity is restricted to its place as a condition in serving the fundamental human interest in forming, revising and pursuing conceptions of the good. Other sorts of assessment of the value of cultural identity may be the concern of citizens, but is not properly the business of the liberal state. Given the rejection of neutralism, this strand of liberal culturalism is not subject to this self-denying ordinance. For Raz, to recall, autonomy is valuable in so far as what the autonomous individual pursues is a worthwhile or valid form of life (Raz 1986: 395). Autonomy is meaningless without the existence of a range of worthwhile options among which the individual may choose. For this perfectionist variant of liberalism, the case for multiculturalism does not rest on the requirement that the state be neutral between different ways of life, or restrict itself to compensating for inequalities generated by membership of a cultural minority. Rather, it bases the claim for recognition on the perfectionist goal of the promotion of individual autonomy, fostering the conditions in which each individual can develop. An important part of these conditions, for which the state has responsibility, is the existence and flourishing of a plurality of valuable forms of life. Autonomy, Raz argues, requires 'full and unimpeded membership in a respected and flourishing cultural group' (Raz 1994: 69), as in the context of choice argument: cultural membership is a condition for individual autonomy. As in Kymlicka's account, this posits a secure cultural identity as a necessary condition of individual autonomy. Respecting a person's autonomy is therefore thought to involve respecting her cultural membership; particular ethnic and cultural identities must not be made marginal or ignored by society. However, the state cannot duck substantive judgement of the ways of life that are pursued within it. Since social diversity, including cultural diversity, supports autonomy to the extent that it provides a plurality of acceptable options among which a person can choose, the state ought to foster intrinsically valuable ways of life within it. For Taylor too (as we saw in the previous chapter) cultural identity is non-instrumentally valuable for a group, and its recognition is valuable as a condition for the undistorted development of the self.[16]

So far I have described ways in which value pluralism and the non-instrumental value of cultural identities are invoked within the liberal culturalist framework. These commitments can of course be invoked outside this framework; for example, by John Gray, who invokes both these claims for anti-liberal ends. Elaborating a claim I have already criticized above, he argues that 'if value pluralism is true at the level of whole ways of life, then the liberal form of life can have no special or universal claim on reason' (Gray 1995a: 142). It is worth noting that Gray claims to be guided by the pragmatic goal of a peaceful *modus vivendi* in his own political prescriptions: 'pluralist political theory is open as to the form of state organization – sovereign nation-state, confederal or federal union, or empire – best able in any given historical context to embody the pluralist regime of a peaceful modus vivendi among different cultural traditions, ways of life and peoples' (Gray 1995a: 140). Strikingly, though, once one moves beyond the minimal value of peace, what has priority in ordering polities is the non-instrumental value of these ways of life: 'the current regime in China might well be criticized for its policies in Tibet; but such criticism would invoke the intrinsic value of the communities and cultural forms now being destroyed in Tibet, not universalist conceptions of human rights or democracy' (Gray 1995a: 140). But why the intrinsic value of cultural identities should have deliberative priority from a pluralist perspective is unclear.[17]

This does, however, bring out an important issue. These three features of this strand of liberal culturalism – the engagement with conceptions of the good in political deliberation, a pluralist conception of value, and permitting a broader range of arguments for the value of cultural identity – raise the question of the *weight* that should attach to cultural identity in political deliberation. Kymlicka, as we saw, aspires to offer a very clear and determinate answer. When what is at issue is a person's secure access to her societal culture, then this consideration has the same kind of basic or 'trumping' force as other basic individual interests, which merit protection through a system of rights. At the same time, it is not the liberal state's affair what she does with this access. That answer suffers from severe difficulties, I suggested in the last section. The non-neutralist alternative allows that cultural identity may have deliberative weight in the political process, and leaves it open as to precisely what weight it has in which circumstances.

Consider the controversial character of Taylor's defence of Quebecois language laws. Canadian political culture, he argues, is partly characterized by a divergence of values, between a procedural conception of liberalism, which emphasizes individual rights, and a more communitarian conception, which emphasizes collective goals. Francophone Quebecois wish to preserve their language, understood as a collective good; anglophone Canadians need to recognize that there is more than one model of liberal society, including ones which promote particular conceptions of the good, and that Quebecois aspirations to have their distinct society recognized express one of these alternatives (Taylor 1993: 177–8; 1995: 245–8). There is no rule which accords rights-based proceduralism unrestricted priority over other forms of liberal politics; there is the need, then, 'to weigh the importance of certain forms of uniform treatment against the importance of cultural survival, and opt sometimes in favour of the latter' (Taylor 1995: 248). As a general principle, the claim that identities are entitled to secure themselves against change – or to secure whatever outcomes they desire – is a dubious one. Would it have been fair for the Catholic Church in the Quebec of the 1950s to have deployed public policy in order to ensure its dominance in perpetuity (Lamey 1999: 14)? Analogously, the Unionists in Northern Ireland could have cited their desire to preserve their identity as a reason to preserve practices found oppressive or threatening by the minority Republican community, such as marching through predominantly Republican areas (Archard 1999; S. O'Neill 2000). In a weaker form, we can understand the claim made as that the preservation of the identity constitutes a value to be considered or weighed among others, but not one which necessarily overrides other competing values. This identity should be protected because it contains within it a genuinely valuable way of life or conception of the good.[18] It may be the case that, all things considered, protecting this way of life would lead to other competing and more compelling values to perish, and that therefore this way of life should not be protected. The point is that, although pluralism suggests that there is no single order of values against which to judge the merits of different ways of life, where there is a conflict of this kind, there is no way to avoid the substantive task of arguing over their value. At the same time, defining the content of the cultural identity to be protected, accommodated or promoted is the subject of interpretative contestation and disagreement.

One response to this tangle of considerations is to cut through it by dismissing the independent deliberative weight of cultural identity in liberal political theory. I discuss this way of proceeding in the following chapter.

## 5.  Conclusion

I have focused my discussion and criticism of liberal culturalism on one key element of it, the claims for the normativity of cultural identity and for the character of rights that are meant to rest on this claim, and I have argued that the liberal culturalist arguments do not establish the pre-emptive claim for the right to cultural identity in the forms discussed here. I have not taken issue with three other core features of this approach, however: namely the protection of basic civil and political rights, the criticism of 'benign neglect', and the support for difference-sensitive rights and policies. In chapter 5, I will set out an argument for the second two of these features in terms of a model of political deliberation as public dialogue. In this sense, liberal culturalism frames what is to follow. First, however, I want to consider a forceful line of criticism of these two features of liberal culturalism.

# 4

## The Way of the World: Two Forms of Negative Universalism

In this chapter I examine the issues raised by those forms of liberalism that exclude the accommodation or promotion of cultural identities from the scope of legitimate state activity. This negative universalism possesses a unitary conception of citizenship as consisting in an identical set of legal, civic and political rights and obligations, with cultural identity understood as a private and extra-political matter. Treating citizens impartially, this form of liberalism insists, involves setting aside their cultural identity for the purposes of law and public policy making. This doctrine comes in libertarian and egalitarian variants, reflecting different and sometimes conflicting accounts of liberal justice. In its libertarian form, exemplified in Chandran Kukathas's work, the state should adopt a stance of neutrality toward different cultures and ways of life, allowing people to pursue their own projects within a framework of liberal rights; at the same time, he allows some sorts of group or association immense latitude in how they treat their members. In its egalitarian variant, as set out in Brian Barry's onslaught on multiculturalism and all its works, a common standard of equal treatment for all citizens enjoins difference-insensitive rights and policies, while the state is permitted to constrain the freedom of association in order to secure the fundamentals of liberal justice: namely, a common set of equal rights and opportunities for all. While these two very different conceptions of liberalism overlap in the 'hands-off' neutrality that they enjoin toward cultural identity, their different foundational accounts of justice provide them with strikingly divergent ways of interpreting what a policy of cultural *laissez-faire* entails.

Kukathas and Barry may seem like an odd couple to yoke together. Neither, it is fair to say, finds much merit in the proposals that the other puts forward for handling multicultural politics (Barry 2001: 131–6, 141–6, 239–41,

318–19; Kukathas 2002 (particularly the indelible comparison of Barry to Marie Antoinette); Barry 2002: 221–2, 230–3; Kukathas 2003: 109–13, 140–8), and these differences will emerge in the discussion below. For this reason, it is worth spelling out what they share. First, each subscribes to a version of the thesis that the state should be neutral or impartial among different conceptions of the good. For both, this rests on a claim that the state ought to respect individual freedom, and that this requires a set of principles that deal fairly with the inherently controversial character of the different interests and conceptions of the good that people have. Second, both argue that the impartiality of these principles does not translate into the equal impact of liberal laws and policies on all those affected by them, and more-over that this inequality of impact should not affect our judgement of the principles' impartiality. Equality or neutrality of impact is a chimera, and it is confused moral reasoning to judge liberal societies by this standard. Third, Kukathas and Barry share the view that liberal principles include a set of basic civil and legal rights, with some permissible deviations from these justified by reference to the importance of freedoms of thought and association – although they differ significantly over the content both of the basic rights and of the character of the deviations permitted. Fourth, this impartiality *does* translate into scepticism both about claims for the normative character of cultural identity and about political recognition or difference-sensitive rights and policies. What I am calling negative universalism may be understood as the strategy of benign neglect in militant and self-conscious mode. In Will Kymlicka's formulation, 'benign neglect' expresses the thesis that the state 'should not interfere with the cultural market-place – it should neither promote nor inhibit the maintenance of any particular culture' (Kymlicka 1995a: 108). He takes this thesis to be incoherent, since he thinks that the state cannot avoid involvement in shaping the cultural profile of society: '[g]overn-ment decisions on languages, internal boundaries, public holidays, and state symbols unavoidably promote certain cultural identities, and thereby disad-vantage others' (Kymlicka 1995a: 198). For negative universalists, however, the distinction between intervention and non-intervention in the cultural life of the society is not the important one. Rather, the claim is that there are reasons, grounded in considerations of impartiality, for not offering recogni-tion to particular cultural groups. While the upshot of this may be that some cultural identities become dominant, this is a price worth paying, or no price at all. Fifth, neither thinks that this impartiality is compromised by the enforcement of particular local norms and conventions in certain important social and political contexts. Cultural minorities who object that such norms impose alien standards need to accept that in some cases it is appropriate to assert that 'this is the way we do things around here' (cf. Barry 2001: 279–91).

Negative universalism should be distinguished from two other sources of scepticism about cultural claims. The first is a prudential claim that the character of politics that results from recognition is 'almost always dangerous' (Kukathas 1998: 692). Instead of contenting itself with managing conflict over material resources, politics becomes concerned with the identity of the society. Conflict over this is inevitably more bitter and less amenable to compromise than the squabble over material goods, undermining the state's commitment to providing order and peace for its citizens. The other source of scepticism also rests on a generalization about the character of culture: that traditional cultures tend to be oppressive, particularly subordinating women according to patriarchal norms (Kernohan 1998; Okin 1999).[1] These points are grist to Kukathas's and Barry's respective mills. But neither of these claims is central to the core arguments that they put forward: even if cultural politics were a tranquil affair, and even if particular cultures were to shed their oppressive characteristics, negative universalism would still claim that it is contrary to canons of liberal justice to offer cultural recognition.

## 1.  Culture and Conscience

According to Kukathas, 'liberalism's counsel is to resist the demand for recognition' (Kukathas 1998: 687). The liberal state should leave people free to pursue their own goals and projects alone or in association, including the project of living by some set of cultural standards, should they so wish. The state is concerned only with providing the conditions of peace and order which are necessary for any such project, but, beyond this, not with a project's success or failure. In the course of upholding these conditions, the state may take measures that intervene in the affairs of individuals and of groups; but liberal politics is not concerned with those affairs in themselves, having no concern for the content of the interests or attachments that people happen to have (Kukathas 1997b: 135; 1998: 695). Accordingly, no specific entitlements accrue to groups by virtue of their identity. Some ethnic and cultural identities will fade, and others flourish; but which do so is not the proper concern of the state. A 'right to culture', such as it is, can be reduced to various individual rights of freedom of conscience, expression and association.

There are two background premisses to this position. The first is a confessedly 'austere' individualism, which is 'content to accept that what matters most when assessing whether a way of life is legitimate is whether the individuals taking part in it are prepared to acquiesce in it' (Kukathas 1992: 124), and which we can call the acquiescence condition. This is articulated through an account of human interests, central to which is an interest in living in accord with the demands of conscience. Conscience is described as a sense of propriety or moral sense that governs a person's conduct. This sense governs and structures human life more profoundly than any other (Kukathas 2003: 48–9).

The interest in 'not being forced to act against conscience' is described as 'pre-eminent among human interests', and to be unable to do what one thinks is right is among the worst fates that a person might have to endure (Kukathas 2003: 17, 55). This is, Kukathas thinks, a universal human interest, 'shared by the remote Aborigines of Australia; the fifteenth century samurai; the Ibo tribesman; the Irish Catholic living in twentieth century Dublin; the Hasidic Jew in New York; and the Branch Davidian in Texas' (Kukathas 2003: 55).[2]

The second background claim, related to the first, is that there exists no public authority which is justified in imposing some particular conception of the good or way of life: the state should be 'neutral with regard to the human good' (Kukathas 1998: 696), and violation of this constraint expresses 'intolerance and moral dogmatism' on the part of the liberal state (Kukathas 1997a: 78). Liberalism ought to be a 'politics of indifference', privileging no particular conception of individual well-being or flourishing (Kukathas 1997b: 135; 1998). The state should avoid imposing a specific moral vision, permitting each citizen to live by the lights of his or her conscience in conditions of peace and order. To implement rules governing the conduct of relationships (including rules setting maximum working hours, banning domestic violence, and enforcing educational standards) is to limit the scope for an individual to live according to conscience. Granting cultural rights also involves this kind of moral dogmatism, which breaches the constraints on legitimate state action. To formally endow a group with a cultural right, then, is to interfere with individual choice and the consequences of that choice.

It follows that a liberal society should be viewed as an 'archipelago' of associations, each with their distinctive conception of human relationships, but none of which aspires to hegemony over the others. In the absence of a consensus on moral fundamentals, the only norms of such a society are those of mutual tolerance and civility, according to which people accept that different groups or communities live by different moral beliefs, but also acknowledge that no group has the right to impose its moral beliefs on the members of other groups. The image of the liberal archipelago represents liberal states as essentially clusters of different authorities and systems of justice, which may include internally illiberal jurisdictions (Kukathas 2002: 191–2; 2003: 27). A society, he writes, is liberal 'to the extent it is willing to tolerate the multiplication of authorities, including authorities which seek to disentangle themselves more thoroughly from the wider society – providing that they are prepared to bear the costs this invariably involves' (Kukathas 2003: 27).

The reason why Kukathas allows for internally illiberal authorities in this archipelago is that, first, having freedom of conscience must mean granting people the right to reject freedom of conscience as a value (2003: 116), and, second, that liberalism ought to protect not only the consciences of dissenters. For the majority can have a conscientious commitment to suppress dissent, and to preserve the religious, ideological or cultural integrity of the group (2003: 37). Hence the importance laid on the individual right of exit.

Kukathas's conception of state neutrality is grounded in the claim that there is no public standpoint from which any particular conception of the good can be vindicated, since there are 'disputes in the realm of public reason itself' (Kukathas 1997a: 81). If liberals are committed to free public reasoning as the only basis for legitimate law making, then they should tolerate the expression of all views, without presupposing that there exist any established principles or canons of public reasoning that impose particular moral or ethical constraints on those engaged in this process.[3] But it is not clear how this picture of free public reason combines with the view of the individual as possessing an interest in association and exit, expressed in his austere individualism. If everything is up for grabs in the process of free public reasoning, then so must be this basic conception of individual interests – in the absence of an account of why these particular interests constitute a point of view that the liberal state is entitled to impose. For the acquiescence condition is just as controversial as any other principle of social life. The alternative to viewing individualism and the claim for public reason as rival principles is to see the commitment to view free public reason as the only source of public authority as itself grounded in the individualist commitment to respect a person's interest in liberty of conscience. Since we respect a person's capacity to acquiesce in her circumstances, and to stop acquiescing when she has had enough, we should circumscribe as little as possible the sorts of thing she can acquiesce in. Similarly: should the state permit or enable liberty of conscience? One response is that it cannot do the latter, since it is controversial what the latter involves. To go in this direction may lead the liberal toward endorsing cultural diversity as a condition for liberty of conscience (e.g. by giving an individual some exit options). But why is enabling more contentious than permitting?

Liberal culturalists such as Will Kymlicka, Charles Taylor and Joseph Raz argue that recognizing cultural identity is an important part of respecting individual autonomy and dignity. For Kukathas's style of liberalism, these are not values with which a liberal political philosophy should be concerned: the state should restrict itself to upholding the framework of law within which individuals may pursue peacefully whatever projects they see fit, and not promote values such as autonomy or dignity (Raz 1994: 70, 72; Kymlicka 1995a: 83–95, 101–5; Kukathas 1998: 691; 2003: 16, 36–7, 101). A person's cultural identity, then, as itself valuable as a condition for her autonomy, dignity or self-respect, drops out of the picture. Kukathas's liberalism is officially agnostic about whether cultural identity in the normative, societal or semiotic sense possesses any value. Yet the emphasis on conscience leads to a picture of agency and a set of arguments that make the normative conception of culture central: 'custom is king' for Kukathas.

## 2.   Libertarianism and Cultural Neutrality

Having outlined some of the basic features of Kukathas's vision, in this
section I will consider his version of the argument on behalf of the cultural
neutrality of the state. In the next section, I turn to consider the most notori-
ous part of Kukathas's argument: the latitude given to voluntary associations
in the treatment of their members, as well as some further issues in his conception of voluntary association. I go on to consider whether his framework
can in fact hold the line against the politics of recognition: I argue that it
cannot, in the sense that his own examples of moral diversity in the liberal
state rely on and embody a conception of political recognition, and that this
is revealed in the account offered of the relationship between members of
different associations.

We can get a firmer grip on Kukathas's conception of cultural neutrality by
considering an objection. This is that a state *cannot* be strictly neutral in this
way, since the institutions and practices of every state are bound to have some
particular traditional cultural character: for example, a particular language,
educational curriculum, set of laws about marriage, public holidays, rules
about property. These rules disadvantage or damage the interests of those who
do not share those rules or practices: to recall the hackneyed example, Sunday-
closing legislation, for example, affects members of different religions
differently. Kukathas accepts that there is no neutrality of outcome, in the
sense that the interests of different groups may be affected unequally by laws
or policies: that 'no political arrangements are neutral in their outcome' is 'the
way of the world' (Kukathas 1998: 693–4). But this is merely the contingent
effect of a policy that is neutral in its justification, in the sense that considerations specific to particular cultures should form no part of its rationale.
Neutrality in this sense is compatible with a state's having a particular cultural character. In defending his conception of the cultural neutrality of the
state, Kukathas aims to redirect the criticism of naivety that is levelled at the
'benign neglect' view of politics and culture back against the critics. The mere
fact that the state has a particular language, set of ceremonies, or public holidays, he argues, should not be interpreted as a sign that the state *affirms* or
*endorses* those practices but only that, given the particular history of that state,
these are its public forms. In other words, it is appropriate for the state to
respond to demands for change in these areas with the retort that 'this is the
way we do things around here', in Barry's resonant phrase – that is the way of
the world. Government will always be conducted in some particular language,
and some days rather than others will be set aside as public holidays, but this
does not compromise the neutrality of the state, since in upholding these traditions the state is not promoting any particular cultural identity or endorsing any particular way of life. In contrast to this, the state fails to be neutral
when it starts taking political action that is responsive cultural identity. The

issue, of course, is whether this is the appropriate context in which to make a purely conventionalist move. The view that the state can be neutral in this sense rests on the assumption that, while a set of rules may systematically privilege some groups and disadvantage others, this should not affect our assessment of those rules' neutrality. But if a rule has these systematic consequences, and some other rule does not, which of the two is neutral? For Kukathas a rule counts as a neutral rule if – and only if – its rationale makes no reference to the religious or cultural identity of citizens. But, once the rule has been challenged on the grounds that it disadvantages some groups, can its rationale remain insulated from considerations of religious and cultural identity? If a particular day is selected as a holiday on the grounds that it suits a certain tradition, but the society contains other traditions that suffer some difficulty as a result, it seems reasonable to raise this point as part of a rationale for revising the legislation. However, to do so counts as a violation of neutrality by Kukathas's lights.

There are two ways to take Kukathas's scepticism about multicultural recognition. The first is to see him as saying that the state is not required as a matter of liberal justice to make multicultural accommodations. For Kukathas, it will be recalled, there is no standpoint from which one could justify any particular distribution of costs (beyond protecting the right of exit) without indulging in moral intolerance and dogmatism. The difficulty with this position is that neither the austere individualism nor the accompanying conception of public reason is inherently non-controversial. Certainly, in itself the 'no public authority thesis' provides no grounds for supporting the *status quo* as a default position where any particular set of rules is concerned. As we shall see, Barry at least raises the issue of the justifiability of particular laws, and indeed of difference-sensitive exemptions, since he is concerned to mete out equal treatment to all concerned – although he claims that on the whole there is no case for exemptions.

Although a purely conventional response ('this is the way of the world'), imposing traditional practice on a recalcitrant minority, is compatible with liberal justice, as Kukathas conceives of it, a prudent or sensible political authority, he thinks, should be open to adjusting features of public life, such as holidays, in order to accommodate the changing preferences of significantly large groups. For instance, if numbers of Muslims in parts of the United States or Britain grow, there may be a case for official recognition of Muslim holy days, and if Islam becomes the dominant religion, then there may be a reason to change the working week. However, so long as there are groups with different beliefs living in a society with shared rules, some will have no choice but to conform, since (short of withdrawing from the society) exit solutions are not possible (Kukathas 2003: 244–5).

This last point seems sensible. However, it leaves open what considerations should count in establishing whether an exemption or a revision of a law is worth implementing. Consider a minority's claim for an accommodation with respect to the working week. Kukathas offers a discussion of a British example, the Ahmad case (*Ahmad* v. *ILEA* (1978), *Ahmad* v. *UK* (1981); see Poulter 1986: 245–52). When Mr Ahmad, a teacher with the Inner London Education Authority, found that his new posting did not allow him to attend Friday prayers without a reduction in pay, he resigned and then claimed unfair dismissal by the ILEA. Kukathas's assessment of this is stark: 'he had to bear the consequences of his beliefs himself, and either miss prayers or lose his job' (Kukathas 1997b: 145; cf. Jones 1994). Missing prayers should be thought of as simply an 'inescapable' opportunity cost that one has to bear in order to hold down this particular job. Yet it is not enough to draw attention to the undoubted fact that *some* opportunity costs are inescapable for Mr Ahmad (or anyone else) in having paid employment: the question is whether having to forgo Friday prayers should be among them. Nor is it the case that a pragmatic solution to avoid this is simply unavailable in the nature either of the job or of Mr Ahmad's beliefs: for example, some elements in the school timetable may be rearranged (and some of the schools where Mr Ahmad had previously been employed seem to have opted for these). In other words, some accommodation is possible without disrupting the running of the school. In this kind of case, claims of conscience on the part of the minority conflict with the conventions found convenient by the majority. The majority has no particular axe to grind about suppressing dissent or communal integrity based on the tenderness of its *own* members' consciences – for Mr Ahmad is not, in Kukathas's sense, a member of that group, and therefore is protected, according to this schema, from such external imposition. So we would seem to have a case, based on the importance that Kukathas attaches to liberty of conscience, for arranging an exemption.[4]

The other, stronger version of his claim for neutrality is that the state is under a duty not to make an accommodation. Kukathas offers two considerations to support this line of thought, the first of which appeals to the hazards of the politics of recognition. From this perspective, any concession to recognition, such as granting an exemption right for a religious or cultural group, as in the Ahmad example, politicizes the cultural identities involved: 'it not only pits minorities against the mainstream society but also brings them into conflict with one another' (Kukathas 1997b: 148).[5] It does so by selecting some groups for preferential treatment over others. So, for example, in the Ahmad case a rearrangement of the timetable may provoke resentment among other teachers whose particular needs and proclivities are not accommodated. The argument in this case runs as follows. Any set of rules (governing employment or languages of education) imposes some opportunity costs. A state needs to enforce some set of rules. Since tinkering with the rules in order to suit particular groups politicizes the rules and the groups involved, it is better to stick with whatever rules have been inherited (cf. Kukathas 1997a: 98).

However, first, in part this last claim contains a contestable empirical assertion about the consequences of difference-sensitive rights: non-neutrality in the impact or outcome of laws and policies may be just as politicizing in its effects (or in the perceptions of its effects), fuelling resentment and providing the raw materials for tribal entrepreneurs. Second, in any case what *counts* as 'preferential' treatment, or rigging the rules to suit a particular group, is what is at issue here. The working week is arranged so that some beliefs carry no burdens, while others do, and the multicultural sceptic about cultural neutrality suggests that this can equally reasonably be construed as a form of preferential treatment for the majority. The response to this, that such rules are a matter of convenience and convention which do not have a culturally peculiar *rationale* is disingenuous. The fact that rules are needed is not culturally peculiar, provided that we think there is generally a good reason to have common holidays, and so on.[6] And so is the thought that it may be very inconvenient to start uprooting all of these and replacing them with a fresh set. But any particular set of rules usually has a specific cultural, religious and societal *history*, which supplied their initial rationale.[7] A third point is that the hazards involved in policies of recognition are irrelevant in some cases. Kukathas's conception of cultural neutrality governs the reasons underlying the adoption of rights and policies, not the specific form of the policies themselves. It rules out reasons for any policy, not just claims for multicultural rights, which make reference to the needs and interests of cultural identities. It excludes, therefore, not only reasons that support claims to exemption, special forms of assistance, and so on, but reasons that support the abolition of a particular rule altogether, on the grounds that this rule unevenly impacts on particular cultural identities (cf. Barry 2001: 39). So, for example, a Sikh may argue not for an exemption from an employer's dress code but for the abolition of that code altogether, if it is not really essential to the kind of work involved. The grounds for this demand are that this dress code makes a demand on those who share this identity, which it does not make on the rest of the population, and therefore unfairly burdens or disadvantages members of this minority. French Muslims who object to the ban on the *foulard* argue that the commitment of the public schools system to *laïcité* unequally affects Muslims. From the republican standpoint, the headscarf threatens the lay status of the school system. In the face of the objection that wearing a crucifix has been found unproblematic, the republican response, now enshrined in law, is to distinguish between discreet and prominent religious symbols. Unsurprisingly, defenders of the right to wear the headscarf find this distinction contrived, and suspect that its purpose is precisely to rule out the public expression specifically of Muslim identity.[8] In both cases, one way of viewing what is at issue is whether the reasoning behind the rule is indeed culturally neutral. For opponents of the rules in question, the reasoning appears neutral only from a particular cultural standpoint.

The other consideration that Kukathas offers in support of the demand that
the state reject all claims for recognition is that the latter naively presuppose
the non-political character of social and cultural identity. He argues that the
politics of recognition makes a mistake in imagining that there is something
external to the political process which can be 'recognized' (that is, recognized
in the political rather than identity-constitutive sense, in the terms outlined in
the previous chapter). Ethnic and cultural communities are not 'fixed and
unchanging entities' that exist 'prior to or independently of legal and political
institutions but are themselves given shape by those institutions' (Kukathas
1992: 110); such communities do not have a fixed identity which is independent
of their interaction with political institutions, and so have no identity which
political institutions can simply recognize. In the United States, for example,
'policies of affirmative action for selected minorities supply incentives for
people to identify themselves as members of those particular groups'
(Kukathas 1998: 693). Once a group has been 'recognized' with respect to eli-
gibility for some benefit, there is an incentive to identify with that group. If the
identity of groups is 'given shape by' interaction with legal and political institutions, this undermines the claim for recognition. However, claims for recognition do not rest on the presumption of a pristine condition in which cultures
exist and which politics ought to preserve. All they need do is establish that
there is a practice or identity which is valuable in the sense that the state ought
to promote or accommodate it. The alleged incoherence is removed if one can
pick out an identity (not always easy or possible, of course), not only if one
can establish that this identity exists independently of all legal and political
institutions. Claims for recognition are not undermined by noticing that in its
current form the practice or identity is controversial or that it would not exist
in the state of nature. (Similar points may be made about the recognition of
many rights.) Furthermore, the validity of a claim is compatible with some
individuals' revising how they think of themselves in the light of changes in
state law. That some people may find it valuable to adopt an identity for
reasons of economic self-interest (e.g. scholarships) does not mean that it
is not valuable to others for other reasons. I conclude that neither of the
reasons put forward for holding that the state ought to refrain from difference-
sensitive accommodation is valid.

### 3.  Harms and Associations

The second thesis is that the liberal state ought to treat cultural communities
as voluntary associations: their members should enjoy the freedom to associate in this way, but the associations themselves should not be given any
formal recognition and should be subject to only the most minimal regulation.
Kukathas lays particular stress on individual freedom of association, since, he

believes, it provides the conditions for communal flourishing which concern proponents of the politics of recognition. Whatever conception members of a cultural community have of their group (as the product of divine edict, compelling belief, or discretionary whimsy), the state should view the group as a voluntary association (Kukathas 1992: 116). It is not the fact that the group has a shared *cultural identity* that means that it is free to organize itself in whatever way its members see fit. For this is justified only by the need to respect each individual's right to live his or her life according to the dictates of his or her own conscience. As he develops the idea, members of such associations are entitled to no special treatment from the state or the rest of society as a matter of justice, in the shape of exemptions, assistance, and so on. All that they can legitimately expect is to be treated with tolerance and civility. Furthermore, these associations are entitled to do as they please in their treatment of their own members, provided that they are genuinely voluntary; that is, that there is a legally enforced right of exit. This latitude is allowed only with respect to an association's own members: *external* harms are not tolerated. So, for example, a group such as the Amish possess no justification for refusing to attach reflective warning signs to their vehicles travelling on public highways (Kukathas 2002: 190; Barry 2001: 186). The right to acquiesce in a life of one's choice does not permit endangering the lives of others.

Provided that 'the interests of the wider community' are not harmed, however, 'cultural tolerance' should be extended to practices that many would deem 'intolerable' (Kukathas 1997a: 70). These practices include the following for him: group customs which restrict the opportunities for women, for example, by denying them education or property rights; child-rearing practices that limit the capacities of children to prepare for life outside the group; the rejection of conventional medical treatments, such as blood transfusions, even where the lives of children are at risk; practices which mandate operations that are physically harmful and may be performed without the fully informed consent of the subjects, such as scarring and clitoridectomy; practices, such as some initiation rights, which expose members of a group to high levels of risk; practices that involve the use of animals – for sport, science or food – in ways that many people find cruel or distasteful; and, finally, practices of punishment within the group, including physical punishment, deprivation and ostracism, that many would regard as inhumane or disproportionately severe. To take one celebrated case, he endorses the right of the Pueblo Indians to ostracize and deny resources to those of their members who convert to Christianity.[9] Since social power within the group is unchecked, more vulnerable members – who tend to be women, children and dissenters, as Kukathas unblinkingly acknowledges (1997a: 88; 2002: 197) – possess no defence, apart from the right to exit, against whatever treatment is meted out by the powerful. This licence for groups is weakly hemmed in by a ban on forcible induction into or imprisonment within a group, since to permit this would violate the individual right of free association. The latitude granted to groups in this way derives from the thesis that there is no public authority which may justifiably impose a particular moral vision on members of the society. The public realm is instead 'an area of convergence of different moral practices' (Kukathas 2002: 196). What allows it to be characterized as a *liberal* public realm is the enforcement of the acquiescence test, in the form of a legal right of exit from any association to which one belongs.

Kukathas's expansive view of what is covered by freedom of association has proved immensely controversial, and I will highlight three difficulties.[10] The first is that this conception allows too much scope for the powerful within a group to oppress that group's members. His anxiety about arbitrary state power, exercised so as to promote some particular vision of the good life, leads him to a highly permissive attitude toward arbitrary social power. Consider, for example, the status of children in this schema, to whom Kukathas devotes some thought and who are not only substantively power-less and dependent but cannot reasonably be taken to have consented to mem-bership. The presumption at work seems to be that power over children lies with their parents: the parents may decide whether or not to deny their child access to medical care or educational resources, for example, or whether to administer severe physical punishment. The parents themselves are guided by their group's practices and traditions, provided that they do not exercise the right of exit. Now this doctrine of absolute parental power does not derive from the right of free association, since children cannot be taken to have con-sented to their treatment, and it is question begging to presume that whatever the *parents* consent to is permitted *vis-à-vis* their children. On an alternative reading, absolute parental power is not Kukathas's doctrine. He has written that 'it is not an implication of my position that parents are entitled to kill their children' (Kukathas 2002: 197; cf. 195); rather, they should obey the law. The question is then what the law entitles them to do. The rules of the asso-ciation to which the parent belongs in this case seem to have absolute power over its members' children. As he puts it, 'no one can live in a society and expect to be able to, say, mutilate his children at will. Unless, that is, this is something accepted as normal or conventional and permissible by his com-munity or by the society at large' (Kukathas 2003: 145). It is not parental but communal power that is paramount. On this reading, his view has the impli-cation that, if someone wants to leave her association, and that group wants to retain custody of her children and is entitled to under its rules, then it may do so, since the judgement of the association is paramount. Of course, this does nothing to assuage the worry that this argument renders permissible any-thing that an association does to its members, provided that they have a legal exit route.

Kukathas's principal line of response to this objection is to point to dangers attaching to the *state's* having the power to determine what counts as an acceptable cultural practice. Who decides where a child's best or even basic interests lie?[11] Should children be given a basic functional education, or a full introduction to the fruits of world civilization? Is their immortal soul the most important thing? Scientists differ over the merits of vaccination programmes. Even when they do not, groups like Jehovah's Witnesses may object to medical procedures such as blood transfusions on behalf of their children. The state will tend to intervene in ways that go well beyond whatever is necessary to ensure the physical safety of children; it will intervene to enforce the views and prejudices of those elites who direct that state. We can distinguish two points here. The first concerns how to define a child's basic interest in health or physical safety. The second is a slippery slope argument: if the state is involved in the business of defending or promoting the basic interests of children, it will tend to go beyond any basic conception to impose a fuller and more specific model of well-being: any such model leads to a dangerous level of state interference, banning sugary foods, video games, and minority languages, perhaps.

On the first point, it is not clear how deep Kukathas's scepticism runs. He does not of course have a generally sceptical view of morality or of human interests. There are indeed various conflicting views of the basic interests of children (and of adults), but there are also various conflicting views of the importance of freedom of conscience, and of its implications. If Kukathas is not a sceptic about the possibility of articulating basic interests (and his own account of liberalism suggests that he is not), then his resistance to the political protection of these standards rests on his doubt about the agency, expressed in the slippery slope argument. Kukathas assumes that, if we accept this argument, this supplies a reason not to enforce basic interests – not to take the first step on the slope. For some, of course, the extension of state power may be a price worth paying for the enforcement of basic interests, and preferable to permitting the torture of children. Another response, however, is to find non-arbitrary ways of discriminating between different points on the slope (cf. B. Williams 1995: 213–23). If we have a sharply defined conception of which interests are basic (and we want to restrict the scope of state activity to the protection or promotion of basic interests), then we can distinguish between the interests that the state ought to be concerned with, and those it should not. Here too, it is worth noting, Kukathas's liberalism relies on the possibility of drawing such a distinction, since he wishes the state to restrict itself only to protecting the interest in freedom of conscience and the conditions that allow for it.

This is compatible with Kukathas's emphatic claim that state power may be abused, and that history is littered with examples of established authorities persecuting dissidents and heretics in the name of a purportedly superior way of life (Kukathas 1997a: 88–9; 2002: 198; 2003: 136). He also presses the point that persuasion is superior to force in promoting the effective transformation of practices (Kukathas 1997a: 89; 2003: 136). Bluntly enforcing liberal norms can promote cultural reaction, alienating the groups whom it is meant to help and strengthening the hand of traditional elites.[12]

The general issue raised in the first point, about trust in state power, is important, and I will probe it a little further in the final chapter. However, here the rejoinder to Kukathas's response is that the dispersal of authority over punishment, how to treat children, and so on is no more mandated by the no public authority thesis than by the concentration of authority. The prudential point about the potential for abuse of state power may be true; but this is so, irrespective of the validity of the thesis about the lack of a common public standpoint from which to assess different customs. Even if there is such a standpoint, we may have reason to be careful about concentrating political power. Kukathas's goal in making the case for absolute power over children seems to be to block the alternative view that there is a role for the state in protecting a child's basic interests, even if these are not taken to be the totality of her interests (cf. Shapiro 1999a: 85–99; 2002; Shachar 2001). The anxiety seems to be that once the state is allowed to intervene in this way, it will impose a particular vision of the good on individuals who may wish to live by other lights. But it is hard to see how either the parental or the communal conceptions of absolute power over children is less morally dogmatic or controversial than a view which allows the state the scope to intervene to prevent harm or promote some basic interests.

The sole constraint on internal harm is the proviso that there exists a right of exit. The exit option stands as the only safeguard against the operation of arbitrary social power against the individual. As noted above, one way of marrying the acquiescence condition to the thesis about public authority is by seeing the latter as derived from the former. Since we respect a person's capacity to acquiesce in her circumstances, and to stop acquiescing when she has had enough, we should circumscribe as little as possible the sorts of thing in which she can acquiesce. So we ought to tolerate a variety of ways of life, even if some of them damage or harm individuals, provided that there exists a legal right of exit from those ways of life. However, the second objection to this vision of free association is that precisely what is entailed by the possibility of exit for a person seems to be subject to the controversies that rage in the public realm about other fundamental matters. For some, the possibility of exit presumes not only a society into which the departing member of the group can enter, but also that they be able to live in that society. On a more expansive interpretation, then, exercise of the right to exit requires 'economic stability, cultural "know-how", language skills, connections, and self-confidence' (Shachar 2001: 69). If Kukathas embraces the first option, then the sting is largely removed from his conception of cultural association, since the state can legitimately specify what the right of exit entails. It is open to the state, then, to underwrite a more interventionist stance in regard to, for example, the health and education of members of a group. Kukathas's own view of what this right entails is minimal: it exists even where the costs are very high (as when the community I want to leave denies me access to vital resources). Kukathas cleaves to the more minimal interpretation in order to avoid the state's becoming involved in judgements about the worth of ways of life or the good of citizens. But its being minimal does not make this interpretation less controversial from the standpoint of public reason, since it embodies its own 'cultural prejudices' or 'moral dogmatism' about what a right of exit entails. If Kukathas embraces the second option, he has to explain how it is in this case that a member of a group with its own laws is allowed to treat a non-member in a way that other non-members are not allowed to treat one another. In other words, the situation seems to be analogous to that of the Amish reluctance to display reflective triangles on the back of their buggies: what is legitimate on their own farms is not legitimate on the public highways.

The third objection is that, if what matters is the capacity of the individual to acquiesce in a way of life and when she chooses to withdraw that acquiescence, and the worry is that a dominant authority will abuse its power to persecute dissenters, then Kukathas's premisses do not lead to where he thinks. Rather, they support a regime of basic civil rights for all, in order to protect dissenters within minority groups, a regime which includes freedom of worship, liberty of conscience, property rights, entitlements to education, and so on. So, for example, it would not be open to a tribal government such as the Pueblo to deny the benefits of membership to Christian converts among them (cf. Svensson 1979: 430–4; Kymlicka 1995a: 40; Kukathas 2003: 137). If we view the Pueblo authority as a sub-state polity, then it should tolerate Christian dissenters, since, as a polity, it lacks a common public standpoint from which to assert a particular vision of religious faith. Kukathas, however, views sub-states in a different way: not as each itself a locus of public reason, to which the 'no public authority thesis' applies, but as entitled to promote and base membership on particular conceptions of the good, including religious conceptions. For the 'archipelago' picture, to recall, presents liberal states as clusters of different authorities and systems of justice, which may include internally illiberal jurisdictions. Kukathas offers three principal considerations in support of this last point. One has already been touched on: namely, the risks associated with centralizing judgement in these matters. The second is that, if liberty of conscience is taken to be of fundamental importance, then it demands not only that dissenters be respected, but also that those who wish to remain loyal to their traditions or practices be respected. Kukathas leans toward supporting the latter against the former, since he views membership of a sub-state polity in a federation as voluntary. Once again, the right of exit is crucial: since Pueblo dissenters can leave, this makes their polities akin to voluntary associations (Kukathas 2002: 192; cf. Kukathas 1997c: 412–16). Setting aside the issue already discussed of how to define the rights entailed in exit, this response presupposes that there is a jurisdiction into which dissenters can move, one that tolerates the beliefs of Pueblo Christians. There is nothing in the structure of Kukathas's federation that guarantees this, however. Instead, there is only a confederative principle of *cuius regio, eius religio* that may leave various individuals and beliefs out in the cold. A society (like Kukathas's 'mytopia') consisting of a bunch of internally illiberal units may have no space left in which dissidents and renegades can form their own associations (Kukathas 2003: 98–9). The paradox of Kukathas's archipelago is that an accessible set of background liberal standards and practices is necessary for the voluntary status, and hence justifiability, of non-liberal components of the federation, but that he claims that there is no standpoint that is not itself intolerant, from which to assert the value of those standards and practices.

The third line of reply is that to impose liberal constraints on the internal governance of associations closes down the kind of authentic dispute about the character of the good life that can occur only when groups are permitted to live according to their own lights, in undiluted versions of their ways of life. The public sphere of a liberal society involves many unresolved disputes, and these should not be eliminated by the imposition of a particular conception of the good life.[13] From the point of view of the realm of public reason, some voices and points of view are muffled if they are not allowed full licence to practice their ways of life. So public reason dictates that internally illiberal groups should be permitted to arrange their own affairs as they see fit, since there is no authoritative standpoint from which to judge the worth of a way of life. This reply also only weakly addresses the objection. We can see how it *does* address it, since it is not hard to see how illiberal, indeed terrible, ways of life may contain elements that are valuable and thought-provoking but not reproducible outside those ways of life. But this does not constitute an argument for the suppression of individual rights. Kukathas already allows that ways of life may legitimately be compromised when the harms that they produce spill over into the rest of society: so the Amish have to compromise with modernity and state law when it comes to ensuring that their buggies are visible at night. This sort of compromise can be justified by reference to the need for mutual tolerance and civility, which is viewed as underpinning liberal society. This does not of course just affect ethnic, religious or cultural groups: a committed neoliberal must compromise his belief in unfettered market transactions in order to live in the liberal archipelago, and a committed feminist must compromise her beliefs about the treatment of girls and women. But the important implication here is that a group's 'foreign policy', so to speak, needs to incorporate a concern for common standards, and may legitimately entail a dilution of the group's way of life.

The notion of an uncompromised way of life invoked in the public reason argument seems to be subject to Kukathas's own objections to the notion of an authentic or pristine way of life, which was rejected by his critique of recognition. The argument there, it will be recalled, was that there is no pristine condition of some cultural identity, independent of political society, which can be politically recognized. Does this amount to saying that there can be no uncompromised identity? If it does, then the thought that identities should be expressed without compromise contradicts it. If Kukathas embraces the idea that there may be uncompromised identities, then the earlier ground for his objection to the idea of political recognition evaporates. Indeed, if it is important that identities present themselves in an uncompromised form before the tribunal of public reason, then we have a reason to support rights and policies sensitively tailored to preserve and promote particular identities.

Kukathas is at pains to point out that the archipelago vision does not imply that anyone can simply secede from the rule of law, and declare her house a private fiefdom: a person is subject to the 'local laws' at pains of 'outlawry', losing the protection of any form of legal community (Kukathas 1997a: 93; 2002: 197; 2003: 134–40). At the same time, 'a liberal society is one in which a diversity of systems of law and morality are tolerated and coexist' (Kukathas 2002: 196). The crucial condition determining whether or not some set of norms should be tolerated is 'the degree to which the cultural community is independent of the wider society', so that '[t]ribal communities of Indians or Aborigines which are geographically remote and have little contact with the dominant society might well live according to ways which betray little respect for the individual'. However, those groups whose members are 'part of the larger legal and political order' will 'not find it so easy' to live by illiberal norms (Kukathas 1992: 251). He has added that remoteness may be a jurisdictional rather than a geographical matter, and that communities can be independent in the relevant sense if governed by different laws, even if physically proximate (Kukathas 2002: 197). So, for example, Jewish, Muslim and Druze communities in Israel, each of which has its own system of personal law, would count as 'remote' from one another in the relevant sense.

Like the notion of an uncompromised way of life, the idea of remoteness is less clear than it may appear. For example, on the one hand, Kukathas defends the exemption of gypsy (Roma) children from some schooling in the United Kingdom's 1944 Education Act. Because their parents often move in search of seasonal work, these children are required to attend only half the number of school sessions that other children do. Since formal schooling is not valued by many in this community, only a minority of children receive any formal primary education. This is justified by the parents' freedom to associate and live according to their own ways (Kukathas 1992: 126). In this case, the community neither possesses its own autonomous legal system nor exists in a state of raw outlawry. On the other hand, he argues that the group of Tennessee parents who sued their local schooling authority for teaching children about matters contrary to their brand of Christian belief in the *Mozert* v. *Hawkins* case are in a different position.[14] In this case, the parents objected to some school textbooks which contained sentiments (such as a belief in the dignity and worth of human beings) held to be 'incompatible with religious faith' (Gutmann and Thompson 1996: 64). Here, Kukathas argues, the liberal state is entitled to impose a particular conception of education on the fundamentalist parents of Hawkins County, since the latter on the whole wish to continue to 'live in mainstream society' (Kukathas 1997a: 96). However, if they shun mainstream society and separate from the state's influence, they may educate their children as they see fit. But, inasmuch as both groups of parents seem to want a *partial* separation from the rest of society, it is not clear why these cases are treated differently.[15] In other words, without some clearer criteria for what constitutes remoteness or withdrawal, we cannot distinguish practices which should be tolerated from those that need not be.

Even with such criteria, the normative significance of remoteness as such is not clear. The vision of political society as a federation of intersecting groups and ways of life with a stable rule of law requires a way of distinguishing those groups or ways of life with a genuine claim to be governed by different rules from those that are merely breaking the law. But Kukathas, as we have seen, rejects the various culturalist strategies for picking out groups or for assigning value to a group's way of life as well as egalitarian claims that there may be good reasons to relieve particular groups of all the costs of their beliefs (cf. Kukathas 1997c). More generally, and underlying this, as we have also seen, he rejects the thought that there is a standpoint from which this kind of judgement can be made. Apart from a general commitment to moral variety in the liberal state, the reasons for granting jurisdictional status in any particular case are unclear.

The underlying point is that the examples of moral diversity tolerated by the liberal state under the rubric of freedom of association that Kukathas offers usually involve what he rejects: namely, legal recognition, in the sense that a named group is given a particular legal status, as in the examples of Muslim personal law in India or Israel, or gypsies in the Education Act. Now we can argue about the justifiability and implications of these claims for recognition, but legal recognition is what these are claims for. They do not derive simply from the individual right to freedom of association, since some standpoint is required in order to judge whether these are instances of that freedom, or merely of unjustifiable deviation from the law.

Yet this approach requires some form of common moral and political framework implemented and enforced by the state, in that the notion of an *external* harm that a group may not impose on another implies a substantive view about what counts as a harm, or perhaps an agreed view, from the perspective of public reason. The public sphere in Kukathas's liberal state is conceived of as a minimal sphere of overlap among the different associations that exist in the state (Kukathas 2003: 131–3). Yet even this attenuated public realm needs a common conception of the overlapping interests that require protection from external harm. Physical harms (crashing into Amish buggies by night) may be uncontroversial, but other harms are more contentious: some associations take a much more relaxed view of proselytizing than others, for instance, for which it can be quite an inflammatory topic. Quite how a common conception is arrived at is not clear. The 'virtual' dialogue among different moral positions that otherwise have as little to do with one another as possible cannot be relevant here. What is required is surely an actual process of discussion and negotiation over how to coexist. However, any actual dialogue seems to require a more substantial conception of the public sphere than Kukathas is prepared to entertain. This consideration leads us toward the topic of the next chapter. But first I want to consider the egalitarian brand of negative universalism.

## 4.   Egalitarianism and Cultural Neutrality

The other strand of negative universalism is egalitarian. Brian Barry in *Culture and Equality* makes a powerful case against multiculturalism, and particularly against cultural protection and differentiated rights and policies. To treat people equally, he argues, is to furnish them with an identical set of rights and opportunities. The repugnance that, in his opinion, should attach to an unequal distribution of these should attach to claims for group rights generally. Claims for cultural rights, where they are not completely vacuous, damage the interests of those they purport to serve, and whatever is valid in these claims can be articulated more coherently in straightforwardly liberal and egalitarian terms (cf. Barry 2001: 8, 118, 317; 1998). This approach is characterized by a commitment, first, to basic liberal civil and political rights. Second, Barry endorses the idea of state neutrality or impartiality. This dictates that the state's reasons for adopting particular principles of justice should not be grounded in any specific conception of the good (cf. Barry 1995). Rather, impartiality consists in giving equal treatment to different cultures, outlooks, religions, ways of life, and so on (Barry 2001: 28–9). This latter idea is in part expressed through the basic set of liberal rights and freedoms: freedoms of conscience and association are distributed in the same way to all religious believers (and non-believers) alike. But the norm of equal treatment also means, for example, that if charitable status for tax purposes or support for religious schooling is granted to one religion, this form of public recognition is owed to all religions. Third, Barry is egalitarian in the sense that on his view the norm of equal treatment requires equalizing the resources that individuals possess in order to pursue their chosen goals and projects, a commitment that calls not only for the basic set of liberal civil and political rights but for substantial and periodic redistributions of wealth, as well as an array of other social reforms. Fourth, Barry's claim is that, on the whole, claims made on behalf of culture cannot be justified in the name of liberal justice, according to this conception, and that the norm of equal treatment requires rights that are insensitive to those differences that multiculturalism encourages us to observe.

Where there exists a good justification for a rule, it should be applied without exception (Barry 2001: 32–50): 'either the case for the law (or some version of it) is strong enough to rule out exemptions, or the case that can be made for exemptions is strong enough to suggest that there should be no law anyway' (Barry 2001: 39). But the egalitarian argument does share with Kukathas's more libertarian stance what Barry calls 'a rather robust attitude' toward cultural diversity. This 'says in effect, "Here are the rules which tell people what they are allowed to do. What they choose to do within those rules is up to them. But it has nothing to do with public policy"' (2001: 32). What matters from the egalitarian perspective is that there exist equal opportunities, which are understood as an identical set of possible choices, for all citizens. People then make choices from this identical set on the basis of their preferences and beliefs. Some of these choices will reflect the chooser's distinctive cultural commitments, but these are a private matter, just like anyone's idiosyncratic or banal grounds for choice. The inequality of impact exhibited by a law or policy does not violate a commitment to equal treatment: only smokers will be affected adversely by laws regulating smoking in public places; the meek will be less adversely affected by a ban on duelling compared with the compulsively violent and status-conscious. But the law exists only to protect some interests against others, and therefore laws will tend to impact unequally on those with different interests (Barry 2001: 34). To consider some examples, Barry offers a firm adjudication on the question of whether Sikhs wearing turbans should be exempt from the rule that requires motor-cyclists to wear crash helmets. We should either accept that it is a valid objective of public policy to reduce head injuries to motor-cyclists, or we should accept that there is a good libertarian case (based on the premiss that motor-cyclists without helmets pose a risk only to themselves) for not regulating headgear at all: Sikhs and Hell's Angels bear the costs of their own decisions. Some Orthodox Jewish and Muslim groups have won legal exemptions in the United Kingdom for the slaughter of animals according to traditional religious precepts, although these methods are denied to the wider society. Barry argues that in such cases there are no grounds for an exemption: if there are good grounds for regulating the slaughter of animals (and animal welfare is here the relevant and powerful ground), then these are strong enough to apply universally. This would unreasonably burden or disadvantage Orthodox Jews and Muslims only if members of these groups were not only required to eat kosher or halal meat but also compelled to eat meat. But since there is a realistic option to be vegetarian, which many members of each of these groups already exercise, they are not so burdened.[16] Consequently, we can hold these groups responsible for the consequences of their beliefs and preferences in this case, and rule that the state has no duty to provide a special exemption for them.

This liberal picture is egalitarian in its recognition that resources will have to be redistributed in order to ensure that the sets of choices people have are in the relevant sense identical. The state's role lies in equalizing the circumstances in which individuals exercise choice, so that, for example, physical disabilities or differentials of income and wealth do not restrict the choice sets of some. But it has no business in ensuring that the *outcomes* of particular choices are successful. This requires a distinction between those features of a chooser's situation which it is the state's responsibility to correct and those for which the chooser herself should be held accountable. What are called 'expensive tastes' are usually held to fall on the latter side of this divide: my love of champagne and fine cigars is something for which I will have to provide, rather than circumstances like disability or poverty for which the state is held responsible. Cultural commitments are then assimilated to expensive tastes, on this schema (Barry 2001: 40; 2002: 215). They are aspects of a person's structure of beliefs and preferences for which the person and not the state is held responsible. It is worth underlining that, in contrast to some conceptions of this distinction between what the state is held to be responsible for and what lies with the individual, the 'origins or revisability' of a person's beliefs and preferences are not held to be crucial in determining on which side of the line responsibility falls.[17] Rather, what matters is 'the justifiability of the range of alternatives with which people are confronted' (Barry 2002: 216). Once people are treated equally in the sense of being presented with a justifiable set of choices, then the question of the state's responsibility (and of difference-sensitive rights) ceases to arise.

Consider again our two rather hackneyed examples. Barry's point is that the range of choices facing a turban-wearing Sikh must be justified, and that considerations of public safety provide the relevant justification. The Sikh, then, has the same opportunity to ride a motor cycle as anyone else, but may choose not to do so, in the light of his religious beliefs. He is in exactly the same situation as someone who believes that riding a motor cycle is too dangerous to be a rational undertaking, and acts on that belief (Barry 2001: 45). Similarly, the Orthodox Jew, confronted with justified regulations on how animals may be slaughtered, has the same opportunity set as the rest of the society: to eat meat produced according to the public regulations or not to eat meat. If she wishes to live by her religious beliefs, she must choose the second option. But she is in the same situation as anyone else whose beliefs tell them not to eat meat.

Having outlined the basics of Barry's picture of equal treatment and the claims of difference-sensitivity, I want initially to chip away at the apparently very solid wall he puts up between these two, starting with four points which he (more or less explicitly) accepts about exemptions within his liberal egalitarian framework. The first is that, as John Horton puts it, 'law is replete with qualifications, special cases, exceptions, stipulative definitions, excusing conditions, assumptions about what is reasonable, implicit *ceteris paribus* clauses, and so on' (Horton 2003: 30; cf. Caney 2002: 85). The emergency services are (usually) exempt from speed limits; conscientious objectors are exempt from military service; churches are exempt from some taxes; some commodities are exempt from sales taxes; on some streets there is no parking except for the registered disabled, and so on. The first point, then, is that the exemptions and exceptions do not in themselves embody a philosophically incoherent or repugnant idea, but a familiar one, designed to accommodate the complexities attendant on having general rules. Barry, of course, accepts that exemptions *exist*: indeed, he allows that there may be pragmatic or utilitarian grounds for extending an exemption to a group, or not abolishing an existing exemption – where to do so would undermine social integration, for example – but argues that exemptions can seldom be justified on the grounds of liberal justice (Barry 2001: 33, 39, 59–60; 2002: 214). For example, an existing exemption for turban-wearing Sikhs from hard hat regulation in the construction industry should not be withdrawn, since there is a 'balance of advantage' in keeping it, for a relatively high proportion of the Sikh community seem to be working in this area, and 'ending this employment' (as Barry puts it) would impoverish and alienate that group. Furthermore, there is no incoherence from the standpoint of liberal justice in an exemption's being legislated, as opposed to being derived from the norm of equal treatment (cf. Barry 2001: 44, 171–2; 2002: 217).

The second point is that there is nothing incoherent about arguing for an exemption on the grounds of equal treatment. Barry's conception of state impartiality as equal or fair treatment is of the sort which allows *justified* exemptions. 'No parking except for disabled drivers' and 'no duelling except for accredited members of the aristocracy' deviate in the same way from 'no parking' and 'no duelling'. But the first is justified from the liberal egalitarian standpoint, and the second is not. In other words, there is nothing wrong *in principle* with targeting rights (or state 'intervention' generally), provided that the rights claimed are acceptable from a liberal egalitarian standpoint. Now in providing this set of rights, etc. to each citizen, the state will sometime treat everyone identically, but will often treat different citizens differently. This is obvious in cases such as the provision of expensive but essential medical care to those who need it, but not to those who do not; or different levels of expenditure on policing in different areas. An alternative instance is the provision of an extra subsidy for rural transport services, on the grounds that there is a smaller customer base, and therefore these services would not survive commercially in the absence of a level of per capita subsidy higher than that for urban services. In this instance, it may be riposted, no one *has* to live in the country (it is *voluntary*), so this is a case of subsidizing an expensive taste. But we are more likely to think that this is not so: that there is a difference between the resources due to rural dwellers and to those, for example, who move to an isolated spot in order to set up a new religious order (Miller 2002: 188–9).

In the light of these first two points, we can see, third, that Barry in fact allows deviation from rules on grounds of justice in cultural cases: this is not incoherent in principle, but simply rare, in his opinion. For example, he considers the case of *Mandla* v. *Dowell Lee*, in which a turban-wearing Sikh schoolboy was refused admission to a private school in Birmingham on the ground that he failed to comply with the school's rules, which prescribed a short haircut and a uniform that included a cap (Barry 2001: 61–2). In this case, he argues, if we accept that the school has a legitimate interest in having such a uniform (rendering the libertarian response unattractive), equal educational opportunity prescribes that a breach with uniformity in a small number of cases is permissible. On the one hand, if the breach is too large, then the interest promoted by the rule is undermined. On the other hand, in this case the boy has an important interest in having a range of educational opportunities equal to that of everyone else, thus justifying the exemption. The interest in equal educational opportunity is sufficiently weighty to mean that he ought not bear the costs of his beliefs, in this case. Second, Barry allows religious institutions some exemption from rules against religious and sex discrimination laws in their employment practices where this is justified as a 'business necessity' (Barry 2001: 167–8, 173–4; 2002: 223–6). The interests in freedom of conscience and association allow that in the case of some religious offices (but not any employment by the church, such as janitorial work), normal anti-discrimination law does not apply. And such a waiver is justified in other cases, such as that of an all-women gym (Barry 2002: 225–6).

Fourth, it is a mistake to identify multiculturalism merely with a regime of rules plus exemptions. In some cases, where there is judged to be a reason to have a rule, there is an alternative (to the original rule, to the rule-plus-exemption, and to the abolition of any rule): namely, to come up with a 'less restrictive alternative form of the law that would adequately meet the objectives of the original one while offering the members of the religious or cultural minority whatever is most important to them. This avoids the invidiousness of having different rules for different people in the same society' (Barry 2001: 39). So, there may be good reasons for having a uniform for hospital nurses: for example, to structure patients' expectations and to symbolize and strengthen the collective ethos of the profession. At the same time, there are good reasons to incorporate flexibility in those rules in order to accommodate Sikh or Muslim dress codes (Parekh 2000: 246–7; cf. Barry 2002: 217).

In discussing culture and job discrimination, Barry employs a 'necessity' test in determining which rules governing employees are justified (Barry 2001: 54–9; 2002: 216). Unless an employer can establish that, say, a specific manner of dress is essential to the performance of a job (for example, wearing a hard hat on construction sites – although, as we have seen, Barry is prepared to grant an exemption here in certain circumstances), there is no justification for the rule in question, since it hampers some people who are equally well qualified for the job from taking it. So an employer is not justified in prohibiting the wearing of a headscarf in an office, since that is not essential to the tasks that the employees have to perform. In other words, it is not adequate in this case to respond to someone who wants to wear a headscarf as a matter of religious or cultural obligation in a conventionalist vein that 'this is the way we do things around here'. Barry presents this as an argument for his libertarian handling of claims for difference-sensitive rules: there is no reason to ban anyone from wearing a headscarf, no matter what his or her motivation. But this is not the only way of dealing with this sort of case. What counts as necessary for the fulfilment of the duties of some job is in some part conventional. What makes it legitimate for a bank to require its tellers to dress soberly is not that this improves their ability to handle money. But what counts as sobriety in dress is open to differing cultural interpretations, and it would be discriminatory (on Barry's criterion of differently impacting on the equally well qualified) to say that standards of sobriety rule out the turban or the headscarf.[18]

In the light of these considerations, the difference between Barry and proponents of the politics of recognition appears a matter of degree rather than of kind. Barry acidly characterizes the latter as theoretically bold but timid in practice (Barry 2002: 230); but in terms both of what he does concede and of what there is space for him to concede, his own thought is rather more sympathetic to what multiculturalism's proponents argue for, particularly in the highly charged areas of education and employment law, than his official rhetoric suggests.

## 5.   Cultural Invisibility

Differences of degree are still differences, however. In this section, I want to consider a stronger line of criticism: namely, that Barry's response fails to deal with the rationale for claims for difference-sensitive rights and policies. The distinctive claim of multiculturalism is that difference-sensitive rights and policies are justified on the grounds of the value or importance of cultural identity; and the previous chapter explored some of the general lines of argument in support of the idea that cultural identity has such value. In outline, Barry's egalitarianism prescribes that a common set of liberal, civil and political rights be distributed to each member of the society: this common set of resources provides a level playing field on which each member of the society can pursue her own particular goals and projects. However, determining what goes into this set involves making judgements about human interests: that is, about what the point of this basic set of rights is, and how they should be ranked in cases of conflict. As several scholars have noted, Barry treats the interests that the liberal rights are meant to serve rather unsystematically in *Culture and Equality* and in a way that is not clearly related to the philosophical architecture of his conception of justice as impartiality (Barry 1995; Caney 2002; Kukathas 2002). Barry in various places alludes to various interests that the common code of liberal rights protects or promotes. People have interests in education (functional and 'for living'), economic resources, being able to change their minds, to form associations and to leave them without heavy external costs, and opportunities for employment (Barry 2001: 30, 35, 106–7, 151, 212, 220, 221, 238, 245).

Now one way of taking the claims for the normativity of culture is to see them (as liberal culturalists do) as marking out an interest that people may legitimately pursue, and therefore that may need legal and political expression. With the exception of the argument for the connection between individual self-respect and the recognition of cultural identity (discussed in chapter 2, section 4 above), Barry does not really grapple with these claims, perhaps because he finds them beneath notice. At the same time, he allows exceptions to the common code for pragmatic reasons (as in the case of the turban-wearing Sikhs in the construction industry) or as a way of reconciling conflicts between the legitimate policies of institutions and the interests of individuals. An example of the latter would be the case of the Sikh schoolboy. While the boy has a right to equal educational opportunity, which he is denied by having to choose between wearing a turban and attending a particular school, the school has a legitimate interest in having a school uniform. Another is the celebrated claim of turban-wearing Sikhs to exemption from the traditional Stetson of the Royal Canadian Mounted Police (Kymlicka 1995a: 177; Parekh 2000: 244–5; Barry 2002: 216).

The obvious way to describe the consideration that supports exemption in these cases is that there exists a legitimate interest in maintaining a cultural identity and in having some control over the way it changes. So, for example, one reason to support the turban-wearing Sikhs in their claim to ride motor cycles without a helmet, or indeed claims for the permissibility of kosher and halal slaughter, is that those putting forward that claim have a legitimate interest in maintaining aspects of their cultural identity. This is not to say in either case that this is an interest that overrides others in general, or that these claims should be acceded to in these particular cases. The point is only that this interest should be taken into account in deliberation about public policy, and that it has an independent weight deriving not just from the preferences of the groups concerned but from the normative character of cultural identity.[19]

In his treatment of educational and employment opportunities, as we have seen, Barry is prepared to let this consideration carry some weight. But it is not clear on what grounds it is dismissed in other contexts. In considering norms of public order, Barry (like Kukathas) supports the imposition of particular local norms, under the slogan 'this is the way we do things around here'. For example, he discusses the decision of an Australian court to uphold an appeal by an Aboriginal woman on grounds of indirect racial discrimination against the decision of a housing authority to evict her. Non-Aboriginal neighbours had lobbied politicians and complained to the police and the media about her, on the grounds that she had living in her small cottage a large number of her unruly grandchildren. Barry objects to the court's decision: the eviction was justified, he thinks, since nobody should be permitted to make the lives of their neighbours miserable through engaging in antisocial activity, 'according to prevailing standards of what constitutes antisocial activity' and providing that this has some 'tangible impact' ('noise, smell, fumes, damage to property or personal injury') and does not consist merely of, say, behaviour that neighbours find morally uncomfortable. In this case, the court handling the appeal 'apparently took the line that, if it was an Aboriginal custom to gather together all one's children and grandchildren, this had to be upheld *regardless* of the consequences for others living in the vicinity' (Barry 2001: 290–1, emphasis added). However, whether or not this correctly interprets the court's decision, there is a different and more plausible reading of it available (Horton 2003: 38). This is that this way of life's having a place in Aboriginal customs and traditions carries some deliberative weight that needs to be taken into account in making a decision. There is no reason to assume that the appeal to culture or custom in this way necessarily trumps the interests of neighbours in a quiet life, by their own lights.

A second instance of the treatment of cultural identity as a matter of convention is Barry's discussion of language policies. As Barry puts it:

> Where language is concerned, a state cannot adopt a neutral stance: it must provide services in one or more languages, decide if a linguistic test for employment is to count as illegal discrimination, and so on. At the same time, it can be said of language as of no other cultural trait that it is a matter of convention. No doubt every language has its own peculiar excellences, but any language will do as the medium of communication in a society as long as everybody speaks it. This is one case involving cultural attributes in which 'This is how we do things here' – the appeal to local convention – is a self-sufficient response to pleas for the public recognition of diversity. (Barry 2001: 107)

While the oppression of speakers of minority languages is condemned (such as the beating of schoolchildren who lapse into their ancestral tongue), it is no concern of liberal political theory if a language becomes marginal or disappears. A language may become extinct 'simply because those speaking it take decisions that in aggregate result in its disappearing. Very many languages have done just that in the past and doubtless many more will do so in the future: two thousand of the world's six thousand languages have fewer than one thousand speakers and are unlikely to survive' (Barry 2001: 65). Liberal states ought not to adopt policies that try to preserve a language when those who speak it prefer in aggregate to let the language perish. But, as in the housing authority case, there is a question-mark both over who the 'we' turns out to be, and over the dismissal of any other claims for the significance of cultural identity.

To view a language as merely a convention adhered to by its speakers is question begging here. For defenders of policies of linguistic preservation and promotion find value in more than a language's generic communicative function. They may view it, as Kymlicka does, as part of the context of choice of an individual, the erosion of which threatens that person's autonomy, as important for a person's identity, or as the repository of non-instrumental value for speakers. From any of these perspectives the loss incurred by the erosion or disappearance of a language is just that, a loss. It does not follow that any one of these interests outweighs a person's interest in making linguistic choices for herself or her children; but even if we view the latter interest as trumping the former, this does not mean that no good or value has been lost in the process of linguistic erosion.

Barry argues that the promotion of the Welsh language in Wales violates liberal principles. Since Welsh is spoken by a significant minority of the population of Wales, there is good reason to ensure that the language is taught in schools. 'At the same time, it has to be recognized that the great majority of people in Wales do not speak Welsh at home, and for them learning Welsh in school from scratch is in direct competition for time with learning a major foreign language. It is therefore scarcely surprising that compulsory instruction in Welsh in the schools has aroused opposition from English-speaking parents' (Barry 2001: 107; cf. Laitin and Reich 2003) – opposition which Barry supports. This abuse of state power is then compounded by another, in Barry's view: policies making knowledge of Welsh a requirement for certain positions in the public sector in Wales. Although Barry does not explicitly say so, it seems that it is not open to the Welsh Assembly to offer the conventionalist retort to the effect that 'this is how *we* do things around here', since compulsory instruction in Welsh restricts the job prospects of students. If we view employment opportunities as the only value relevant to judging language policies, then this may be the case; but it is question begging to assume that this is the only dimension on which to assess these policies. If there are other legitimate interests defended by the language policy, and the loss of employment opportunities is offset by the rigging of the public sector job market, then a marginal loss in job prospects may be justifiable. My point is not that this must be the case, but that Barry's way of setting up the problem once again renders invisible the concerns of those he is considering.

## 6. Conclusion

These two different versions of negative universalism express two different models of liberalism. On the one side, there is the liberalism deriving from

Montesquieu's *thèse nobiliaire*, which emphasizes the importance of 'interme-diary powers', local authorities and customs (indeed, customs authorities), viewing them as important bulwarks against the impudence of centralized state authority. On the other side, there is a 'Jacobin' strand of liberalism which views the state as an instrument for the elimination of petty absolut-isms. The first, in Kukathas's presentation, empties out the public realm of as much significance as it can. The second tries to shield the public realm from the depredations of particularity. From the libertarian perspective, the com-mitment to equality of resources in the service of a fundamental interest in being able to form, pursue and revise a conception of the good is a Trojan horse for the politics of recognition. For if one views it as the state's business to provide what is necessary for sustaining this fundamental interest on fair terms, then it is a relatively short step to regarding cultural identity as one of the conditions that may require political protection. Barry's egalitarian version of the negative position tries to hold the line against this conclusion – but not successfully, I have argued. We must look next at arguments that try to move beyond pre-emption.

# 5

# Cultural Accommodation and Political Dialogue

Understood as a model of political deliberation, liberal culturalism embeds an interest in cultural identity in the foundations of liberal political theory, and in doing so generates a problem of how to evaluate this interest in the process of political decision making and how to accommodate the politicization of cultural identity. Identities are not monoliths displaying clear, distinct and uncontested inscriptions of their character. Rather, power shapes identities in multifarious ways, and cultural identity is subject to disagreement, reinterpretation and negotiation. Impressed by the latter point, negative universalism, in both libertarian and egalitarian guises, tries to expunge questions of recognition, cultural normativity and difference-sensitive rights from the scope of political deliberation, but it does so only at the price of the distortions traced in the previous chapter.

For the conception of political deliberation as public dialogue, it is the public or democratic character of political dialogue that is crucial to allowing these claims for the recognition of cultural identity to be handled in an acceptable way. Such claims must aim to withstand the test of the exchange of public reasons in processes of political discussion and argument. From this perspective, the focus of theoretical debate shifts away from justifying a pre-emptive judgement of cultural normativity, recognition and the value of difference-sensitive rights toward considering what forms of public dialogue could fairly deal with the relevant array of claims and counter-claims, what fairness means in this context, and who should participate and on what terms.

There is now no shortage of subscribers to the belief that public deliberation holds the 'key for securing just relations among ethnic or cultural groups' (James 2003: 157). For instance, Seyla Benhabib advocates 'complex multicultural dialogue', arguing that 'a deliberative model of democracy, based on discourse ethics, can offer compelling answers to the challenges posed by multicultural demands' (Benhabib 2002: 101, 106). James Tully endorses a conception of democratic freedom as consisting in 'intersubjective and open-ended practical reasoning' as a way of generating just political relations among cultural groups (Tully 2002b: 217). Bhikhu Parekh also argues for 'intercultural' dialogue over disputed practices (such as arranged marriages, polygamy, and kosher and halal butchery), oriented around a society's 'operative public values' and a 'principle of dialogical consensus' as a basis for political action (Parekh 2000: 264–94; 1999).[1] This agreement over the importance of political dialogue emerges from the overlap of quite different positions, and papers over some significant disagreements about the meaning and political implications of democratic deliberation.

This chapter proceeds as follows. In section 1, I set out some of the basics of this position, and, since this raises a large range of questions, I also briefly indicate some of the areas that this chapter won't be exploring. In section 2, I look at some of the distinctive issues raised by cultural claims for this basic conception, distinguishing what I call equality, importance and compromise arguments for cultural recognition. The process of public discussion may bring to the surface forms of disagreement and dissent within groups that call into question the character and demands of cultural identities. In section 3, I look at the cultural costs and risks of this process, and consider the charge of cultural bias. I develop this charge further in section 4, which examines the problem of underdetermination: public deliberation seems to rest on the existence of a common standard of acceptability for proposals, but how to flesh out this core notion is problematic. I argue that, although there is force in the charge of cultural bias, it does not provide a reason to reject a suitably understood view of public deliberation.

## 1.  Political Deliberation as Public Dialogue

The theory of public deliberation expresses an ideal of democratic decision making as a process of reasoned public discussion of arguments for and against some proposal, with the aim of arriving at a judgement which is generally acceptable. This approach views a set of democratic arrangements as deliberative when the decisions arrived at are the result of a process of discussion to which each participant is able to contribute freely, but in which each is also committed to listening to and taking seriously the point of view of other participants. The decisions reached should reflect this process, and rest not simply on the prior opinions, interests and positions of those who take part, but on their considered judgements made after reflection on the arguments presented. Even if processes of discussion and argument aim at agreed outcomes, there is seldom, if ever, consensus, and particular decisions are likely to require procedures, such as a vote, in order to be reached.[2] These procedures can themselves be discussed deliberatively, criticized, endorsed and revised, however, and they may also be evaluated by reflecting on how they promote or hamper other aspects of the deliberative process.[3]

The central and complex normative claim of public deliberation is that it makes decisions that are rational, legitimate and inclusive. Public deliberation aspires to be reasoned in the sense that the decisions reached are determined by the reasons given in deliberation or deliberatively adopted. Participants are viewed as committed to responding to the reasons and arguments of others *qua* reasons and arguments. What is meant to matter in political deliberation is not bargaining power, but only the force of the better argument: participants give their reasons 'with the expectation that those reasons (and not, for example, power) will settle the fate of their proposal' (Cohen 1997a: 74; cf. Miller 2000: 77–8). This commitment exerts a crucial equalizing constraint in the deliberative process. If participants are not under this constraint, then they are free to respond to the relative bargaining strength of others, with the result that those positioned so as to stymie the process of decision making, to help build a coalition, or to offer an attractive deal, will benefit at the expense of those who lack such bargaining resources. This commitment, then, means that the arguments and point of view of the weak are taken into consideration, although there is no presumption that a position of weakness itself confers any particular authority on arguments or points of view.[4]

The responsiveness to reasons of the deliberative process makes it attractive, on the surface at least, to some supporters of the claims of culturally marginal groups. For example, Melissa Williams writes that 'the only hope that marginalized-group presence will have a lasting effect on policy outcomes is that decisions are based not only on the counting of votes but on the sharing of reasons' (M. Williams 2000: 125). For groups that are marginal in the sense of being poorly politically organized, or unable to muster a majority of votes, will tend to lose out in decision-making processes that are sensitive principally to powerful political interests or to majorities.[5] Furthermore, the exchange of reasons and arguments opens up the different arguments and points of view in play to scrutiny, leading to examination of familiar and unquestioned assumptions. Public deliberation is critical, in the sense that decisions reached, and the reasons underlying them, are arrived at through a process of critical reflection and viewed as subject to revision.[6] The outcomes are provisional and fallible, and the process must include the critical scrutiny and discussion of those reasons, not simply the tacit acceptance of communal norms. Further, although deliberation may construct a new set of political ends or goals on which to act, these are themselves fallible and not insulated from scrutiny, criticism and revision. In any particular case, as Tully puts it, 'the dissenters may turn out on reconsideration to have been right after all' (Tully 2001: 28).

Deliberation aspires to be legitimate, in that the process of discussion is framed so that each person who takes part can see and understand the reasons for the policy adopted, even if she is not personally convinced by those reasons or a supporter of that particular outcome. This may a tricky and demanding condition to meet (cf. Festenstein 1999; Bohman 2003). On the one hand, the reasons and justifications offered for public policies should actually justify those policies. On the other hand, these reasons and justifications need to be in a relevant sense intelligible or accessible to everyone bound by the policies.[7] So in public deliberation we should not appeal to reasons that are intelligible only to, or can be affirmed only by, some particular group of participants. Nor should participants make exclusive appeal to the interests of some particular group.[8] In some cases, of course, I can make sense of reasons even if they are not ones that I myself would accept. So, for example, an unbeliever can make sense of a religious denomination's argument that it should be granted permission to build a temple on a particular spot, since granting this will promote social harmony, reflect numbers of local worshippers, or in some fashion treat this group equally compared with others, even if these are not in this case wholly *persuasive* reasons for the unbeliever. For these are norms and values that she can make sense of, even if in this particular case she disagrees with their application. But she may not find acceptable a reason that presupposes the truth of this religious outlook – say, that the site chosen has been granted to this group by their god. The underlying intuition is that there is a variety of ethical perspectives, conceptions of the good, and so on, with no prospect of agreement among them. This variety may be not only a *de facto* plurality of values but *de jure* pluralism, deriving from reasonable or justifiable differences in values, world-view and so on.[9] For some proponents of political deliberation, particularly those influenced by the political liberalism of John Rawls, finding a common meeting ground in the space of public reasons protects citizens from alienation from the social and political order in which we live and constitutes a form of reconciliation to this order.[10]

Participants in public deliberation are accordingly viewed as committed to offering arguments persuasive to all other participants in the deliberative process.[11] On the standard conception of deliberative democracy, participants in the deliberative process are required not only to offer arguments but to offer arguments persuasive to all: there is no presumption, then, that some members of the deliberating body do not count. As Joshua Cohen puts it, deliberation aims at finding 'reasons persuasive to all who are committed to acting' on its results, and participants are committed to 'providing reasons that they sincerely expect to be persuasive to others who share that commitment' (Cohen 1997a: 75–6). This is not of course to impose the impossible requirement that a participant's reasons and arguments should be compatible with all the beliefs of one's interlocutors: the point is precisely to change their minds, at least with respect to the proposal at hand. There is plainly a question here about the limits to the duty to offer generally persuasive arguments: if I persist in failing to draw the simplest inference from your arguments, or base my reception of them on bizarre or horrible assumptions, how long should you pour resources into trying to communicate with me? But I want here to accept this commitment provisionally as an intelligible, as well as an essential, component of public deliberation.

Finally, public deliberation aims to be inclusive in the sense that every member of the political community can take part on an equal basis. Deliberative theorists have emphasized the need for inclusiveness and equality of access to the process. If, as Bernard Manin writes, 'a legitimate decision . . . is one that results from the deliberation of all', the need to ensure that all in fact do or may take part in the deliberative process becomes paramount (Manin 1987: 352).[12] It is a little ambiguous (an ambiguity which I do not hope to clear up here (but see Festenstein 2004)) whether proponents of public deliberation support inclusiveness for concerned individuals for its own sake or on the grounds that it is only through discussion conducted inclusively that a wide range of *issues* relevant for political decision making can be discerned: for example, that the true extent of the diversity of interests and identities in a society can be grasped. The epistemic benefits of public debate as a means of pushing those who take part into greater understanding of the predicaments of others and overcoming the limited horizons of individual points of view have been stressed within the liberal tradition by John Stuart Mill, John Dewey and others. As Melissa Williams argues, 'the partiality of our own experience' limits our capacity to see how current laws and practices affect the fundamental interests of others. So 'we need to confront the actual particularity of others' experience to reflect on what our just obligations toward them may be' (M. Williams 1995: 80; cf. M. Williams 2000: 129; Deveaux 2003: 782–3). Or, as Peter Jones puts it, 'the best authorities on what a particular culture requires are, indeed, likely to be those whose culture it is' (Jones 1998: 57). In actively seeking the points of view, or 'voices', of different groups, and different members of different groups, public deliberation aspires to a level of epistemic sensitivity necessary to address the problems and conflicts posed by cultural identity. Accordingly, deliberative theorists debate the design of institutions and spaces for the expression of this diversity – and of all the other sources of diversity in interests, preferences, points of view, perspectives, conceptions of the good, and so on.[13]

## 2.   Dialogue and Recognition

Public deliberation may appear inhospitable to multicultural rights. The public deliberation position builds an argument about the character of citizenship and public debate in a democratic society. The justificatory standard for a claim, to recall, is that the policy, right or entitlement on behalf of which the claim is made should be supported by a reason or argument that has been subjected to a process of public scrutiny and discussion, and is accessible to all. For a test for a claim that hinges on a commonly acceptable reason seems to suggest that claims on behalf of a particular group for some form of special right will inevitably appear as the kind of special pleading that the public deliberation model aims to reduce in the sphere of democratic reason giving. Yet a positive argument for difference-sensitive rights and policies can be made within the framework of the public deliberation, as it is set out here. To understand how this is so, we need to distinguish two ways in which a claim in deliberation can be partial. First, there is a claim to an entitlement that is specific only to one group, as in a dress code exemption for Sikhs. For, first, we should not confuse the character of the entitlements claimed with the scope of the reasons supporting that claim. An exemption from a dress code, for example, can be made on grounds that do not purport to be valid only to some particular group, even if the exemption applies only to some particular group. The reasons for permitting Sikh members of the Royal Canadian Mounted Police to wear non-standard headgear are not non-public, in the sense that only a member of that group can feel their force. The second sense of partiality refers to a reason or justification that is available only to one group: for example, Catholic arguments against abortion. By 'available', we do not need to mean 'compelling', or uncontroversial – available to other citizens *qua* citizens. The Catholic case against abortion is emphatically not for an exemption or some other differentiated entitlement for a particular group; nor does it refer to a group-specific interest.

With this general point in mind, I want now to distinguish three forms of argument that can be accommodated within the public deliberation perspective for the recognition of cultural practices. Each form of argument submits itself to the discipline of common acceptability, while working to a different template. The first form of argument aims to support differentiated treatment on the grounds of publicly acceptable reasons of equality. To consider a familiar non-cultural example initially: special rights of access to public buildings, including commercial premises, can be claimed for the disabled, in the form, say, of designated parking spaces. This claim can be supported by reasons that are publicly accessible: that there is a general interest in equal access to these buildings, and that the disabled have the same interest in access to supermarkets and libraries as the able-bodied. Within the sphere of claims for cultural rights, arguments for exemptions from dress codes at school and work, for alteration of the standard working week, and so on, take this form. The core idea is that people with a particular identity have a legitimate interest both in not giving up the practice that is made problematic by a general rule, and in participating in, or having the opportunity to participate in, the practice that this rule governs. Similarly a claim for an assistance right, such as special provision for the education of a group of children in their first language, if it is not the language of the state, can be based on publicly accessible claims about what a citizen is normally entitled to. To be sure, this can rest on what is sometimes a contentious empirical claim, that children who speak their minority language at home will be disadvantaged if educated in majority language.[14] In particular contexts, there is plainly room for disagreement, but the point to underline here is that the form of the argument is public: it makes an appeal to a general interest to equality of educational opportunity, on premises that all can find intelligible – even if they disagree with the particular policy. Similarly, what constitutes a *burden* to be rectified may sometimes be culturally constituted. So, for example, a particular shame may attach to some physical injuries or forms of slander for some groups that ground a claim for compensation or for a higher level of compensation than would otherwise be the case (Poulter 1998: 64). The point in each case is not that there cannot be counter-arguments that also meet this standard, only that we should not pre-emptively judge one way or the other. There is an ample tradition of granting differentiated rights on the back of arguments that meet the public deliberation standard, and a range of claims made on behalf of culturally differentiated citizenship can do so too.

Now equality-based arguments of this sort require some kind of affirmation of the cultural identity of those on behalf of whom a claim is made. So, for example, if we want to distinguish the cases of Sikhs demanding exemption from crash helmet legislation and Hell's Angels making the same claim, we need to affirm something about the religious, conscientious or cultural character of the former group. But this need not amount to anything as strong as public validation of that cultural identity, only that turban wearing is the sort of commitment which it is not reasonable to those who have this identity to renounce. Against this background understanding of what it is reasonable or unreasonable to expect citizens to renounce or change in particular social contexts, decisions about how to deal fairly with the problems posed by the relationship of particular identities to general social roles and rules can be made. But this form of argument does not require that the public *endorses* the particular identity in question, in the sense that it judges it to be valuable, or to possess normativity in terms of the categories outlined in chapter 2. The second form of argument aims to establish publicly the *importance* of some feature of an identity. This is an argument for exemption or support for a practice not on the grounds of equality, but on account of that practice's having the significance (for practitioners, perhaps for others) that may make it a candidate for exemption or support.

In part, this is a matter of presenting or describing practices so that they fall into the categories relevant for equality arguments; so, for instance, the wearing of a turban comes to be seen to be part of a Sikh man's identity in such a way that it would be unreasonable to demand that he renounce it. Comparison, redescription and analogy are important parts of the discursive armoury here.[15] The scope of importance arguments is wider than merely providing the basis for an equality argument, however. So, for example, a minority linguistic group may argue for education in its own language on the grounds that its members do measurably less well in the absence of such provision, and for reasons that can be traced to and remedied by minority language education. But it may also argue (in terms of the arguments for the normativity of a cultural identity canvassed earlier in this book) that the language has importance for its members, and that this merits protection. For some proponents of public deliberation, reasons and arguments that appeal to the normative character of cultural identity are thought to be characteristically too controversial to act as reasons in the public arena (cf. Fraser 2001; Miller 2002). Of course, this may be the case with any particular argument. But, first, it does not follow from the controversial character of some culture-based claims that the equality-based arguments make no assumptions about what sort of activities are important, or count within the scope of those things that person may not reasonably be compelled to give up. Rather, these assumptions themselves can be held up to the light, disputed, revised and so on. Second, what counts as important in this sense changes (for instance, in relation to technological changes or to a looming environmental crisis), and new considerations can be introduced and discussed. Third, and finally, the potentially controversial character of any particular consideration is not a reason to restrain it from entry into debate, or even for someone who believes in this consideration to restrain herself.[16]

The third form of argument aims not at establishing the importance of a consideration nor at establishing what equality requires in a particular context, but at achieving a compromise among conflicting points of view. Indeed, for some, compromise is the 'bread and butter of democratic deliberation' (Richardson 1997: 352; 2002: 143–61; Bellamy 1999: 12–13, 37–8, 93–114). Compromise may take the form of splitting the difference, as in a wage dispute, or a log-rolling arrangement in which each party revises its support for some proposal in order to win the benefits of co-operation with others. Or we may compromise in the sense that we settle on a proposal that means different things to different participants. Compromise of these kinds may seem to be an inevitable but regrettable feature of public deliberation, since it seems to appeal only to the overlap of the separate strategic interests of different participants, rather than to a common standard of acceptability. Yet public deliberation allows for a distinctively deliberative compromise, which takes the form of an arrangement that seeks to recognize the arguments on each side of the dispute, as they emerge and change in the process of public deliberation. This second sort of compromise affects the underlying ends, interests and goals that shape particular policy preferences, in response to the arguments and point of view of other participants. This may happen through one party's coming to share the reasons of another, through the first's finding the reasons of the second persuasive. It may also be motivated by a commitment to the shared enterprise of deliberation or to other participants *qua* citizens. Deliberative compromise, then, takes the form not of reciprocal back scratching, as on the strategic view, but is 'a modification in one's practical commitments that one would not have made but for one's concern and respect for the other or for the joint entity or enterprise one shares with him or her' (Richardson 2002: 146). A compromise in this sense is not a matter of working out an egalitarian formula for the treatment of bearers of different cultural identities. Rather, it is a matter of finding a set of commonly acceptable and provisional terms to solve the problem of conflicting practical commitments.

Sometimes the construction of a compromise is necessary because the content of a claim to equal treatment in some particular respect is so indeterminate. So, for example, a claim for group representation in order to realize a value of political equality gestures toward a wide variety of possible forms of government, the precise specification of which will hinge on the concrete political geography of the claimants and others in a shared political space. In other cases, compromise is required not in order to specify an outline conception of what equality demands in some particular case, but simply where practical commitments or claims to recognition conflict. Claus Offe discusses this case:

> On March 29, 1990, Slovak deputies of the Czechoslovak Federal Parliament entered a motion that the name of the state should from now on be hyphenated as 'Czecho-Slovakia' (as it was written in the inter-war period) rather than Czechoslovakia. The Czech majority voted in favour of the compromise that the spelling proposed by the Slovaks should be used in Slovakia, but the unhyphenated version should be used in the Czech Lands and abroad. This decision was perceived by the Slovak public as deeply insulting, and the elimination of the hyphen was protested the next day at a mass rally in Bratislava by a crowd of 80,000 people. In this case, a compromise could actually be found. On April 12, the parliament changed the official state name to Czech and Slovak Federal Republic. (Claus Offe, quoted by J. Levy 2000: 156)

Where there is sufficient commitment to a shared association (as ultimately of course in this case there wasn't), space can be found to base a compromise on recognition of the reasons or points of view of others.

To affirm the place of compromise in political dialogue is not to forget that compromise sometimes means paying a high price. Living with political arrangements which in some respects you reject or find loathsome is not easy, and to engage in a process of compromise puts at risk goods and values held dear. Furthermore, public deliberation, as we saw, requires not only a willingness to compromise but a preparedness to dissent from and criticize procedures and outcomes. These considerations bring us to the topic of the next section.

### 3.   Culture versus Public Deliberation

Conceptions of public deliberation are often criticized on the grounds that they cannot accommodate social pluralism. Who participates? On what terms? Who is included, silenced, or given more or less time and resources to articulate their case during the course of public discussion? In this section I want to consider the ways in which public deliberation may be thought to exclude or be biased against cultural minorities. In focusing on cultural sources of exclusion, I want to bracket at the outset discussion of what is probably the most important source of exclusion from public deliberation. Proponents of public deliberation often allude to compensation for those 'background inequalities' that disadvantage some participants in the processes of negotiation, discussion and persuasion (Gutmann and Thompson 1996: 134). As Benhabib puts it, 'participation in . . . deliberation is governed by the norms of equality and symmetry; all have the same chances to initiate speech acts, to question, to interrogate, and to open debate' (Benhabib 1996b: 70). If a group lacks the resources to put across its point of view, there is little chance that this point of view, and perhaps this group's interests, will be embodied in the outcome of public dialogue. The goal of inclusion requires a pre-deliberative process of equalizing access to resources and capacities relevant to effective participation.[17] In bracketing this large set of questions, I want to focus not on the material conditions of participation but on what has been called 'the unfreedom of assimilation', the risks of cultural bias and exclusion in the deliberative process. A group may be excluded, or compelled to assimilate, when the dominant language and symbols of public discourse make it necessary for a group with a different style of participation either to conform or not to take part.[18]

> When formerly excluded people are "included" in practices of democratic deliberation, they often find that the practical knowledge of the practice [of deliberation, argument, negotiation] is different from the ones to which they are accustomed. This is often overlooked by dominant groups, for it is their customary way of reasoning together; or if it is noticed, it is often presented as canonical, as universal or the uniquely reasonable, modern or 'free and equal' way of deliberating, as if there were only one way of exercising democratic freedom. If one wishes to be heard, then, it is necessary to act in accordance with the dominant practice of reasoning together and resolving differences, and, as a result, to gradually develop the form of identity and comportment characteristics of participants in this kind of practice. This is the unfreedom of assimilation for one is not free to challenge the implicit and explicit rules of the dominant practice of deliberation, but must conform to them and so be shaped by them. (Tully 2002b: 223; cf. Laden 2001: 8, 132; Young 2000: ch. 2; Sanders 1997)

In one sense, this is an empirical issue. Deliberative theorists respond that there is no shortage of skilled advocates among marginalized groups, capable of making use of and remoulding prevalent discursive norms (Gutmann and

Thompson 1996: 132–3; M. Miller 2000: 153; Williams 2000: 135–6). Their presence in turn may have the effect of opening up the deliberative arena to different styles of speech and argument (cf. Phillips 1995; M. Williams 1998). Further, where there are divergences in styles of reasoning and argument, devices such as mediators and moderators can be deployed to assist in negotiating these barriers (Deveaux 2003: 790–5). The underlying point is that while this is a difficulty for public deliberation, it is one that this model seeks to overcome through devices to foster inclusiveness. Furthermore, those (like Tully or Iris Marion Young) who attack 'the unfreedom of assimilation' in this sense argue for the admission in public deliberation of a variety of modes of speech and argument. But this makes sense as an aspiration only if one believes that these various forms of speech and argument can bridge semiotic differences. Certainly an a priori pessimism seems as unjustified as a blithe hopefulness that all these differences and accompanying 'residues of misunderstanding, non-consensuality and injustice' (Ivison 2002: 73) will assuredly be laundered out through the process of public discussion.

A different concern is that for some forms of life, as James Bohman remarks, '[t]he cost of interaction in the public sphere may well be the loss of some cultural forms of authority' (Bohman 1996: 146). So, for example, if a religious group argues for the right to educate its children in denominational schools, the public justification of this proposal may throw open to scrutiny the character of the religion, the elements of a proposed curriculum, the way it treats boys and girls, and so on. Those members of this group who advanced the proposal will not be able to exercise firm control over the scope of such discussion, with the result that 'the self-interpretations of such cultures and their traditions will be thrown open beyond their authorised interpreters to a wider set of participants, even to non-members with whom they engage in dialogue' (Bohman 1996: 146). To open up an identity for discussion in this way creates space not only for disagreement about the demands of such an identity (as in disagreements about what its canonical texts prescribe, what claims are part of specific cultural traditions, and so on) but for dissent: that is, for disagreement within a group about how children should be educated. The public discussion of identity may in this way lead to identities being politicized. To recall Jones's comment, 'the best authorities on what a particular culture requires are, indeed, likely to be those whose culture it is' (Jones 1998: 57); but whose account of that culture has authority may become a political issue. Further, to the extent that the adherent to public deliberation hopes for the inclusion of all participants and issues, she will encourage precisely those processes that elicit such disagreement and dissent: '[d]emocratic legitimacy is not secured by merely soliciting the views of established leaders in communities, but rather requires that a plurality of group members with divergent interests and circumstances be included in deliberation' (Deveaux 2003: 790; cf. Spinner-Halev 2001: 108; Benhabib 2002: 114–19; Phillips and Dustin

2004: 545–6). Inclusion of this range of voices may tend to (indeed, is only really necessary if it does) challenge 'community leaders', and so may tend to generate political rifts within as well as alliances across identities.

Finally, for some groups, interaction in the public sphere is at best a necessary evil, which secures conditions for their living in a generally withdrawn and insular fashion. In one sense, public deliberation is compatible with the withdrawal from public life of a group (such as the Amish in the United States or ultra-orthodox Jews in various democratic states) from large areas of common social life. What the public deliberation model does claim is that the practices of such groups are not immune from external assessment (as they are on Chandran Kukathas's voluntary association model), but that the assessment arrived at needs to take account of the viewpoint of members of these groups. To adopt this conception of politics does not mean embracing the view that the only desirable form of life is one spent in the forum, but what it does imply is a commitment to offer justifications for reasons and policies, where these are needed, with the aim of arriving at a commonly acceptable proposal. It is this requirement, rather than the non-instrumental value of political participation, which is meant to make the 'costs of interaction' acceptable for those who pay them. Yet the formal compatibility of withdrawal with the commitment to public deliberation seems to be subverted by the commitment to elicit inclusion in the political process of members of those groups (mainly women) who are traditionally left out. In sum, then, the objection is that, by not only allowing but fostering disagreement, dissent and engagement in public life, the public deliberation model seems to be biased against those ways of life that value tradition and separateness.[19]

One response here is to distinguish the possible effects of discussing the character and requirements of an identity and those of seeking to include traditionally excluded members of groups in public discussion from the rationale for this style of discussion. The goal of conducting political dialogue on these terms is not to transform traditional cultural identities, and framing political dialogue in this way involves no judgement of the merit or otherwise of a particular way of life. In some instances, this seems a reasonable response. Yet in other instances, this will not be the case. Where the identity-based claim is for the marginalization of women in the public sphere, for example, then the active attempt to include them conflicts directly with this claim, not merely as a matter of its consequences.

An alternative response to this is to see putatively authoritative spokespeople on behalf of an identity in public deliberation as committed to allowing the expression of internal disagreement and dissent on pain of a sort of pragmatic self-contradiction (Tully 2001: 9, 16). For representatives of a group to advance a claim (say, for separate schooling) for consideration and debate by the polity rests on their having the right to speak, and to call into question prevailing arrangements on behalf of the identity that they (claim to) represent. In exercising that right, however, they must allow it to others, and there are no grounds for excluding members of their own group from the ambit of that right. So, as we have seen, debates over such matters as family law, membership and the place of women in some communities often lead to the expression of internal differences within particular communities and the formation of groups across cultural lines. As Tully puts it, 'the citizens for whom the demand is made' by community leaders 'must themselves accept the proposed identity and support it from a first-person perspective'. This in turn 'requires democratic negotiation and agreement which ensures that minorities *within* the group have the opportunity to have a say in the formulation of the demand so that it accommodates the other aspects of *their* identity that matter to them' (Tully 2000b: 474). Yet this pragmatic *self*-contradiction arises only if one assumes that the principles guiding negotiation and discussion in the wider polity must be identical with those guiding relations in a community, and conservatives within a group may not be committed to *that* belief.

Perhaps, then, the potential costs and risks of interaction in the public sphere will, with good reason, seem dangerously high for some traditionalists. I want to make two points about this conclusion. The first is that this suggests that public deliberation cannot in itself guarantee the reconciliation for all citizens to the public reasons that govern them, as some Rawlsians hope.[20] The second is that there may nevertheless be a pragmatic case for participation in public deliberation, even for the kind of conservative discussed here. For the alternative to attempting to include all participants and issues is to attempt to include only a select number, and there is no guarantee for the conservative that hers will be among them. Participation, even in this necessarily costly form, may well be better than no opportunity to participate at all.

## 4.    The Underdetermination of Public Deliberation

Important though these concerns about cultural bias and exclusion are, there is a deeper worry about the character of public deliberation. We can understand it this way. Public deliberation requires some recognition prior to the process of discussion of who counts as a participant and what counts as a commonly acceptable reason within deliberation. But why should disagreement not go all the way down, to encompass these areas too (cf. Tully 2002b: 218)? Public deliberation requires us to come up with arguments to back political action that meet the standard of common acceptability. Yet, as a standard, this radically underdetermines the content of the arguments and reasons on the basis of which political action can be taken, saying nothing about this beyond that such reasons must be arrived at through a particular kind of process.

Here we can consider the conception of 'reasonableness' found in the later work of Rawls and deftly applied to the issues under consideration here by

Anthony Laden. Modern societies are viewed as characterized by reasonable disagreement among a plethora of ethical outlooks, this disagreement stemming from the various ways we can reasonably interpret and weigh the facts available to a 'common human reason'. From the Rawlsian perspective, 'only public reasons are properly invoked in political deliberation' (Laden 2001: 99–100). These are those reasons that 'all citizens as free and equal may reasonably be expected to endorse in light of principles and ideals acceptable to their common human reason' (Rawls 1993: 137). What makes deliberation political is its covering only a certain sort of subject matter, taking place in a specifically political forum and engaging only the political identities of citizens. For Rawls, public reason governs only 'the constitutional essentials and matters of basic justice', and not the mundane stuff of democratic decision making or public policy (Rawls 1993: 214ff). Second, political deliberation 'takes place in properly political fora: in legislative debates, electoral campaigns, political demonstrations, and the decisions of appeal courts' (Laden 2001: 100; Rawls 1993: 215–16; 1999: 577). What makes reasoning public is that it is taken to be responsive not to truth or right, but to 'an idea of the politically reasonable addressed to citizens as citizens' (Rawls 1999: 574). I abstain from asserting that it is the truth of my point of view that provides a compelling reason to adopt my preferred proposal, but instead rely on canons of reasoning whose specific content is given by the points of view of other citizens, themselves respectful of the same constraint. The conception of what constitute fair terms of co-operation at which a society arrives cannot be pre-empted by a judgement prior to the process of public discussion.[21] A and B must recognize one another as possessing minimally reasonable conceptions of what are fair terms of co-operation, even if they disagree over which is more reasonable. So, for public reason to operate, A offers fair terms of co-operation Fa to B, sincerely believing that it is reasonable for B to accept Fa (cf. Rawls 1999: 581).[22] Fair terms of co-operation are hammered out through a process of exchange of public reasons, understood in this way.

It is not the case, as some critics of this Rawlsian perspective believe, that this makes no space for the possibility of differentiated citizenship. Some critics of Rawlsian public reason who are keen to press the claims of multiculturalism object that it blocks the possibility of claims for difference-sensitive entitlements. For instance, Monique Deveaux argues that 'the accounts of reasonableness and public reason so central to Rawlsian liberalism stand in tension with some claims for cultural recognition' (Deveaux 2000b: 92). Particular communities may legitimately invoke 'partialist' beliefs and norms, rather than appeal to widely acceptable political norms. For instance, the Inuit peoples of Nunavut, she argues, made indispensable appeal to their community's distinct history, ways of life, and special requirements for cultural survival in justifying claims for land use and language rights. Similarly, Parekh views this model of public reason as 'inhospitable' to cultural plurality in the sense that it does not accommodate groups which aspire to 'cultural auton-omy and hence some departure from the conventional liberal preoccupation with a homogeneous legal and political structure' (Parekh 2000: 89). However, on the account of public reasons set out here, there is no necessary incompat-ibility between the constraints on participants to offer public reasons, at least to the extent that they wish to authorize the use of state power, and the claims for differentiated legal, political or constitutional arrangements.

By making the use of public reason a necessary condition for reasonable political deliberation, this line of argument authorizes a particular response which can be made within political deliberation as a way of outflanking some kinds of argument advanced in that process. If some participants in public deliberation urge an argument for a particular view that does not satisfy the principle of public reason, Anthony Laden writes, 'we can now, as a legitimate move within the debate, point out to them why their argument fails to meet this criterion of reasonableness and why as a result it does not carry the weight they thought it did' (Laden 2001: 125). As Cohen argues, 'it will not do simply to advance reasons that one takes to be true and compelling. Such considera-tions may be rejected by others who are themselves reasonable'. Rather, we have to seek out reasons that are compelling for others, in the knowledge that those others have reasonable commitments of their own that differ from ours and 'knowing something about the kind of commitments that they are likely to have – for example, that they have moral or religious commitments that impose what they take to be overriding obligations' (Cohen 1997b: 414). The kind of reasons which this public deliberative process may block includes, then, the view that 'some are worth less than others or that the interests of one group are to count for less than those of others' (Cohen 1997b: 414). If the Muslim schoolgirls of Creil demand an exemption from the school's dress code on the grounds that conforming to that code will offend Allah, it is open to others to respond this is not a *public* reason. Given the depth of reasonable disagreement, the assumption that everyone else will find their reasons author-itative in virtue of their citizenship is definitive of unreasonableness on this view (Laden 2001: 104–5; Rawls 1993: 48–54, 61).

Further, it is wrong for the state to act on reasons only valid within some or other idiosyncratic standpoint. If we consider a practice that is the subject of dispute, such as the wearing of the headscarf in a secular school system, we may respond that there is scope for reasonable disagreement over the significance of this practice: for some it constitutes proselytizing, for others a manifestation of patriarchy, for yet others a means to negotiate a transition to a new society, and so on. For the state to act on only one set of reasons is for it to take a controversial position that fails the test of common acceptability. Now it does not follow from this that the case for abolishing the rule or for an exemption is *justified*. Rather, a certain kind of argument for the original rule is deemed illegitimate as the basis for that rule. On Laden's view, the French state's response to the headscarves' affair itself embodies a denial of the plurality of public reason. It imposes a particular, partial or biased conception of citizenship on Muslims (and others), irrespective of the reasons that they can, as citizens, understand as theirs (Laden 2001: 106; Quong 2004: 50–2). For example, when being a citizen requires endorsing a set of comprehensive philosophical beliefs or taking part in a set of non-political cultural practices, then people who do not endorse those beliefs or who do not follow those practices are burdened or face a choice that does not confront their fellow citizens (Laden 2001: 132 and chs 6–7 *passim*; Tully 2002b: 221–5; cf. Tomasi 2001: 91–7). In the latter case, citizens can argue that they are unfairly burdened by laws or practices that interfere with the capacity of people 'to be able to rule themselves in accordance with their own customs and ways' (Laden 2001: 173; Tully 1995: 4). The demands of citizenship impose a burden on some people, by virtue of their non-political identities, that others do not have to bear.

But the problem with the reasonableness response is that it reproduces the problem with which we began, since what counts as reasonable is subject to the same lack of determinacy. As Melissa Williams writes, the issue then turns on the contingency of the judgement that another's arguments are reasonable, and this judgement can be conditioned by group membership, other beliefs, interests, etc. (M. Williams 2000: 137). Consider, for example, the opposing positions of the French state and the Muslim students and their supporters in *l'affaire du foulard*. For those satisfied with the distinction between discreet and proselytizing religious symbols, there is no unfair burden on the identity of the students involved in banning the latter, and hence the headscarf; the appearance of unfairness to the students and their supporters is a matter of the construction that they are putting on the state's policy, not of the policy itself. What counts as an instance of 'reasonable disagreement', of pluralism within the bounds of the state is itself open to re-evaluation. My objection is not that no sense can be made of the distinction between reasonable and unreasonable disagreement. It is that the 'criterion of reasonableness' does not fulfil the role assigned to it: we cannot use it to show other citizens why a particular argument they put forward fails to meet this criterion and therefore does not carry the weight that they thought it did. If what *counts as* a public reason is constructed through a particular process of public discussion, then we cannot also appeal to it as a standard in that process of discussion. To do so amounts to the kind of *ex ante* assumption that 'there's no talking to these people' considered in section 2, which in practice works in the kind of exclusive way discussed in the last section.[23]

A second unsatisfactory response to underdetermination is to appeal to the authority of procedures which are deliberatively endorsed – that is, which are supported by an argument that rests on public reasons.[24] Yet, while procedures may reduce practical underdetermination, furnishing a particular decision, they do not eliminate the theoretical problem. Consider an example of this line of argument offered by Shane O'Neill in his discussion of opposition to the Good Friday Agreement of 1999 in Northern Ireland. Even those opposed to particular measures and outcomes of the Agreement, he argues, must accept that (in the terms used earlier) they have been *included* in the procedures that legitimate it, so it is *legitimate* for them. 'Legal validity is concerned with procedural legitimation and the relevant procedures in this case were the election of negotiating representatives and the referendum on this Agreement itself. If opponents of the Agreement are to reject the legitimacy of the institutions, then they also have to reject the legitimacy of these procedures,' and 'since most of those who do reject the Agreement are inclined to extol the virtues of majority rule, it seems rather difficult for them to deny powers of legitimation to a majoritarian decision-making procedure like the referendum' (S. O'Neill 2003: 84–5; cf. S. O' Neill 2000, 2001, 2002; Newey 2002).

Yet this does not follow at all. First, it overlooks those who do not extol the virtues of majority rule. Second, it overlooks those who think that there sometimes have to be substantive constraints on what majority rule is entitled to do. Third, it overlooks those who do not agree with referenda as legitimate expressions of the principle of majority rule, perhaps on the grounds that referenda may be open to governmental manipulation. Fourth, it overlooks those who disagree with a referendum *in this* case. Fifth, it overlooks those who endorse the principle of majority rule but believe that it should be expressed through elected representatives rather than plebiscites. Sixth, it overlooks those who disagree with the drawing of the constituency boundaries for this vote. For this argument to work, deliberatively endorsed procedures have to be so endorsed through public dialogue – it is not enough to note that people have participated in them, or that they have expressed support for procedural resolutions of disputes. Yet (as in this example) procedures themselves are subject to myriad levels and kinds of disagreement.

If we cannot see the 'criterion of reasonableness' as *guiding* public deliberation, the process may seem vulnerable to domination by sheer power, or more subtly by the norms and assumptions of dominant groups (M. Williams 2000). Of course, as I have suggested, if the process is conducted with attention to the conditions of rationality, inclusion and legitimacy, this will not be the case. But there is nothing in the conceptual character of public reason as such to imply that public deliberation cannot simply be a mask for domination. Before we arrive at this sceptical conclusion, we need again to consider what the suggested comparison is. If public deliberation is just one regime of power among others, then we still need to make a decision about which regime of power we should choose (unless we think that there is really *nothing* to choose between dictatorships and democracies), and the public deliberation model offers some criteria for such a choice. These criteria do not determine how they are applied in every case, of course, but the general sceptical point can be made about any criteria proposed to answer this problem of choosing among regimes of power.[25]

## 5.   Conclusion

I have argued that public deliberation can accommodate a wide range of arguments for the importance of cultural identity and for differentiated rights and
policies. I outlined the core claims of public deliberation to offer reasoned,
inclusive and legitimate political decisions, and went on to distinguish three
sorts of argument for cultural recognition for which this conception makes
space: equality-based, importance and compromise arguments. Yet I also
argued that political deliberation risks bias, and the perception of bias, and
puts received interpretations of identities under a public spotlight, which may
legitimately worry members of groups claiming those identities. Furthermore,
the conception of public deliberation supported here makes no claims to be
able to reconcile different groups, identities and individuals to this process
through the use of public reason alone, for the content of the latter is underdetermined and always open to contestation. This raises the question of what
can or does sustain the political trust required by public deliberation in a culturally diverse society, and I turn to this in the following chapter.

# 6

## Deliberative Trust: Ethos, Identity and Institutions

In the previous chapter, I raised the point that the concept of political deliberation as public discussion requires trust among participants. They must recognize each other as participants and be prepared to bear and indeed
sometimes actively connive in the losses and compromises of this process. In
the present chapter I try to increase understanding of the character, sources
and effects of such trust. I suggest three main ways of filling this deficit for
political deliberation, rooted respectively in ethos, identity and institutions. I
argue that, while (in the right form) each has its merits, none conclusively
resolves this problem. Furthermore, I argue that there are tensions between
each of these approaches to addressing the problem of deliberative trust which
make it difficult simply to add them together.

This chapter proceeds as follows. In section 1, I pay closer attention to the
concept of trust in order to bring out its significance for the conceptions of cultural diversity and political deliberation that we have examined, and introduce
some relevant conceptual distinctions. Deliberation as public discussion, I
argue, has a particularly heavy investment in trust. I consider three candidates
for the source of trust for this view of deliberation: namely ethos, cultural identity and institutions. I go on to look at and to appraise the claim that features
internal to the process of public deliberation may suffice to create and stabilize
relationships of trust. In section 2, I discuss cultural sources of distrust and
trust, and begin to examine how some of the claims for cultural identity and
difference connect to the problem of trust. I argue for caution in ascribing distrust among individuals and groups to specifically cultural sources. This lays
the ground for consideration in section 3 of a position that has been waiting in
the wings: namely, positive universalism. For the positive universalist, there are
reasons grounded in the structure and requirements of political deliberation to

foster a common national identity. I discuss communitarian, civic and culturalist forms of this position. In section 4, I consider some of the ways in which
institutional stratagems may be deployed to mitigate distrust and to create conditions in which valuable trust relations can develop. As my approach in this
chapter suggests, my argument is that there is no single royal road to the valuable form of trust relations that deliberation as public discussion requires.
While ethos, identity and institutions can each play a role in the construction
of valuable trust relations, I argue in conclusion, each has its pitfalls and ambiguities, and further, the processes and mechanisms that each of these accounts
posits may not in practice cohere with those posited by the other accounts.

## 1.   Trust, Politics and Deliberation

Trust is a protean and logically complex concept. As a starting point, we can
view trust as a form of judgement, which may be tacit or habitual, on the part
of an agent to grant another discretionary power over some good for that
agent.[1] Surrounding this is a large periphery of debates over who or what may
count as an agent for the purposes both of trusting and of being trusted, to
what extent and in what ways the character of agents' interests, motivations
and competences matter in defining a relationship as a trust relationship, and
what kinds of value or virtue attach to trusting and to trustworthiness. Here
I want to focus on tracing how trust matters for the overall stance toward the
politics of cultural diversity discussed. Trust appears before political theory in
two guises: as creating a problematic relationship of power and vulnerability
and as the 'social cement' that is needed in order to render political relationships workable. Let me explain.

What Mark Warren calls the generic problem of the relationship between
trust and politics is that political relationships throw the very conditions of
trust into question (Warren 1999a: 312). For politics is a realm in which the
interests as well as the identities of other actors may differ and conflict with
ours. If we view trust as based upon a judgement, then the problem of vulnerability that arises from acting on trust can be viewed as arising, first, from the
possibility of a conflict among people's interests and identities, and secondly,
from a problem of mutual opacity, hindering the formation of warranted
beliefs about the trustworthiness of others. Given that I know that our interests and identities may conflict, how can I know that you will act so as to secure
my interests, and so can rest satisfied with the habit of reliance upon you?[2] It
is worth underlining that, while politics may be a realm of instrumental and
strategic agency, this is not the only source of distrust in politics. The opacity
of others and the difficulty of assessing the consequences of agency can also
lead us to doubt their competence to fulfil entrusted tasks, in the absence of
mechanisms of monitoring and control.

Yet this cautiousness about the motives and competences of other agents does not release us from the vulnerability that we are exposed to in any case by virtue of our dependence on others. The dominant thrust of modern political thinking has been to emphasize, as John Dunn puts it, 'that in the extraordinarily complex division of labour on which modern social life necessarily depends no one could rationally dispute that human beings need, as far as they can, to economise on trust in persons and confide instead in well-designed political, social and economic institutions' (Dunn 1990: 38). So the central response within liberal political thought to the vulnerability implied by trust relations has been to limit the scope for judgements of trustworthiness and the need to act on trust by circumscribing what political agents can legitimately do. Residual trust can be built up only on the back of the provision of effective and predictable constitutional safeguards against abuse, and distrust is rational where these safeguards are absent or ineffective. From the liberal perspective, trust is rational wherever institutions ensure that it is in the trusted's interests to be trustworthy. As 'precommitment strategies', well-made constitutions remove from the scope of political discretion and negotiation courses of action that would otherwise damage the interests of citizens. This focuses attention on the constitutional procedures of accountability and the rule of law, and mechanisms of redress when those who are meant to be acting on our behalf fail in their responsibilities: 'we should not ask about a politician whether we would buy a second-hand car from him but whether we would be adequately protected by a Sale of Goods Act if he sold us a bad one' (Parry 1976: 142; cf. P. Johnson 1993: 18). In a liberal democracy we rely not on the elite's 'ethic of responsibility' but rather on the constitutional 'machinery of accountability' (Parry 1976: 141). The less we trust those with power over us, in other words, the more we will be motivated to put in place monitoring procedures and systems of sanctions and incentives in order to make them accountable to us.

Yet precisely because of the complexity of the social and political division of labour, this is not to say that liberal political theory can dispense with trust as a category, or see it as merely supervening on the confident expectation that political agents will fulfil their institutionally prescribed roles. This can be made clearer if we consider briefly the linked themes of democracy, representation, political decision making and collective agency. Consider first democracy, which renders us vulnerable to the votes of fellow citizens. On the one hand, we can understand democracy as the institutionalization of a form of distrust, designed to keep rulers in check and perhaps requiring the cultivation of habits of suspicion among the citizenry, as well as other features such as a strong political opposition (cf. Ely 1980; Hardin 1999a, 2002a; Pettit 1998). On the other hand, democratic thought is accompanied by an anxiety about the tyranny of the majority and the vulnerability of minorities and losers in votes to the will of majorities. In part, this vulnerability can be mitigated by restricting the scope of democratic decision making; however, so long as democratic decisions involve the important interests of citizens, a degree of vulnerability remains. As Claus Offe puts it:

> distrust in . . . fellow citizens, the fear that they are guided by dangerous motives, manipulated into supporting disastrous political forces, or are allowed to engage in collectively damaging conflict, is as old as the theory and practice of democracy . . . Obviously a lot of trust, i.e. the confident expectation that my fellow citizens are neither ignorant nor follow vicious intentions, is needed in order to overcome [a] gloomy perception of the realities of democracy. (Offe 2001: 173)

This problem is reiterated if we consider political representation.[3] In seeking election, representatives may present themselves as trustworthy, and representation as a trust. Yet, unless constituency boundaries closely follow lines of identity and interest (if that is conceivable), representatives will often need to pursue the votes of various sorts of interest and identity groups which will make them less than perfectly reliable custodians of particular interests and identities. Furthermore, where the discipline of political parties is strong, they may have to answer to other pressures. The very fragility of trust in this situation may serve to *enhance* its importance. For what we want are representatives who are trustworthy precisely in the sense that they can negotiate the inevitable compromises entailed by these structural pressures. Similarly, trust arises as an issue in spite of well-designed institutions if we consider problems of 'dirty hands'.[4] As Peter Johnson argues, the problem of trusting politicians to act so as to achieve desirable goals effectively raises the issue of relying in the public realm on those who may well be untrustworthy in the private world: 'it is no longer sufficient to speak of trusting the institutional constraints on rulers; procedural rules governing the decisions of officeholders are now penetrated by ambiguity and uncertainty' (P. Johnson 1993: 12). Finally, trust can play a role in desirable forms of political agency: a flourishing democracy also requires a sufficient level of trust among citizens to allow them to form associations and act collectively: 'it needs active citizens, ready to get engaged in the democratic institutions, as well as the associations and organisations of civil society . . . [This] requires some measure of trust in the political regime, the fairness of the rules, the potential effectiveness of their efforts' (Sztompka 1999: 147) – and, we can add, in those with whom they co-operate as equals, leaders and followers, to act in this way. Political trust, I would suggest, weaves a path between reliance on institutional devices to mitigate distrust, through monitoring and constraining political agents, and those forms of personal trust which are necessarily incompatible with the demand for accountability.

We can consider the different models of political deliberation about cultural diversity in terms of the conception of the sources, character and role of trust in politics that they suggest. As I noted in chapter 3, we can interpret the argument that Will Kymlicka frames in terms of equality of resources on behalf of cultural self-determination for national minorities as a response to a problem of trust. In the case of liberal culturalism, an individual's interest in secure access to a societal culture is judged to be so weighty that it grounds a right, taking control of this interest out of the sphere of political decision making, deliberation, bargaining and negotiation. This form of right to culture in turn grounds a claim to self-determination for the group or province that can stake a claim to this societal culture. We can view this line of thought as a response to a minority group's distrust of the majority or (to view the problem in institutional rather than interpersonal terms) the political process to safeguard this cultural identity, and the interest that they have in it (cf. Weinstock 1999: 301). In a case where what is claimed as the expression of the underlying right to a secure cultural identity is a self-government right for a group, the problem of vulnerability entailed by the residual trust inherent in sharing political space is dealt with by 'repatriating' control over the good that the group may view as entrusted to the wider political community or political process. Furthermore, as I suggested earlier, one way of interpreting the particular link that he makes between the interest in culture *qua* context of choice and the right to self-government is as resting on a claim about the trustworthiness with respect to cultural goods of governors who share a cultural identity with the governed. I will develop and examine this last claim in section 3 below.

For the libertarian Kukathas, trust is rooted in individual assessment of risk in conditions of opacity and conflict of interests, beliefs and identities. The response is to minimize opportunities for trust or distrust by minimizing non-voluntary dependence, particularly political relationships. The state and its officials are often opaque, and anyway have interests that may never harmonize with those of many citizens. Projects of cultural construction and accommodation, whether through the politics of recognition or through nation building, only present fresh grounds for distrust of state power: in taking responsibility for the cultural character of the society, the state will violate the consciences of those who wish to live according to customs and in ways incompatible with the vision imposed. The only solution is to minimize the scope for state intervention. Yet this generates two profound problems of trust. The first is that the *de facto* powers of self-government granted to conscience-based associations re-create the problem that liberal mechanisms of accountability were designed to address: namely, the risk of arbitrary and tyrannical government, particularly with respect to dissidents. The second is that the basis for mutual trust required in order to arrive at conditions of toleration and civility, as well as a clear and agreed-upon conception of the limits on such associations' actions, is left unexplored. Associations, unlike archipelagos, tend to lack natural boundaries, and the framework for handling disputes seems to require the form of trust in a public realm that Kukathas wishes to minimize. I argued in chapter 4 that Brian Barry's exclusion of cultural identity as a relevant consideration in political deliberation is less clear-cut than at first appears. He argues that supporting a particular cultural identity is not only inevitable but desirable when such an identity is instrumentally valuable in fostering the relations of trust and solidarity that can aid co-operation in redistributive projects of social justice (Barry 1991a: 156–86; 2001; and see chapter 2, section 2). This raises a related point to Kymlicka's, to which I will also return, in considering forms of liberal nationalist argument.

Finally, the public deliberation model seems to require and benefit from trust in several ways. First, public deliberation rests on the recognition of one another among participants in which trust plays a part. Communication and the free exchange of reasons and arguments are made easier where there is trust that others will listen to and respond to arguments. This is particularly so, given that the underdetermination of public reasons and arguments, as I emphasized in the previous chapter, poses a major problem of trust for this process. Where we are both *constructing* standards of publicity as well as *appealing to* them, we need to trust one another to pursue this path precisely when common standards are called into question and become problematic. Second, we can carry on playing the democratic game of exchanging public reasons and arguments, to recall James Tully's Wittgensteinian image, only if we are confident that others will not tear up all the rules as we go along – that they will accept the binding character of a vote, for example, even if they continue to dissent from the outcome achieved. Third, compromise, which I have argued is a central feature of the model of public deliberation that I would defend, is facilitated by trust in other participants not only to play by the rules of the game but also to retain a sense of reciprocity: 'the whole of government is but a continual series of . . . sacrifices' (Bentham, cited in Wolin 1961: 326), and some participants will be prepared to make sacrifices if they are assured that others will do likewise at the appropriate time. Fourth, as Warren observes, an important political function of trust is that it can mitigate the problem posed by the demanding and time-consuming character of this kind of deliberation: as he puts it, '*if* I can trust food inspectors to do their jobs and scientists to set appropriate standards, then I can minimize my worries about the risks of food and turn whatever deliberative resources I have (time, security, expertise, etc.) to other issues' (Warren 1999a: 337–8, emphasis original). For these reasons, then, the public discussion model, while it addresses lacunae in the other conceptions, seems mortgaged to trust more heavily than these other conceptions.

One response to this problem of trust posed for the public deliberation model is to argue that there are features inherent in the practice of this form of deliberation that may help to create or strengthen the ties of trust necessary for its own working. Once under way, in other words, public deliberation fosters dispositions in participants that help to hold in place the trust relations that it needs in order to flourish (Warren 1999a: 339–42). First, narratives of distrust, conspiracy, fear and betrayal in which other groups are demonized thrive in the absence of public discussion. Public deliberation provides a way for individuals and members of groups to present themselves in such a manner as to dispel these demonizing images. The concrete experience of co-operation in the form of public discussion with others has a reassuring effect on all concerned, at least in comparison with the stereotypes and misrepresentations that can flourish in the absence of this process. Second, public deliberation can act so as to diminish the opacity that causes a problem for trust by the emphasis on public argument and reason giving. Public deliberation should tend to mitigate perceptions of betrayal on the part of representatives and the political process by providing reasons that justify compromises in interests and identities. Even when political representatives must compromise interests and identities, if they can put their reasons on display, then this is likely to be perceived less as betrayal but more as inevitable compromise in a situation that pragmatically requires it: 'what provides the basis for trust here is not that we agree necessarily with decisions taken on our behalf, but that we follow the process of moral thinking by which they are reached. We trust the rules of the game and so distrust is not our automatic response if we regard any particular outcome as undesirable' (P. Johnson 1993: 12). Even where we do not support a decision arrived at, to recall from the last chapter, the public character of the arguments supporting it make this form of decision making legitimate in the way a more opaque process cannot be. Third, the need for civility and persuasiveness in these deliberative settings can also help to generate trust. Even if one disagrees with what the other person says, one recognizes her as a speaker whose views should be treated carefully and deliberatively.[5] Such displays of civility can generate trust and a mutual commitment to the deliberative relationship that can have some of the beneficial consequences (such as easing compromise) that are desired.

These effects may be real, but they are fragile and conditional, however. For public deliberation requires a disposition to co-operate on deliberative terms – not to filibuster or ignore awkward participants. As I have emphasized, this is particularly important at the margins, where conceptions of reasonableness and common acceptability are challenged.[6] Publicity is ambivalent, and may sometimes inflame differences. The politicization of cultural differences through public debate may lead not to mutual respect and accommodation but to a hardening of attitudes and a deepening of mutual suspicion. Indeed, the intensity and publicity of the *foulard* debate in France arguably led to a far more entrenched and polarized state of affairs than the more local and behind-the-scenes accommodations to religious differences within schools (and elsewhere, over such matters as butchery and crash helmet legislation) in Britain (Favell 1998; cf. Phillips 1999: 131; Barry 2002: 213). As Stephen Holmes in particular has argued, one motive for a liberal constitutionalism replete with 'gag rules' to keep certain matters off the political agenda is that open debate of these matters (such as slavery in the antebellum United States) may make destabilizing social conflict more likely (Holmes 1995). This latter is a powerful objection, which strikes at the heart of the public deliberation model's assumption that contentious social matters should be dealt with by throwing them open to public debate. Of course, there is a danger on the other side that a policy of public silence may simply entrench an unjust *status quo* and vest power over the political process in those with a manifest threat advantage. Furthermore, not all forms of social conflict are destabilizing, and it may be better to allow the expression of opposition and conflict than to pre-empt it. Finally, while it may prove necessary to construct good fences in order to make good neighbours, for these fences not to seem merely arbitrary (violating what we called the legitimacy condition in the previous chapter), some public discussion seems an important prerequisite. Yet it remains the case that public deliberation may sometimes undermine trust among participants, for communication and transparency can bring out into the open disagreements and conflicts of interest that would otherwise have remained hidden.

## 2.   Culture as a Source of Trust

I want to start this section by fleshing out the intuition that a common cultural identity fosters trust, initially calling on some of the conceptual distinctions drawn earlier.[7] So one way in which the problem of opacity can be diminished is through a set of semiotic practices. Such a form of common culture creates familiarity between truster and trusted, through shared and mutually understood practices and symbols, allowing members to understand and predict each other's behaviour with greater accuracy than may be possible in the case of the behaviour of non-members. This familiarity on the semiotic dimension permits, although it does not itself constitute or create, trust relations, since it reduces the problem of opacity: if A cannot 'read' B's behaviour, he is unlikely to be disposed to trust B. Moreover, a familiar symbolic landscape may help to provide the security that allows someone to act on trust.

Along the normative dimension, a shared culture also allows common understandings of norms, values and roles.[8] A shared set of norms also serves to enhance the translucency of other agents, but is significant in other ways. Trust relationships often involve an important component of discretion, in which B will have room to fulfil A's trust in various ways. A framework of shared understandings about what is appropriate allows A to trust B: in the absence of such a framework, there will be disagreement over what counts as successfully safeguarding A's interests and a corresponding difficulty in establishing a relationship of trust. Shared norms also create the conditions for so-called symbolic credit – that is, 'relations between actors which are based not on the direct, conditional, but on the indirect, long-range, give-and-take of services or resources and on the setting up of "titles" or entitlement to such

resources or services' (Eisenstadt 1995: 345, cited in Seligman 1997: 80).[9]
There is an example of the latter, rolling together signs, norms and symbolic
credit, in Andrea Levy's novel *Small Island*:

> So I had to give him the sign. All we Jamaican boys know the sign. When a man
> need to be alone with a woman, for reasons only imagination should know, the
> head is cocked just a little to one side while the eye first open wide then swivel
> fast to the nearest exit. Even the most fool-fool Jamaican boy can read this sign
> and would never ignore it in case it should be they that needed it next time. (A.
> Levy 2004: 20)

In a similar vein, but in a different context, Francis Fukuyama conceives of
trust as rooted in '*inherited ethical habit*' (1995: 34, emphasis original), and
consisting in 'the expectation . . . within a community of regular, honest, cooperative behaviour based on communally shared norms, on the part of other
members of that community' (Fukuyama 1995: 26).

Yet we don't always trust those with whom we share cultural practices by
virtue of that sharing. On the semiotic side, the familiarity of shared symbols
and practices may help trust, but it does not in itself say anything about the
trustworthiness of those with whom we share practices. Indeed, we can be
more cynical and less trusting, the greater our sensitivity to the nuances of the
cultural languages at work: 'if I trust my society, I recognise the symbolic language of the society as expressive of my own genuine values and concerns. If
it sounds shallow or untrue, I do not wholly trust my society. I believe at least
a certain perhaps healthy distrust of society is the attitude of most adults in
most societies' (Lagenspetz 1992: 14). Shared symbols and practices may
allow us to monitor and assess the actions of others more effectively, but, as I
have argued, that is not the same as trusting them. Perhaps, though, such a
capacity can be the basis of a valuable form of trust relationship; I will return
to this point in the following section.

On the normative side, a shared culture can be a source of distrust with
respect to some matters. The *content* of cultural norms can promote distrust
or only the most 'particularized' forms of trust, as in Edward Banfield's
famous study of 'amoral familism' in Montegrano, where 'any advantage that
may be given to another is necessarily at the expense of one's own family.
Therefore, one cannot afford the luxury of charity, which is giving others more
than their due, or even justice, which is giving them their due' (Banfield 1958:
110, quoted in Uslaner 2002: 19). The norms in this society may be genuinely
shared, but what these norms enjoin is mutual distrust within that society, as
soon as one steps outside the family group. Further, we may trust those with
a different cultural identity more than we trust those who share ours: this may
be for a reason rooted in something about their cultural identity (perhaps we
have read Fukuyama and know that they come from a 'high trust culture'), or
for some other reason.

Furthermore, claims about the reasons that a cultural identity gives to act in a particular way raises those issues around the hermeneutic contestability of the character of culture, and the importance of cultural ties as against other aspects of identity or reasons for action, raised in chapter 1. What needs adding here is that the claim about the cultural source of trust raises a further question of the warrant and value of trust relations. The power and vulnerability inherent in trust relations make the question of what *warrants* trust crucial. This follows not merely from the fact that to trust opens up the possibility of betrayal through ill will or a failure of competence on the part of the trusted. Even where the trusted *dependably* performs her role, this may flow from motives that render her actions morally suspect, such as fear, coercion, confusion about her own interests, and so on. Accordingly, Baier suggests an 'expressibility test' for trust relations: they are 'morally decent only if . . . knowledge of each party's reasons for confident reliance on the other to continue the relationship' can be entrusted to the other: '[t]o the extent that mutual reliance can be accompanied by mutual knowledge of the conditions for the reliance, trust is above suspicion, and trustworthiness is a nonsuspect virtue' (Baier 1986: 259–60). If those who give their trust to others come to see that it is being exploited by the guile of its recipients, or if those who are trusted come to see that this rests on nothing more than fear of the truster, the relationship is 'morally corrupt' (Baier 1986: 255). Failure of expressibility is not the only way in which a trust relation may not be valuable. What is further required is that the goods or interests entrusted be such that they should be protected or fostered, where this expectation is grounded in something more than the truster's trust. In other words, we need to be able to make some positive judgement of the value of the goods or interests at stake. Trust relations based on *omertà* and other elements of an honour code may be warranted within the Mafia, but the relation is not thereby valuable. Similarly, for a Marxist, contractual relations in a capitalist society may be impeccably adhered to, but the resulting relationship of exploitation is not deemed to be a valuable one. So particular instances of cultural trust may be problematic, masking relations of domination and exploitation. These very general points establish only that culture (in the sense under discussion here) is fallible as a source of, or aid to establishing and sustaining, trust relations, not that it can't be or is reducible to something else.

## 3. Liberal Nationalism

We are now in a position to evaluate the claim that only a shared national identity can provide the source of deliberative trust. I have closed in on this claim from two directions: first, by suggesting the forms and limits of the public deliberation claim to offer endogenous sources of trust, and, second, by offering some general theoretical cautions against the presumption that cultural identity is a source of trust, or cultural difference of distrust. It is time to confront the nationalist thesis more directly. In doing so, we also consider the third principal conception of culture: namely, the societal view of culture as a set of encompassing social and political institutions, but only as one conception of national identity.[10] The general position is that a shared national identity fosters conditions for widespread social trust and common commitments (Barry 1991a: 156–86; Miller 1995; Canovan 1996; M. Moore 2001). The trust and loyalty that citizenship requires is generated in the modern state by national identity. Crucial to this are those symbols and practices that give a nation a focus of identity and allegiance, and in particular the education of citizens into an awareness of their common identity. A key text here is Rousseau's *Considerations on the Government of Poland*, in which he offers an array of suggestions as to how to instil a distinctive national consciousness into a politically vulnerable state. As well as such measures as the wearing of national dress and special national festivals and games, Rousseau lays particular emphasis on education:

> It is education that must give souls the national form, and so direct their tastes and opinions that they will be patriotic by inclination, passion, necessity. Upon opening its eyes, a child should see the fatherland, and see only it until his dying day. Every true republican drank love of the fatherland, that is to say love of the laws and of freedom, with his mother's milk. This love makes up his whole existence; he sees only his fatherland, he lives only for it . . . (Rousseau [1772] 1997: 189)[11]

While not every adherent of positive universalism is quite as committed to the exclusive love of the political community, they all share the belief in the need to foster a common sense of identity in order to provide the underpinnings for mutual commitment. This positive universalism, as I understand it here, is not to be identified with any particular set of policies, but with an overall goal, to inculcate this common sense of identity in the citizens, and a belief that a significant national culture is required in order to achieve this goal. So it may be that, as David Miller suggests, 'in large-scale societies, where people look and sound very different from one another trust is a problem'. From this it may seem only a short step to conclude, as Miller himself does, that it is only where we have a shared national identity with a sufficiently rich and determinate cultural content that we can reasonably expect the mutual trust necessary for democracy to prosper: for, where there is such an identity, although 'we may disagree politically with the other side, we may even despise much of what they stand for . . . we know that they still have a good deal in common with us – a language, a history, a cultural background. So we can trust them at least to respect the rules and spirit of democratic government' (Miller 2003a: 117).[12] For John Stuart Mill famously, the presence of multiple nationalities in a state generates 'mutual antipathies' and a society in which none feel that they can rely on the others for 'fidelity' (J. S. Mill [1861] 1991: 429). He expresses a particular worry that 'soldiers, to whose feelings half or three-fourths of the subjects of the same governments are foreigners, will have no more scruple in mowing them down, and no more desire to ask the reason why, than they would have in doing the same thing against declared enemies' (J. S. Mill [1861] 1991: 429). Well over a century later, Miller too emphasizes 'the important role played by trust in a viable political community', which he relates to national and cultural homogeneity (Miller 1995: 90). The level of commitment needed to sustain schemes of just social redistribution in modern economies is not feasible without the sense of trust and reciprocity supplied by a common national identity. The mutual trust fostered by nationality allows us to see beyond mere sectional advantage so that we are prepared to bear costs on behalf of others, in the knowledge that they will reciprocate should that be necessary: bonds of national identity make redistributive obligations appear for members 'as expressions of who they are rather than arbitrary burdens' (Ripstein 1997a: 209; Barry 1991a: 174–5; 2001: 79; M. Moore 2001: 3–6; 2002: 80–5). For Miller, 'only a common nationality provides the sense of solidarity' that democratic politics requires (Miller 1995: 98). In particular, deliberative democracy 'can only succeed where there exists a fairly high level of mutual trust in the deliberating body, which is why I argue that a shared national identity is close to being a necessary prerequisite' (Miller 2003b: 365). If we share a common nationality, we will possess the motivations to overcome other sorts of social difference in order to co-operate on a deliberative basis.

The nationalist argument performs a delicate balancing act between trust as passion and trust as policy (cf. Dunn 1990: 26–7). It seeks to mobilize an unchosen disposition toward 'liking in groups' as the basis for a claim about belief and choice. For the nationalist, the nation is regarded as a privileged locus of political trust, in that it encompasses within a territorially bounded frame a variety of more particular identities. Trust on a national scale is 'generalized' rather than 'particularized', in the sense that it allows us to trust people outside the narrow group of those who look and sound very similar to us, or who share a geographical location, a set of religious beliefs, an economic interest, or some other particular feature. At the same time, the scope of this generality is limited to those within the nation. The trust I feel is specifically directed toward fellow nationals. Others *in this group* can be relied on to treat you fairly, even if they deeply disagree politically with you and differ too in many other aspects of their interests and identities.

I will consider three lines of argument, based on three conceptions of national identity: respectively, a communitarian, a cultural and a civic argument. For the first, a nation is a form of community, containing valuable goods which its members should foster and sustain. In the second case, national identity is viewed as a matter of sharing certain objective cultural attributes which facilitate political relationships. For the third line of argument, national identity is viewed as identification with a set of common values, given particular expression in a country's history and traditions. The communitarian argument for the value of national identity is based on the claim that a shared national identity constitutes a valuable ethical relationship. In the terms of the discussion of the normativity of identity, a shared nationality itself constitutes an 'irreducibly social good' or 'participatory' good, and the nation is a community with a common good of this sort.[13] This value is the basis for obligations that fellow nationals owe to one another, but not to outsiders. These 'special obligations' derive from valuable features of the particular social relationship that holds among the agents bound by these obligations to one another.[14] Yael Tamir, for example, writes that 'deep and important obligations flow from identity and relatedness' (Tamir 1993: 41).[15] The latter idea requires a normative (or, as Andrew Mason puts it, 'moralized') conception of the relevant social relationships, the goods of which put its participants under those obligations necessary to sustain it (Mason 2000: 32–3, 99–112).

In one version, the relevant common goods are contextually defined: it is up to each nation to define the goods that are common for it (Miller 1995; cf. Miller 2002). For Miller, this need not mean that any and every goal or value promoted by a nation constitutes a common good, no matter how horrendous or banal that goal or value may be. What common nationhood is thought to supply is a concrete form of social and political identity, which is valuable to its members in such a way that it generates special obligations. The argument made by the nationalist need not be that national identity of any sort or character will entail these obligations. Miller assuages the concern that the emphasis on nationality as the basis of political community leads to the 'sanctification of merely traditional ethical relations' by arguing that 'to the extent that national identities, and the public cultures that help to compose them, are shaped by processes of rational reflection to which members of the community can contribute on an equal footing, this no longer applies' (Miller 1995: 70).[16] In being so shaped, they possess a more than merely subjective standing *vis-à-vis* the judgements of particular members of the community '[t]he culture in question *is* a public phenomenon: any one individual may interpret it rightly or wrongly' (Miller 1995: 69).[17]

The objectivist alternative finds this procedural test too thin. Taking as central the thought that a community that is organized around vile or worthless goals is valueless, it responds by arguing that a national community has value when the goods it holds in common possess objective value (Taylor 1995; Hurka 1997). This value may be 'agent-relative', in the sense that it holds only for the participants in the relationship, since it derives from the participation itself; but this does not impugn its objectivity. So, for example, the Quebecois may feel that their language and culture are goods of this kind; and Canadians may feel that a national system of public health care is a good of this kind

(Hurka 1997: 153–4). In the case of either sort of argument, the link with trust runs through the generation of special obligations. A shared set of obligations directed toward sustaining a common good may seem to provide a sound basis for trust, since we know that each member of this community possesses *ex hypothesi* a reason to act so as to sustain commonly valuable relations. So we have a reason to view one another as mutually trustworthy.

These communitarian claims are compatible with the relevant community's being *imagined* in the sense which Benedict Anderson made famous: 'all communities larger than the primordial villages of face-to-face contact (and perhaps even these) are imagined' (Anderson 1991: 6). At the same time, the nation is 'imagined as a *community* because, regardless of the actual inequality and exploitation that may prevail in each, the nation is always conceived as a deep, horizontal comradeship' (Anderson 1991: 7, emphasis original). While the relationships that are often invoked as analogies of the national community (friendships, family relationships, orchestras and sports teams, and so on) often do involve direct or face-to-face contact, the crucial point is that the relationships produce the goods claimed. Further, both versions of this argument allow for the failure of the relationships to produce these goods, and so for the nation to fail to constitute a community, in the normatively valuable sense. On Miller's contextualist account, a nation can fail to instantiate the goods that are part of its tradition, and, on Thomas Hurka's objectivist account, a nation can fail to produce objectively valuable goods at all. There is room, then, on either of these accounts for coherent social criticism of a national identity, and indeed for the failure of a national identity to produce the shared goods that this argument requires.

For many people, the thought that a nation constitutes a community generating a set of objective or intersubjectively recognized goods is far-fetched. Nations (France, Turkey, Mexico, Iraq) may have many valuable features, but the nation itself is hard to conceive of as a community, rather than an assemblage of different identities, interests, goods and so on. However, even if we set aside cases of manifest failure of a national identity to generate any particular goods, and follow the hypothesis that some nations may do so, there are two objections to this position. The first concerns the weight and significance that we attach to the obligations that are meant to flow from the fact of relatedness. Let us accept that a commonly achieved good generates an obligation for those who are part of that community to play their part in its upkeep; to take a now familiar example, a shared language can be viewed as such a good. The issue is whether the obligation to sustain this good is weightier than other reasons an agent has not to sustain this good – to assimilate to another culture, for example, or to educate her children in a different language. The *pro tanto* reason supplied by the common good argument leaves the question of the overall weighting of reasons unsettled.[18] Within the communitarian framework, this is a particularly pressing difficulty if we believe that a nation may be only one among other communities that may make claims on our loyalty. If the weighting of reasons both for myself and for others is unsettled, the mutual trustworthiness that the communitarian argument arrives at is undermined.

The second objection is that for the link to trustworthiness to be made requires not only that there are such common goods as generate obligations on us but also that we converge in our understandings of those common goods, and particularly of how they should be fostered and sustained, and that we know we do so. To consider the objectivist line of argument first, the issue that arises is whether or not everyone else sees the shared goods and common values in the way that I do. If they do not, and if I know that they may not, this may lead to *distrusting* them. For example, the linguistic purist will distrust the eclectic coiner of phrases drawn from other languages; or (to take a non-cultural example) the advocate of 'contracting out' health care services from the national scheme will distrust the advocate of public control of such services.[19] In the case of the contextualist argument, the epistemological situation is more delicate, since the character of the common good is intersubjective and depends on the outlook of others. But here too the same problem of disagreement arises, calling into question the special obligations as a basis of trustworthiness. If the possibility of criticism and reform of a conception of the common good is to have any bite, then others must be capable of erring, of being on the wrong side in these debates, so the difficulty faced by the objectivist recurs here.

We can view the second, cultural line of argument as addressed less to the notion of trustworthiness as such than to the issue of mutual opacity and transparency that raised a difficulty for the formation of a warranted belief about the trustworthiness of others. A shared national identity commonly includes certain objective features that facilitate the public discussion that is central to deliberation. The obvious feature to which to appeal here is language. In particular, 'if people are to engage in political deliberation, they need to be able to understand one another: they need to speak the same language . . . well enough to follow arguments, appreciate alternative points of view and be persuaded to change their minds' (Canovan 2002: 152).[20] Or, as Mill put it, '[a]mong a people without fellow-feeling, especially if they read and speak different languages, the united public opinion necessary to the workings of representative institutions cannot exist' (J. S. Mill [1861] 1991: 428). The lack of a shared language may not just be evidence of the lack of fellow-feeling; but it makes it harder to create fellow-feeling. We are more opaque to one another, and less likely to be able to generate bonds of trust through the discursive ethos described in section 1. This is not, strictly speaking, an argument for a supportive relationship between a shared national identity and a sense of mutual deliberative commitment. Rather, a shared language is seen as a condition for the collective discussion that this commitment requires and which deliberative theorists believe reinforces the sense of commitment. If democracy is conceived as a public space in which different points of view can be discussed and compared, and in which entrenched perspectives may be modified, then linguistic unity becomes an important good. Those not fluent in the language of political communication are at a disadvantage, since they are unable to take part with the same ease as native-speakers. Where there is no common vernacular for politics, bilingual or multilingual elites take on a more prominent role, at the cost of the relative exclusion of those who do not speak the dominant language or languages of political discourse.[21] Furthermore, the nationalist can thicken out this claim for the importance of a shared language by pointing to a similar value that may attach to other shared features of a national identity: a common sense of history, for example, can provide a shared set of reference points in discussion. National identities are not simply congruent with linguistic identities (consider Austria, Germany and Switzerland, or Canada and the United States). The mutual familiarity that national identity in a wider sense supplies need not have any strong normative content, but may be 'banal' (say, common memories of school textbooks or of jokes), but such cues and symbols can grease the wheels of communication, and allow the generation of discursive trust.[22] So, it is not merely the language, but the presence of the wider societal culture, that plays this role.

Here we can distinguish a stronger and a weaker version of the nationalist claim. In its stronger version, political trust is possible only between those who share a national culture: in 'states lacking a common national identity . . . politics *at best* takes the form of group bargaining and compromise and at worst degenerates into a struggle for domination. Trust may exist within groups, but not across them' (Miller 1995: 92, emphasis added).[23] In this version, the national culture should be valued as a necessary condition for the creation and stabilization of trust relations. In a weaker version, a shared national culture is valued only *instrumentally*, for increasing the prospects for valuable forms of political trust among those who share it.[24] In the latter case, something else logically may substitute as a means to this end.

It is in turn worth distinguishing both of these from what may be called the extreme version of this claim. For the latter, a shared national culture must be interpreted in essentialist terms: the culture is understood as a fixed and distinctive set of features, characteristic of, and marking out, a particular group.[25] Secondly, the nationalist thesis claims that there exists almost full transparency within a group, with none across groups.[26] On the first of these points, as I argued in chapter 1, the cultural claim need not be given an essentialist interpretation. In this nationalist form, it is compatible with the boundaries of an identity being both vague and permeable. The edges of an identity can be ragged and diffuse: for example, a minority national group within a multinational state may view itself as in part its own 'public', and in part overlapping with that of the larger state or majority nation. Nevertheless, the nationalist can argue that such a partial overlap among 'nested nationalities' can still make a contribution to creating the conditions of communication and trust (Miller 2000). Second, the nationalist thesis does not need to suppose that members of the nation are always necessarily transparent to each other and opaque to outsiders (or for that matter that there are no bilingual members of the nation, members of the nation who feel themselves more at home among foreigners, and so on). The point is only that a shared language and aspects of a national culture tend to create the conditions for greater mutual translucency among members of a particular national group than is possible in the absence of such conditions, and so provide the conditions for greater levels of communication and for the form of trust required by the process of public deliberation.

Yet a reformulation of this second point poses a serious difficulty for what I called the strong version of the nationalist claim: that a shared national culture is a necessary condition for political trust. For it is clearly no more than a questionable empirical hypothesis that the relevant conditions for political trust in principle cannot be generated in the absence of the kind of shared linguistic and cultural identity posited by the nationalist. Multinational polities are not always deserts for public deliberation, and the constitutive version of this argument comes to hinge on what counts as proper or flourishing public deliberation. The alternative is to view a shared national identity as instrumental for the creation of these conditions. Where such identities exist, according to this line of argument, we have reason to affirm or endorse them, since they can ease communicative trust. There may in principle be other routes to such a common sense of trust, but this does not detract from the instrumental value of nationality as one, socially powerful and widely intelligible route. The objection to the instrumental argument is that the price of emphasizing the value of mutual familiarity grounded in a shared cultural identity as the basis of political trust is that unfamiliarity then becomes particularly problematic. Challenges to the familiar are then viewed not merely as disagreement or dissent, but as eroding the conditions for public deliberation. To base our understanding of trust on a shared national culture, then, can have the perverse consequence of reducing mutual trust in public dialogue. So, for example, if a group wishes to change the educational curriculum – perhaps how history is taught in schools – to take the view that a common understanding of such matters underpins the very process of public deliberation renders a challenge to this aspect of the societal culture particularly threatening. Here the nationalist may respond that some challenges may indeed be particularly threatening to the conditions for mutual political trust, understood in this way. So we have a dilemma. Either some matters are taken off the agenda, since they are viewed as threatening the cultural conditions for political trust, or we allow them on the agenda. The difficulty with the first is that this seems to drive a coach and horses through claims on behalf of minority or unfamiliar cultural identities. The difficulty with the second is that conditions for continuing the political conversation are put at risk. If we accept the force of the instrumental argument – that in some

cases a shared national culture can promote the conditions for political trust –
then this is a genuine dilemma. Yet, given the points made throughout this
book about the contestable character of cultural identity, it seems hard to
clutch at the first horn of this dilemma in good faith. For an *ex ante* constraint
on the scope of public deliberation based on the presumed requirements of a
cultural identity seems unjustifiable. This leaves a cultural conception of a
national identity in the same boat as cultural identities generally, exposed to
the risks and costs of interaction in the public sphere.

This suggests the third form of nationalist argument that I want to examine.
National identity may be viewed as a shared patriotic identification with a set
of civic values, traditions and practices. Rather than viewing a national identity as resting either on a shared common good or on a shared set of cultural
features, the civic conception sees as central the existence of a shared set of
political values, with which the national populace is meant to identify, as the
basis of national unity.[27] With such a common set of values, the nationalist
may then argue, we begin to address the problem of trust. For although there
may be conflicts of interest, identity and opinion, we possess a common political vocabulary with which to discuss them. The difficulty with invoking civic
nationalism in this context is that to do so presents the same problem as that
which we are trying to solve. For the problem that such a civic nationalism
faces is in explaining how the active identification with such values is created
and maintained in a populace that diverges in so many other ways.
Furthermore, even if we can find common reference points in political values
and practices, the problem of underdetermination confronted by the theory of
public deliberation looms. So, if we agree on the importance of religious
freedom, we may disagree on how to reconcile this value with a common
school system. Here of course some critics of civic nationalism charge it with
being in bad faith: any invocation of a particular national identity is bound to
bring with it a specific cultural heritage, and so the problems raised by the culturalist argument. For our purposes, this difficulty of underdetermination is
enough to establish that civic nationalism takes us no further in addressing the
problem of trust in public deliberation, since it is one of the central problems
confronted by the latter idea in any case.

## 4.  Institutions: Mitigating Distrust

The third perspective I want to consider focuses on the way in which many of
the institutional measures claimed under the rubric of differentiated citizenship can serve to repair trust relations where these have fractured along the
lines of cultural identity. In different ways these measures take as their starting point not the construction of trust relations, but the repair of relationships
of political distrust, where members of a particular cultural group have *qua*

members of that group come to distrust major features of their own polity. Judgements of what will or will not repair trust relations in a given society are necessarily severely contextual, and what follows is intended only as an outline of four principal approaches to this problem. I concentrate too on the factors relevant to considering the relations among culturally identified groups, where of course there are various other important dimensions to the disrepair into which trust relations can fall that I do not explore here, such as poverty or racial discrimination.

The first strategy to mitigate distrust is through providing for the self-determination of groups. For instance, one method of containing identity-based distrust of a majority in a democracy is through federalism, redrawing the boundaries of the political community in order to keep the depth of division manageable. This requires that the minority in the multinational state becomes a majority within the federal unit, in order that it eliminate the vulnerability and distrust created by exposure to democratic decision making. This requires a reasonably durable agreement on the division of powers between the centre and the federal unit, however, and therefore sufficient underpinning of a deliberative commitment to arrive at a legitimate, inclusive and reasoned arrangement. Furthermore, this solution raises the problem of residual members of the majority within the territorial unit (Spanish/Castilian speakers in Catalonia, for example), and of their relationship with the federal state. Finally, territorial federal solutions are unsuitable wherever ethnic, linguistic or cultural groups are dispersed (such as the Romany in Central and East European states).

An alternative model aims to reduce the relationship of dependence which generates a trust relationship with respect to a particular feature of a group's identity (cf. Weinstock 1999: 301). So, for example, where a group distrusts the state in some respect, control over a specific aspect of a public policy can be ceded to it, or the group can be granted control over a certain area of its own affairs, such as language policy or family law. As set out by Ayelet Shachar (and in a different way by Ian Shapiro (1999b, 2002)) a 'joint governance model' aims, on the one hand, to allow groups a degree of self-government necessary to maintain and promote their ways of life, while, on the other, to protect important interests of those rendered vulnerable to local tyrannies by such arrangements, particularly women and children. The idea is to reap the benefits of co-ordinated interaction among the different sorts of authority claiming membership over an individual. Individuals are members of more than one group or authority, and each controls certain aspects of the situation: for example, while marriage may be sanctified by the '*nomos* group', the state retains the authority to allocate assets in the event of divorce. For such a model, neither the individual nor the state holds exclusive authority over a contested social arena that affects individuals both as group members and as citizens (Shachar 2001: 121).[28] For example, traditionally some groups have used family law to demarcate insiders and outsiders, controlling membership as well as the character of the group. Accommodating the demands of groups for jurisdictional powers over matters of marriage and divorce with regard to their own members tends to impose a particular burden on women and children, who have less power in shaping the character of these laws and are often subject to discriminatory burdens. Invoking the exit option pushes women 'into a cruel zero-sum choice: either accept all group practices – including those that violate your state-guaranteed individual rights – or leave' (Shachar 1999: 100; cf. Shachar 2001: 41).[29] Her proposal is to distinguish between the demarcating and the distributive functions of family law. The first concerns who is a member of a group, and the second governs such matters as property relations and child custody (Shachar 2001: 51–4). The 'no monopoly' rule requires that certain aspects of a given matter or dispute fall within the group's jurisdiction, while linked aspects fall within that of the state. So, for example, the group gets to determine membership status, 'allowing the state to address societal concerns surrounding distribution (i.e. the effect on women, children, employers, taxation, and social services)' (Shachar 2001: 121). Alternatively, the group may retain control over distribution, while the state has authority over the demarcating function, determining membership in disputed cases.

Identities are not merely entrenched but are themselves meant to be subject to a benign dynamic of change, or what Shachar calls 'transformative accommodation' (Shachar 2001: 117–45). The institutional structures and procedures proposed provide each authority with an opportunity to increase its accountability and sensitivity to otherwise marginalized members of groups, since each entity must now compete with others for individuals' continued adherence. Shachar argues that her proposals allow women to gain more power within their communities, because they will have state protection for their property during divorce proceedings (Shachar 2000: 220). So we can view this approach as offering to minority groups a form of accommodation designed to build their trust in the state, while building in liberal safeguards against the abuse of trust for vulnerable members.

Yet there is an obvious imbalance in the relation between state and *nomos* group, in the way that this model is set up. For proponents of separatism, the 'reverse' or 'choice' options run only one way: any individual may appeal to the state, but the scope of the *nomos* group's jurisdiction is restricted to members. Moreover, the benign liberalizing dynamic of these arrangements relies on the state's retaining a stronger bargaining hand. The pressure to transform identities is also one-sided: the state is less likely to adjust its system of criminal punishment or marriage laws. Accordingly, we may suspect that to a considerable extent the identity-based problem of trust needs to have been overcome in order for these arrangements to be acceptable to the relevant *nomoi* groups: as Jeff Spinner-Halev puts it, 'the moral authority of the United

States to tell Native Americans how to run their own affairs is rather weak'
(Spinner-Halev 2001: 105). Shachar suggests that 'there are incentives firmly
in place for both parties to engage in constructive dialogue once they have
embarked on a path of joint governance' (Shachar 2001: 130), but the incentives (and sanctions) are overwhelmingly directed toward the *nomos* group,
since the state or majority in the political community could, if it chose, enforce
state-wide family law (for instance), where nothing like this background threat
is usually available to a minority *nomos* group.

A second family of strategies for mitigating distrust is through promoting
the representation of some different groups in law-making, judicial and other
public bodies. This may have the effect of increasing the accountability of
those bodies to members of those groups, or it may principally have the symbolic function of affirming the membership of this group in the society. For
example, ensuring the representation of ethnic minorities on a public board
that monitors policing may have the effect of reducing suspicion of the police
in that group and of extending to its members a sense of inclusion in the
society. Group representation comes in various forms and is a notoriously
ambiguous device, however. Sometimes group representation involves ensuring that a member of a particular group is given public office. In other cases,
it involves drawing electoral boundaries so that voters from a group are given
particular weight in affecting the outcome. Given the points I have already
emphasized in this book about the scope for disagreement over the character
of a cultural identity, it would not be sensible to support group representation
on the grounds that the outlook and interests of all members of a group, and
thus of a representative and her constituents, are necessarily identical or even
very close (Phillips 1995: 53). I do not think that this means that the rationale
for group representation is incoherent, however, even if we set aside the important component of symbolic inclusion. As I noted in section 1, mechanisms of
accountability require some degree of trust of representatives. Where the
shared history of groups has generated distrust on the part of a minority, then
this can lead members of a minority group to withhold trust of representatives drawn from a majority or dominant group. Such distrust can be self-
perpetuating, as even trustworthy majority representatives will not be trusted
by the minority, who may not believe it worthwhile even to attempt to communicate their interests. Group representation is one way of re-establishing
links of trust between representatives and the represented necessary for sustaining the machinery of accountability.[30]

A striking example of the ambivalence of group representation is offered by
consociationalism. Consociational approaches to governing divided societies
aspire to avoid the risks of exclusion for minorities, which might then become
militant. Democracy can be maintained only through constitutional devices
that share power among the elites of the principal rival groups, and which
protect the smaller of these groups from being perpetually outvoted. These

mechanisms include territorial federalism, but, more distinctively, minority vetoes, rules for the proportional representation of groups in public offices, and prescriptions for coalition government. The latter is the 'primary characteristic' of consociational democracy, according to Arend Lijphart: 'the political leaders of all significant segments of the plural society cooperate in a grand coalition to govern the country' (1977: 25). Critics argue that the approach is unstable, except in quite particular circumstances (cf. Barry 1991a; Horowitz 1991; Shapiro 1999b; Arel 2001: 66–7). For this arrangement encourages citizens to see themselves as primarily members of their own group, with interests opposed to those of other groups. This in turn puts an immense pressure on politicians, who must both appease their own constituents (and head off the danger of a challenge from someone claiming to represent this group more authentically) and co-operate with other groups. However, supporters of consociationalism argue that even with these tensions 'an extended period of inter-group cooperation should reduce divisions rather than maintain or deepen them' (McGarry 2002: 466). Relationships of political trust must build on something, and this may sometimes be a fruitful starting point. The elaborate political framework created in Northern Ireland by the Good Friday Agreement puts at the centre devices to reassure Unionists and Nationalists that decisions cannot be made without the joint consent of both. Yet, while such devices can mitigate distrust and perhaps create the climate for co-operation, they are far from creating sufficient conditions for deliberative trust.

The fourth approach that I want to consider involves *creating* relations of dependence across groups: for example, by constructing electoral mechanisms designed to encourage politicians to 'fish' for votes in groups other than their own. In contrast to consociational power-sharing models, this border-crossing model emphasizes the need to construct an electoral system that encourages politicians to cross the borders of different ethnic groups in search of support. This supplies aspirant political leaders with incentives to avoid mobilizing support along ethnic group lines, and encourages accommodation among different groups. Border-crossing aims to permit and encourage flexibility of identities, and to form political identities which cross ethnic or cultural boundaries. It provides a mechanism for doing so, grounded not in the altruism of the politicians, but in their interest in election. This same mechanism aims also to protect against inflexibility of identities and hostilities, by creating a community of interest, which runs athwart identities. While some minorities may benefit from this kind of arrangement, designed to achieve stability rather than inclusiveness, others may be excluded by the redrawing of boundaries in order to create heterogeneous constituencies. This may reproduce the problem of democratic trust within the domain of each constituency. Furthermore, parties may proliferate within politicized groups, and some parties may be forced into more extreme positions in order to hold on to their core support (Shapiro 1996: 145–7).

Hedging about these four forms of institutional solution with reservations in this way does not mean that specific solutions are unavailable in particular contexts. But it does suggest that we should be cautious about what to expect from implementing such proposals: '[w]hatever constitutional devices there are need to be understood from the point of view of the actors who are affected by them, and the commitments and values that those actors bring to their perception may well be decisive' (Weale 2003: 81). This returns us to the conditions for forging such beliefs, perceptions and commitments that are the focus of those approaches that take ethos and identity as central.

## 5. Conclusion

What I have examined in this chapter is how to conceive of the sources of the trust necessary for political deliberation in circumstances of cultural diversity. I have tried to show that each offers a fruitful but also fragile and conditional account of the sources of political trust. Furthermore, the three conceptions of the sources of political trust that I have discussed are to some extent in tension with one another. Institutional arrangements to mitigate distrust, such as self-determination, vetoes and group representation, may reduce opportunities for public deliberation and incentives to deliberate across group boundaries. From the side of public deliberation, there is the worry that 'it would be ironic if a preoccupation with the rational basis of system trust resulted only in the encouragement of a more calculating disposition and an inability to act in the public domain unless securely supported by sanctions, insurance policies, or safety procedures' (P. Johnson 1993: 171; cf. Allen 2004: 82). Solutions to the problem of trust that appeal to a shared cultural identity share with those supported by proponents of the deliberative ethos a scepticism about the power of constitutional forms. Yet shared identity responses are necessarily tempted to constrain deliberation in order to protect the integrity of the identity, as we saw in the discussion of liberal nationalism. Furthermore, institutional measures to carve out areas of self-determination for groups or to guarantee group representation may undermine the common sense of identity that the liberal nationalist values as a necessary condition of political trust, and the circumstances in which trust can be generated by the creation of relations of dependence are quite limited. These difficulties flow not only from the problem of establishing the trustworthiness of some political actors, but also from the character of trust as itself a form of perception or recognition, and the difficulty in engineering perceptions. The conditionality of these approaches and the tensions among them clearly suggest serious obstacles to achieving the political trust necessary for public deliberation. Yet they do not give a reason to suggest that this is impossible or cannot be achieved to some significant degree.

# Conclusion

This book has discussed different ways in which the concept of culture has been used in political theory, particularly when it has been thought to put pressure on liberal conceptions of citizenship. I distinguished normative, semiotic and societal usages, and tried to clear this discourse of culture of the accusation of a necessary essentialism. I went on to spell out the character of arguments in defence of the normativity of cultural identity, before turning to the question of how these issues and claims should be handled in political deliberation. To see cultural identity as part of practical reason is not to take it to be the crucial element. Once we break from the confident and essentialist romantic fusion of person with nation or linguistic group (and its counterparts, for example, in some forms of Marxism), and conceive of the latter in essentialist terms, the question of how to understand the multiplicity of claims made on us by our practical identities, and perhaps sometimes to reconcile these claims, becomes central to our account of practical rationality. I have been concerned here principally to clear the cultural claim from charges that it is necessarily confused or malign.

In working through some central theoretical statements of the relationship between culture and citizenship, I argued against pre-emption of the political process in this area.[1] Pre-emptive accounts which *support* a right to culture, as in liberal culturalism, obscure the internal disagreement and contested character of cultural identity, while pre-emptive accounts which *block* consideration of the normativity of cultural identity or the possible grounds for differentiated citizenship unjustifiably neglect morally relevant considerations. I argued for a conception of political deliberation as public dialogue, and tried to bring out how this can accommodate some of the peculiar features of cultural claims, without ducking the reality and importance of disagreement over the character, importance and requirements of cultural identities or of dissent within groups over these and other matters. Finally, I traced the ways in which the practice of political deliberation on these terms relies on trust, and examined accounts of the potential sources of such trust, grounded in participants' ethos, identity and institutions.

In some ways, this only scratches the surface of these issues. In particular, there is ample scope, of course, to think through the relationship of this sort of analysis both to empirical inquiry and to institutional recommendations, in far more detail than I have tried to do here. Further, the focus on culture in this book is not intended to substitute for the exploration of other dimensions of power and exclusion – of poverty, for example. Nor have I said anything about how to conceive of and question the boundaries of the community engaged in political dialogue. Some choices of boundary, for example, notoriously exclude a group from possessing an effective stake in the polity to which it belongs, entrench distrust, and undermine the stability of the unit, by rendering each election an 'ethnic census' (Hardin 1999b: 277–80). More positively, some of the values of public deliberation may be promoted by appropriate boundary drawing, and used as a standard for assessing boundary drawing.[2]

The kind of critical standard embodied in the conception of public deliberation that I have outlined here draws attention to the density and particularity of relations of exclusion and the vulnerability of identities in processes of political deliberation. I have emphasized the contingencies of this conception, and the delicate relationships between compromise and criticism, distrust and trust, that this conception rests on. Some proponents of multiculturalism may feel that what is given with one hand is taken away with the other: 'it is all very well to have it suggested that I confide in a process', they may say, 'but it is not the process but specific forms of identity, recognition and disadvantage in which I have an interest'. Yet I do not think that the fragility of public deliberation furnishes a good reason for proponents of multiculturalism to adopt either a more thoroughly instrumental or a pre-emptive conception of the politics of cultural diversity. To promote a politics merely of the pressing of sectional interests is unlikely to benefit politically weak minorities. And to turn to a politics of pre-emption, as I have tried to argue, is also likely to freeze injustice in place, unless we are very trusting of those powerful groups who set the terms for pre-emption.

# Notes

## Chapter 1    Approaches to Cultural Identification

1   Raymond Williams says of 'culture' that it is 'one of the two or three most complicated words in the English language' (R. Williams 1983: 90). See Kroeber and Kluckhohn 1952, who pick out 171 uses; Geertz 1973; Kuper 1999; Wedeen 2002.

2   'The concepts of identity-building and of culture were and could only be born together' (Bauman 1996: 19, cited in Kuper 1999: 236). On the 'weak ontological' turn in political theory, see White 2000: 3–17.

3   'Something important is missing from a description of any individual's life which does not include reference to the collectivities to which they belong' (Graham 2002: 66n); cf. Taylor 1989: 36; Bell 1993: 94.

4   Sandel 1982, 1996; Taylor 1985, 1989, 1995; MacIntyre 1981, 1988.

5   Rawls 1972: 17–22, 583–6. For helpful analyses of the liberal–communitarian debate sensitive to these distinctions, see (from a compendious literature) Buchanan 1989; Caney 1992; Taylor 1995: ch. 10; Mulhall and Swift 1996.

6   For comparable relational accounts of identity, see Connolly 1991; Mouffe 2001; Honig 1992, 2001.

7   And see, e.g., Walzer 1983: 314; Tamir 1993: 35–6; Miller 1995: 10–11; 2000: 27; Raz 2001: 35.

8   Korsgaard coins this phrase in Korsgaard 1996b: 100–7. As the quotation here suggests, her conception is independent of any particular claims on behalf of the social thesis. The notion of practical identity is combined with a version of the social thesis in Neuhouser 2000: 93–100 (explicating Hegel); Laden 2001, 2003. Compare MacIntyre 1981: 204–5; Sandel 1982: 179.

9   This conception of importance figures particularly in philosophies of 'recognition': below, ch. 2, sects 4, 6.

10  For discussion of some of the issues in conceptualizing groups, see L. May 1987; M. Gilbert 1996; Bickford 1999; A. Mason 2000; Graham 2002; as well as Young 2000; Connolly 1991; and Mouffe 2001.

11  For early modern understandings, see Hont 1987; Pagden 1982. For a classic analysis of the moralized conception of culture in the first of these senses, see R.
Williams 1961, and Mulhern 2000 for a discussion of this motif. For the second,
the canonical statement is Herder's: 'Men of all quarters of the globe, who have
perished over the ages, you have not lived solely to manure the earth with your
ashes, so that at the end of time your posterity should be made happy by European
culture. The very thought of a superior European culture is a blatant insult to the
majority of nature' (Herder [1784–91] 1969: 311). Herder is a contentious figure
for authors concerned with the politics of recognition and multiculturalism
(compare Parekh 2000: 67–79; Markell 2003: 47–61).

12  The term derives from Cover 1983.

13  Discussions that make the normative dimension particularly significant also
include Spinner 1994; Spinner-Halev 2000b; Heath 1998; and (in part) Deveaux
2000b; Laden 2001.

14  See Parekh 2000: 249–54; Galeotti 2002: ch. 4; Benhabib 2002: 94–100, 117–19;
Moruzzi 1994.

15  Geertz is citing Clyde Kluckhohn here, in order to reject this view in favour of
what he sees as the analytically sharper semiotic conception. See P. Gilbert 2000:
33–4, 37–8; J. Johnson 2000: 408.

16  See in addition, e.g., Kymlicka 2001a: 25–8, 53–5; Margalit and Raz 1990: 443–7;
Jones 1998: 29.

17  Cf. Miller 2000: ch. 8. Compare McCrone 1998; Keating 2001.

18  This also misses the mark as a criticism of the particular conception of societal
culture offered by Kymlicka, since the presence of a coherent system of beliefs is
no part of this conception; rather, this objection is properly directed at what I am
calling the normative conception.

19  See J. D. Moore 1997: ch. 19; Kuper 1999: ch. 3.

20  For a sense of the debate over this constellation of ideas and its significance, see
Geertz 1973, 1983, 2000; Clifford 1988; Turner 1993; Carrithers 1992; Moody-
Adams 1997.

21  So-called 'thick' ethical concepts would be one example of this. See B. Williams
1995: 140–3.

22  Michael Walzer in *Spheres of Justice* (1983), for instance, combines societal and
normative accounts. As several commentators noted, the boundaries of political
community or societal culture may not line up comfortably with shared normative
boundaries.

23  As Sherry Ortner puts it, 'a deeply sedimented essence attaching to, or inhering in
particular groups' (Ortner 1997: 8–9, quoted in Wedeen 2002: 713).

24  Is this true of the semiotic account? If we view it as tied to the kind of hermeneutic presuppositions discussed in the previous section, this seems to be the hardest
case to make out.

25  For a powerful development of the rational choice approach, see Hardin 1995 and
the criticisms in Cunningham 1997. See also Brubaker 1996, 1998; Ensminger and
Knight 1997; J. Johnson 2000; Scott 2003.

26  In a different vein, Richard Rorty offers a general argument about the 'priority of
democracy to philosophy', and the subordinate status of this kind of ontological
claim: see R. Rorty 1991: 175–99; Tully 1999; Festenstein 2001, 2003.

27   Compare Brian Barry: '[t]he gravamen of my complaint against academic sup-
     porters of multiculturalism and multinationalism is that they have failed to pen-
     etrate what is, in essence, an ideology in the strict Marxist sense: an otherworldly
     rationalization of a distasteful reality. Whereas in recent decades, historians and
     social scientists have concentrated on unmasking the pretensions of these move-
     ments, political philosophers have been willing to act as intellectual accomplices'
     (Barry 1998: 313).
28   The ethical and political ambivalence of the social thesis is now well established:
     e.g., see Taylor 1995: 181–203.
29   It should be noted that this bald view is rejected in Parekh 2000: 176.
30   See the discussion of recognition below, ch. 2, sect. 4.
31   The following discussion is indebted to Graham 2002: 113–15, and Hollis 1998:
     111–23.
32   See below, ch. 4, sect. 2.
33   Laden develops this account of the notion of practical identity as a way of broad-
     ening Rawls's notion of a 'conception of the good' to refer not only to a set of
     beliefs (religious, ethical, philosophical and so on) but also such aspects of self-
     hood as 'my gender, ethnicity or race, where these are understood not as objective
     facts about me but as social ones' (Laden 2003: 145). But this putative broaden-
     ing in fact narrows the concept, since it limits it to only those aspects of an iden-
     tity that a person values or endorses.
34   Of course, we may view a 'principle of self-identification' as an important politi-
     cal principle, but that is a different point.

## Chapter 2   Culture and Normativity

1   See above, Introduction, and below, ch. 3, sect. 1.
2   For Chandran Kukathas, for example, it is a mistake for the state to become
    involved in the evaluation of the merits of cultural identity, as we will see. That is
    to say, this version of negative universalism rests not on the *denial* of an argument
    for cultural identity, but on an argument for the irrelevance of any such assess-
    ment to politics. See Festenstein 2000, and below ch. 4, sect. 1.
3   See below, esp. ch. 6, sect. 3.
4   Compare Kymlicka (1989: 241) on groups rather than cultures: 'Groups have no
    moral claim to well-being independently of their members – groups just aren't the
    right sort of being to have moral status.' For an opposed point of view, see
    Graham 2002.
5   Mason (2000: 43–5), following Korsgaard (1996a) distinguishes the instrumental/
    non-instrumental distinction from the distinction between intrinsic goods – those
    which possess value by virtue of their intrinsic properties – from extrinsic goods
    – those which have value by virtue of their extrinsic properties. Extrinsic proper-
    ties are those which depend for their character on the existence or character of
    something else, not merely their intrinsic character. See also J. O'Neill 1992;
    Musschenga 1998. I am grateful to Paul Gilbert for discussion of this issue.
6   See Raz, in *The Morality of Freedom* (1986), though he is more equivocal in later
    thinking.

7   On the 'relativism of distance', see B. Williams 1981: 132–43; 1985: 160–3.

8   This is culture according to what was called a semiotic conception: above, ch. 2, sect. 2.

9   For sceptical responses to Taylor on the intrinsic value of culture, see Hardin 1995: 66–9; J. Johnson 2000: 407.

10  Pettit 1993: 287: 'While [some] goods are not properties of individuals, they are still properties that make an impact on individuals; persons will fare differently, depending on whether they belong to a fractured or solidaristic community.'

11  For examples and discussion of this position, see Hurka 1997: 148; Graham 2002: 96–7.

12  The claim for the value of cultural belonging needs to be distinguished, then, from the claim that eclecticism necessarily constitutes a defective form of life. Parekh departs from his usually generous and nuanced formulations in writing of cultural eclecticism: '[l]acking historical depth and traditions, it cannot inspire and guide choices, fails to provide a moral compass and stability, and encourages the habit of hopping from culture to culture to avoid the rigour and discipline of any one of them', argues Parekh, ominously concluding that, '[a]s Hegel showed in his analysis of the French Revolution, culturally unbounded and unguided freedom, the culture of the pure will, destroys both itself and the world around it' (Parekh 2000: 150–1). This kind of argument mirrors the doubt about arguing for the non-instrumental value of a cultural identity, namely, that this line of argument may usher in a coercive and illiberal imposition of cultural identities.

13  The striking character of this formulation derives from Weinstock's claim that 'appealing to the intrinsic value of *languages* is actually a way of ascribing rights to languages or linguistic communities against their own members' (Weinstock 2003: 255, emphasis original). Yet it is not obvious that an ascription of non-instrumental value is actually an ascription of a right.

14  Compare, e.g., Hoover on 'the harm of a truncated subjectivity, a diminishing of one's capacities for self-development and self-understanding' (Hoover 2001: 205).

15  As well as texts already cited, see the discussions in Fraser 1997, 2000, 2001; Fraser and Honneth 2003; M. Cooke 1997; Zurn 2003; Markell 2003.

16  For an interesting discussion of Taylor's relationship to Herder in this connection, see Markell 2003: 39–61.

17  On Ellison, see Allen 2004.

18  For some subjectivistic conceptions of national identity, national membership consists not in the possession of any objective attributes (a shared language, territory or ethnicity, for example), but in recognition by others that you are a fellow national. For this account, objective attributes may be *causally* relevant in bringing about the relevant state of mind among the population: for example, the fact that we all live in the same patch of territory or that we speak the same language may be relevant in explaining why we recognize one another in the way that we do. But it is our state of mind – the mutual recognition of one another as fellow nationals – which constitutes the relevant identity, *making* us members of the same nationality. So, for example: 'A portion of mankind may be said to constitute a nationality if they are united among themselves by common sympathies, which do not exist between themselves and any others – which make them cooperate with each other more willingly than with other people, desire to be under the same

government, and desire that they should be governed by themselves or portions of themselves, exclusively' (J. S. Mill [1861] 1991: 427). 'Any territorial community, the members of which are conscious of themselves *as* members of a community, and wish to maintain the identity of their community is a nation' (Cobban 1944: 48). 'The simplest statement that can be made about a nation is that it is a body of people who feel that they are a nation; and it may be that when all the fine-spun analysis is concluded this will be the ultimate statement too' (Emerson 1960: 102).

19   Cf. Honneth 2001b: 52; 2001a.
20   Compare Gellner on nationalism:

> It is this which pushes people into nationalism, into the need for the congru-ence between their own 'culture' (the idiom in which they can express them-selves and understand others) and that of the extensive and interconnected bureaucracies which constitute their social environment. Non-congruence is not merely an inconvenience or a disadvantage: it means perpetual humilia-tion. Only if such a congruence does obtain, can one feel 'at ease in one's skin'. Only then is one's personal style of being accepted and endorsed by the environment, only then is one allowed to 'be oneself' without impedi-ment. Nationalism is not explained by the use it has in legitimising moder-nisation – a view with which I am mistakenly credited – but by the fact that individuals find themselves in very stressful situations, unless the nationalist requirement of congruence between a man's culture and that of his environ-ment . . . [Nationalist] passion is not a means to some end, it is a reaction to an intolerable situation, to a constant jarring in the activity which is by far the most important thing in life – contact and communication with fellow human beings. (Gellner 1996b: 627–8, quoted in Hall 1998a: 11)

21   See Rawls 1993: 316; 1999: 171; Barry 2001: 266; Weinstock 1998: 298. On Barry, see the excellent discussion in Caney 2002: 93–5, and see below, ch. 4, sect. 3.
22   I return to this point in chapter 5, to consider some harder cases.
23   See above, ch. 1, sect. 4.
24   This is a major theme of Markell 2003, although I am not sure that the recognition project necessarily carries with it the full range of pathologies that he identifies.
25   For the first formulation, Raz 1994: 175; 1986: 369–70, 408; for the second, Kymlicka 1995a: 80.
26   Cf. Raz: 'options presuppose a culture' (Raz 1994: 176); Margalit and Raz 1990: 449; Patten 1999a, 1999b.
27   See P. Gilbert 2000: 35–8 for some interesting reflections on the sociological pre-suppositions of this line of thought.
28   See above, ch. 1, sect. 2, for a related point on societal culture and social identity.
29   This is not to say that the notion of societal culture exhaustively *explains* these differences, although it may figure in an explanation.

### Chapter 3   The Limits of Liberal Culturalism

1   There is an alternative, of course, which is not to publicly recognize any holidays, and to 'disestablish' them on the model of the liberal disestablishment of religion.

The question, then, is whether there is an overriding, legitimate interest in having 'common pause days'. Only if there is, does the problem for the benign neglect strategy arise. The structure of this kind of decision is discussed below, in ch. 4, sect. 4.

2   For example, in Charles Taylor's work: see the discussion of this line of thought, and an argument against allegedly illiberal implications, above in ch. 2, sect. 2, and conclusion.

3   In reply to criticism from Andrea Baumeister (2003b), Joseph Carens (2004) resists the argument that procedural fairness requires that Quebec offer the option of an education in English to native French-speakers and immigrants, since this is available to English-speakers, and this latter group also has the option of an education in French. This is a mistake, he argues, as the objection applies to Quebec a conception of procedural fairness that does not apply at the level of the state. Canada offers a constitutional guarantee to a public education in English or French only to those with a parent who has received an education in that language in Canada. Provided that we take Canada's rules to be a reasonable interpretation of what procedural fairness requires in this case, we cannot object to the Quebecois interpretation. Quebec's language policy matches Canada's, in other words: Anglophones are provided with an accommodation to fit their special circumstances, without this generating an obligation to provide this option to others who don't share those circumstances. This, he says, 'presupposes that a non-state political community like Quebec can matter morally in much the same way that a state can' (Carens 2004: 132; and on Catalonia cf. Costa 2003). But there is a further question about what kinds of policy this stance toward sub-state political communities supports, and what powers such communities should and should not have.

4   On 'even-handedness' within and across particular contexts, see Carens 2000; Spinner-Halev 2000a.

5   In terms of Kymlicka's own self-understanding, I think, Monique Deveaux (2000b: ch. 4) is mistaken to interpret both Raz and Kymlicka as perfectionists. Her account conflates two distinctions, between political and comprehensive liberalisms, and between neutralist and perfectionist liberalisms. Kymlicka disavows the 'political turn' taken by John Rawls in later work, but this does not put him in the perfectionist camp. At the same time, we may wonder how the account of primary goods is shielded from itself being a theory of the good (even if a 'thin' theory relative to some others).

6   See above, ch. 2, sect. 2, and ch. 3, sect. 6.

7   See above, ch. 3, sects 5 and 6.

8   For the contentiousness of this identification, see above, ch. 2, sect. 2.

9   See above, Introduction.

10   For scepticism about this distinction, see Parekh 1997; Young 1997b; Kukathas 1997c; Festenstein 1998; Carens 2000: 52–88.

11   On the case of religious isolationist groups, see Spinner-Halev 2000b.

12   Here too there is an issue of how to understand and assign responsibility: refugees and economic migrants may have little real choice about emigration, but some choice over where to migrate to.

13   'Other theorists have sketched some concepts or principles which they think should govern liberal approaches to ethnocultural demands (e.g. Raz, Taylor,

Habermas). But these are more outlines than systematic theories. It is impossible (for me at least) to tell what their abstract concepts imply for specific debates about the particular claims of particular groups' (Kymlicka 2001a: 50).

14  We should

> look upon life as affording a plurality of values, equally genuine, equally ultimate, above all equally objective; incapable therefore of being ordered in a timeless hierarchy, or judged in terms of some one absolute standard . . . The fact that the values of one culture may be incompatible with those of another, or that they are in conflict within one culture or group or within a single human being at different times – or, for that matter, at one and the same time – does not entail relativism of values, only the notion of a plurality of values not structured hierarchically; which, of course, entails the permanent possibility of inescapable conflict between values, as well as incompatibility between the outlooks of different civilisations or stages of the same civilisation. (Berlin 1990: 79–80)

Influential expositions of pluralism include Berlin 1969, 1979, 1990; Chang 1997; Crowder 1994, 2002; Gray 1993: 287–306; 1995a, 1995b; Hampshire 1983, 1999; Kekes 1993; Larmore 1987, 1996: 152–74; Lukes 1991, 2003; Moon 1993: esp. 13–35; Nagel 1979: ch. 5; B. Williams 1981: ch. 5. For relevant statements from Raz and from Taylor: Raz 1986: ch. 13; 1994, 1999, 2001; Taylor 1994: 250–1; 1995: 34–60.

15  'Can we not in good conscience consider our own moral universalism as superior to earlier and very different tribal moralities, while acknowledging that thereby we have lost the possibilities of good they embodied? The weighing of heterogeneous goods is not likely to yield a cardinal ranking. But surely we can have reason to believe that some goods are more important than others, in the given circumstances or overall, and even a lot more important' (Larmore 1996: 162).

16  See above ch. 2, sects 2 and 4.

17  For critical discussion of Gray, see Crowder 1999, 2002; Weinstock 1998.

18  This is compatible with Stephen White's suggestion that we should see Taylor as here supporting the need to maintain space for 'alternative modernities' which allow for the exploration of different sorts of value (White 2000: 74). The flourishing of this exploration is to be sought in societies where the polity can act, within limits, to 'enhance the congruence' of cultures within it and so 'honour affiliations with some depth in time and commitment' (Taylor 1989: 513). The point is not that the world should be refashioned in the image of Taylor's second sort of liberalism, but that a world that accords a place to societies that pursue this form of liberalism does better justice to the depth of diversity that characterizes modernity. Cf. Gutting 1999; Smith 2002.

### Chapter 4    The Way of the World: Two Forms of Negative Universalism

1  I discuss the first of these sources of scepticism in chapter 1, and the second (although not fully) in various places, including ch. 5, sect. 3; ch. 6, sect. 4. On the latter, see Benhabib 2002; Deveaux 2003.

2   It is worth pausing on this, although a full exposition and study of Kukathas's position is beyond the range of this chapter. What does acting against conscience mean? This seems to engage the full panoply of arguments over the concept of liberty. Can a person think she is acting against conscience but not be (consider someone who is not sure if what she is doing is sinful). Her own judgement would seem to be final (see the quotation from Pierre Bayle at Kukathas 2003: 131n), but is it her judgement after any reflection? Is she forced to act against conscience by lack of opportunities to do otherwise, only by physical coercion, or by some other constraint?

3   Kukathas develops this through a reading of O. O'Neill 1989: 29–50, on Immanuel Kant (Kukathas 2003: 127–8).

4   I am not of course saying that this is the end of the debate: just that these are relevant reasons, and indeed that they are acceptable ones within the framework offered by Kukathas.

5   I should note that this point is made specifically against Iris Marion Young's vision of democratic group representation; see Young 1990. But I do not think it distorts the tenor of Kukathas's thought to apply it more generally against claims for recognition.

6   Of course, we may not think this.

7   See above ch. 1, sect. 3.

8   See Silverman 1992; Favell 1998; Galeotti 1993, 2002: 115–36; Moruzzi 1994; Gaspard and Khosrokhavar 1995; Jennings 2000; Carens 2000: 155–9; Parekh 2000: 249–57.

9   Kukathas 1992: 121; and see Kukathas 1997a: 88–9; Svensson 1979; Kymlicka 1992, 1995a: 164–6.

10  See, e.g., Kymlicka 1992; Green 1995; Festenstein 2000: 72–7; Mason 2000: 75–7; Shachar 2001: 68–70; Barry 2001: 141–6, 238–42, 318–19; Okin 2002: 215–16.

11  On this distinction, see Shapiro 1999a: 90–1.

12  Does such persuasion itself constitute an external harm?

13  'A commitment to discovering what is true about the good life or about proper moral practice requires a social order whose fundamental disposition is to toleration' (Kukathas 2003: 134).

14  See Gutmann and Thompson 1996; Macedo 2000; Tomasi 2001.

15  On the notion of partial citizens, see Spinner-Halev 1999.

16  Some members of these groups argue for the compatibility of their sacred texts with more humane methods of slaughter.

17  Cf. Dworkin 2000; Heath 1998; Matravers 2002; and cf. Mendus 2002; Kelly 2002a; Barry 1991b.

18  In a scholarly study, Simon Caney (2002: 83–4) points out that Barry in various writings also allows for self-government rights and external rules such as the cultural protection of a local film industry (Barry 1991a: 156–86; cf. Barry 2001: 117, 226).

19  Barry accepts this point about freedom of religion. For example, he considers whether UK laws penalizing those who carry knives in public places should cover the Sikh ceremonial knife, or *kirpan*. He argues that it should not be exempted, since there is a public order interest in not having some of the population carrying offensive weapons, but also concedes that denial of the exemption abridges

freedom of religion for Sikhs: '[w]e can disagree about which of these two values should prevail in this particular case, but it would not be sensible to deny that, whatever the outcome, something valuable will be lost' (Barry 2001: 152; cf. 51, 53).

### Chapter 5    Cultural Accommodation and Political Dialogue

1   As well as the texts cited already, the following contain arguments promoting the idea of an elective affinity between multicultural claims and various forms of deliberative or communicative democracy: Tully 1995: 183–4; 2001, 2002a, 2002b, 2004a, 2004b; Bohman 1996, 2003; M. Williams 1995, 1998, 2000; Young 1990, 1997a, 2000; Deveaux 2000b; 2003; James 1999a, 1999b, 2004; Dryzek 2005; Phillips 1999; Baumeister 1999, 2003a; Festenstein 1999, 2000; Laden 2001; Squires 2002; Goodin 2003; even J. Johnson 2000 and Barry 2002. More generally, the efficacy of deliberation in this context has been pressed by Chambers 1996; O'Neill 1997; Habermas 1998. For a more practical context, see also the Runnymede Trust Report on the Future of Multi-Ethnic Britain (the Parekh Report) (Runnymede Trust 2000: 223, 234). For the background, other important texts include Dryzek 1990, 2000; Benhabib 1992, 1996a; Nino 1996; Bohman and Rehg 1997; Bohman 1998; Elster 1998; Miller 2000; D'Entrèves 2002.

2   Cf. Manin 1987: 359–60. See also Knight and Johnson 1994; Miller 2000: 8–23.

3   For a stimulating discussion of electoral systems in this connection, see James 2003.

4   For some critics this is a defect in this conception. Cf. M. Williams 2000: 145.

5   Cf. Chambers 2001: 99: 'voice, rather than votes, is the vehicle of empowerment'.

6   See Misak 2000; Festenstein 2002a, 2004.

7   Cf. Jeremy Waldron on a 'distinctively liberal' attitude: 'If life in a society is practicable and desirable, then its principles must be amenable to explanation and understanding, and the rules and restraint that are necessary must be capable of being justified to the people who live under them . . . the liberal insists that intelligible justifications must be available in principle for everyone' (Waldron 1993: 44).

8   That is: we may appeal to such a reason in the course of discussion, but we should not expect such a reason to serve as the basis of a commonly agreed-upon outcome. I discuss this point further in sect. 3.

9   As Amy Gutmann and Dennis Thompson write, 'moral disagreement is a condition with which we must learn to live, not merely an obstacle to be overcome on the way to a just society' (Gutmann and Thompson 1996: 26). See above, Introduction and ch. 3, sect. 4.

10   On these Hegelian themes, see Hardimon 1994a and Neuhouser 2000, both of whom see this as a concern of Rawls's political liberalism (1993); Habermas 1998: ch. 2; Laden 2001.

11   This is compatible with, but does not require, a view, such as Tully's, of political participation as non-instrumentally valuable: 'the intersubjective activity of striving for and responding to forms of mutual recognition is an intrinsic public good of modern politics which contributes to legitimacy and stability, whether or

not the form of recognition demanded is achieved' (Tully 2001: 5). For Tully, 'the democratic-constitutional citizen' is 'akin to the young Olympian athlete who greets the dawn's early light with a smile, rises, dusts herself off, surveys her gains and losses of the previous days, thanks her gods for such a challenging game and engages in the communicative-strategic agon anew' (Tully 2002b: 219). Part of the argument, in sect. 3 particularly, will be that we should not expect or require such equanimity on the part of all participants in public deliberation.

12  See Dryzek 1990: 43 ('No concerned individuals should be excluded, and if necessary, some educative mechanisms should promote the competent participation of persons with a material interest in the issues at hand who might otherwise be left out'); Benhabib 1996b: 70; 2002: 134; Knight and Johnson 1997; Young 1996, 1997a, 2000. For a divergent view which offers arguments to distinguish participation from the inclusion of relevant issues and interests, see Goodin 2003: esp. 194–208.

13  For differing perspectives on this set of issues, see Dryzek 1990, 2000; Fishkin 1991, 1992; Shapiro 2002; Smith and Wales 2002; Goodin 2003.

14  For discussion of this issue, see Barry 2001; S. May 2001; Kymlicka and Patten 2003.

15  Gutmann and Thompson discuss the African-American Senator Carole Moseley-Braun's impassioned appeal to the Senate against legislation that would have renewed a patent on an emblem of the organization the Daughters of the Confederacy. The emblem included a representation of the Confederate flag, the racist symbolism of which made granting the design patent offensive and divisive (Gutmann and Thompson 1996: 135–6; and see M. Williams 2000; J. Levy 2000: ch. 8). Moseley-Braun took the floor with an 'oratory of impassioned tears and shouts': '[h]er passionate – some said extremist – rhetoric was probably necessary to provoke the Senate to take the issue seriously. With her rhetoric, she turned the routine into the notable, and provoked deliberation that almost certainly would not otherwise have occurred' (Gutmann and Thompson 1996: 135, citing 'Ms. Moseley-Braun's Majestic Moment', *New York Times*, July 24, 1993).

16  'I think it is a serious mistake to approach the problem of intercultural deliberation *first* with the idea of deliberative discipline and the exclusion of certain lines of argument . . . Our first responsibility in this regard is to make whatever effort we can to converse with others on their own terms, as they attempt to converse with us on ours, to see what we can understand of their reasons, and to present our reasons as well as we can with them. The a priori conviction that stalemate is bound to result and that "there is no talking to these people" is itself a violation of the duty of civic participation. (And, one should add, it is a violation most often committed by members of the majority or dominant culture in the kinds of societies we are talking about.)' (Waldron 2000a: 163–4).

17  'Explorations of deliberative or communicative democracy often refer rather grandly to a principle of equal access to decision-making assemblies or substantive equality in resources and power, but they do not give much attention to how these conditions would ever be achieved' (Phillips 1995: 154).

18  It is tempting, but, I think, mistaken to hold that this corresponds to the 'semiotic' conception of culture, and the line of criticism explored in the following paragraphs broadly addresses what I called the normative conception of cultural

identity. For there can be norms governing modes of speech and participation that are relevant to 'assimilation' in the sense discussed here.

19   Compare Alan Keenan, discussing the *œuvre* of Ernesto Laclau and Chantal Mouffe:

> Thus although the contingency of identity makes hegemonic struggle possible, it also makes it particularly hard to convince different groups/identities to enter into a hegemonic project with others precisely *because* that overall struggle will require them to change 'who' they are now. Often a terrifying prospect in itself, such change is particularly risky in the absence of any guarantees that the situation a person will ultimately find herself in will be an improvement over her present state . . . Although a discourse of equality and justice is necessary to persuade people to accept such risks, what justice requires can itself only be judged from some particular vision of the community, and thus its effectiveness requires something of the sense of trust and commonality whose 'foundation' is exactly what must be built. (Keenan 2003: 123)

20   See above, n. 10.

21   In some of Rawls's writings, the presumption seems to be that the content of public reason derives from a social agreement on a particular liberal conception of justice (cf. Waldron 2000a, b; Parekh 2000; cf. Rawls 1999: 430n, 582). In later work, this is not his intention, since he describes the content as given by a 'family of reasonable conceptions of justice', which includes, but is not subsumed by, his own political liberalism (Rawls 1999; cf. Laden 2001). Reasonable disagreement penetrates even the common standpoint from which the exercise of political power is to be justified. Apart from the works discussed here, see for scrutiny of the idea of public reason D'Agostino 1996; D'Agostino and Gaus 1998; Gaus 1996, 2003; Macedo 2000; Tomasi 2001; Horton 2002.

22

> Citizens are reasonable when, viewing one another as free and equal in a system of social cooperation over generations, they are prepared to offer one another fair terms of cooperation according to what they consider the most reasonable conception of political justice; and when they agree to act on those terms, even at the cost of their own interests in particular situations, provided that other citizens also accept those terms. The criterion of reciprocity requires that when those terms are proposed as the most reasonable terms of fair cooperation, those proposing them must also think it at least reasonable for others to accept them, as free and equal citizens, and not as dominated or manipulated, or under the pressure of an inferior political or social position. Citizens will of course differ as to which conception of political justice they think most reasonable, but will agree that all are reasonable, even if barely so. (Rawls 1999: 578)

23   But cf. Laden 2001: 124.

24   'If citizens consent to the rules that govern such procedures, then they can be said in an important sense to endorse the reasons for the policies the procedure generates, since the reasons for supporting such policies include the fact that the policy resulted from a legitimate procedure legitimately applied' (Laden 2001: 122).

25  Cf. Parekh 2000: 269, 294; and Tully, drawing on Wittgenstein, in Tully 1995, 1999, 2000a, 2000b, 20004b; Wittgenstein 1958; Owen 1999.

## Chapter 6    Deliberative Trust: Ethos, Identity and Institutions

1   See, e.g., Baier 1986: 235; Warren 1999b: 1; 1999a: 311; Giddens 1990: 34; Hardin 2002b: 11–12. There is now quite a substantial literature on trust and questions in political theory. As well as the works already listed, the following are particularly valuable: Allen 2004; Baier 1994; Braithwaite and Levi 1998; Cooke 2001; Dunn 1985: 34–54; 1990: 26–44; 1996: 91–9; Fukuyama 1995; Gambetta 1988; Hollis 1998; P. Johnson 1993; Luhmann 1979; Macedo 2000; Seligman 1997; Sztompka 1999; Uslaner 2002; Weinstock 1999; M. Williams 1998.

2   'Where there is politics, then, the conditions of trust are weak: the convergence of interests between truster and trusted cannot be taken for granted' (Warren 1999a: 312). But cf. P. Johnson 1993; Mara 2001.

3   In James Mill's economy of trust, for instance, there was no problem of mutual opacity, and the problem of trust for politics really did derive from the instrumental and strategic character of human action: the uniformity of human motivation meant that we could rest assured that others would sacrifice our interests as soon as it was expedient to do so. For Mill, government, like other social relationships and institutions, should be viewed in instrumental terms: it is essentially a means of reducing human insecurity in the light of the individual selfishness that Mill sees as the fundamental human motivation (J. S. Mill [1819] 1992). For Mill, the purpose of government is to promote the happiness of the individual and the whole community. The main way in which it does this is by providing for individual security and by constraining the extent to which some members of the community illegitimately live off the labour of others. In the absence of public authority, we would all be vulnerable to the unrestrained use of terror on the part of those seeking to use us to advance their own interests and desires. Government is required, since there is no limit to the terror that we are prepared to inflict on one another in pursuit of our chosen ends. Even that paragon, the English gentleman, when in possession of unchecked personal power over others, as in the case of the slave-holders in the West Indies, is capable of blood-freezing cruelty. However, given the uniformity of human motivation, any governors we set up over us will themselves be inclined to use their power in order to exploit the rest of the populace. The solution is to make governors representative, subject to election with short terms of office. As his essay on *Government* makes clear, Mill is incongruously optimistic about the extent to which the interests of those represented are harmonious, a position in conflict with the assumptions of self-interest and potential mutual antipathy from which he sets out. Warranted trust reappears, then, when he suggests that the interests of women happily converge with those of their husbands or fathers, for example, allowing the franchise to be restricted to men, and the interests of men below middle age and the very poor too may also be satisfactorily represented by others. Compare Warren 1999a: 314–16.

4   P. Johnson 1993; and see more generally the essays collected in Hampshire 1978; Hollis 1982; Walzer 1973.

5 On civility and speech see Kingwell 1995; Allen 2004.

6 'The challenge is thus not to presuppose a moral conception of respect for others, but to focus on the processes that help us *move to it* in different ways' (Ivison 2002: 88, emphasis in original). See above, ch. 5.

7 See above, ch. 1.

8 On this point, see Baier 1986: 245 ('awareness of what is customary affects one's ability to trust'); Hawthorn 1988: 114.

9 Cf. Coleman 1990: 91; R. D. Putnam 1993: 182–3. For a different account of the empirical evidence, see Uslaner 2002: 229–42.

10 See above, ch. 1, sect. 2. Recent discussions and defences of nationality include Miller 1989; Buchanan 1991; Tamir 1993; Miller 1995, 2000; Canovan 1996; P. Gilbert 1998; Clarke and Jones 1999; Archard 2000; M. Moore 2002.

11 For the view that this statement provides a bridge between an earlier republican conception of citizen's loyalty to the polity and a later nationalist emphasis on the cultural and spiritual unity of the people, see Viroli 1995.

12 See also Miller 1995: 140; 1998: 48; Barry 1991a: 174–7; Kymlicka 1996a: 131; 1997.

13 See above, ch. 2, sect. 2.

14 For discussion, see Hardimon 1994b; Horton 1992; Tamir 1993; Parekh 1993; Miller 1995; Dagger 2000.

15 Cf. Horton 1992: 357; R. Rorty 1989: 195; and (specifically in the context of this set of questions) Frost 2001: 492–3.

16 For the charge of conservatism, see P. Gilbert 2000: 157. For a different line of criticism, see Archard 1996.

17 This position belongs to the same family as the argument about the character of hermeneutic contestation of cultural identity, above ch. 1, sects 2 and 3.

18 On *pro tanto* reasons, see above ch. 1, sect. 4, and Hurley 1989: 130–3.

19 For a comparable objection to this line of argument, see P. Gilbert 1998: 84.

20 'As far as linguistic homogeneity is concerned, we can . . . press the view that, for democratic politics to work, the citizens must be able to communicate with one another, and must have access to the same forums of political debate' (Barry 1991a: 178); 'democracy within national/linguistic units is more genuinely participatory than at higher levels that cut across language lines . . . democratic politics is politics in the vernacular' (Kymlicka 2001a: 213).

21 Compare the debate on the 'European public sphere' between Dieter Grimm and Jürgen Habermas: Grimm 1995; Habermas 1998: 155–61.

22 On 'banal nationalism', see Billig 1995. But cf. Levinson 2003.

23 Miller's example of such a state of affairs is Nigerian politics. Yet when Miller draws the contrast between a state with a functioning national identity and Nigeria, for example, he needs to separate out those features of the Nigerian political situation which causally contribute to the lack of national identity, those which constitute it, and those which are effects of it, from a list that would include poor economic performance; ineffective, uncompromising or militant political leaderships; social and economic inequality; the lack of civil society institutions; the character of the state control of the economy; the character of the armed forces and their involvement in politics; international economic, financial and diplomatic pressures; and the character of the constitution and the electoral system.

24  See above, ch. 2, sect. 1.
25  See above, ch. 1, sect. 3.
26  For an interpretation of this argument in these terms of '(mutually exclusive) "entities" whose boundaries are neatly specifiable and overwhelmingly impenetrable', within which a 'realm of almost fully transparent mutual comprehension and communication' is possible and outside of which 'there cannot be significant (i.e., politically relevant) mutual comprehension or communication', see Abizadeh 2002: 502.
27  For discussion and criticism of civic nationalism in this broad sense, see, e.g., Viroli 1995; 2002: 79–103; Yack 1996; Habermas 1996; P. Gilbert 1998: 75–90; J. Levy 2000: 84–91; Canovan 2000.
28  On the '*nomos* group' and normative conceptions of cultural identity, see ch. 1, sect. 2.
29  Sceptical but sympathetic responses include Benhabib 2002: 122–9; Spinner-Halev 2001; Okin 2002.
30  See M. Williams 1998; Mansbridge 2000.

## Conclusion

1  For a fiercer and more general case of resistance to pre-emption, see Raymond Geuss: '[r]ights-discourse is a way of trying to immobilise society, to freeze it in an idealised version of its present form; not of course in its present *real* form, given that even recognised rights are rarely ever fully implemented in any society at any time. It is an attempt to ensure that the ghostly hand of the present is able to throttle the future' (Geuss 2001: 154).
2  But not the only one, or one without ambiguities: for some further discussion, see Festenstein 2002b.

# References

Abizadeh, A. 2002: Does Liberal Democracy Presuppose a Cultural Nation? Four Arguments. *American Political Science Review* 96: 495–509.

Allen, D. 2004: *Talking to Strangers: Anxieties of Citizenship Since Brown Vs. Board of Education*. Chicago: University of Chicago Press.

Anderson, B. 1991: *Imagined Communities: Reflections on the Origins and Spread of Nationalism*, rev. edn. London: Verso.

Appiah, K. A. 1994: Identity, Authenticity and Survival: Multicultural Societies and Social Reproduction. In A. Gutmann (ed.), *Multiculturalism: Examining the Politics of Recognition*, Princeton: Princeton University Press, 149–64.

Archard, D. 1996: Should Nationalists Be Communitarians? *Journal of Applied Philosophy* 13: 215–20.

——1999: The Ethical Status of Nationality. In Clarke and Jones 1999: 145–66.

——2000: Nationalism and Political Theory. In N. O'Sullivan (ed.), *Political Theory in Transition*, London: Routledge), 155–71.

Arel, D. 2001: Political Stability in Multinational Democracies: Comparing Language Dynamics in Brussels, Montreal and Barcelona. In A.-G. Gagnon and J. Tully (eds), *Multinational Democracies*, Cambridge: Cambridge University Press, 65–89.

Baier, A. 1986: Trust and Anti-Trust. *Ethics* 96: 231–60.

——1994: *Moral Prejudices*. Cambridge, Mass.: Harvard University Press.

Banfield, E. C. 1958: *The Moral Basis of a Backward Society*. New York: Free Press.

Barry, B. 1991a: *Democracy and Power: Essays in Political Theory I*. Oxford: Clarendon Press.

——1991b: *Liberty and Justice: Essays in Political Theory II*. Oxford: Clarendon Press.

——1995: *Justice as Impartiality*. Oxford: Clarendon Press.

——1998: The Limits of Cultural Politics. *Review of International Studies* 24: 307–19.

——2001: *Culture and Equality*. Cambridge: Polity.

——2002: Second Thoughts – and Some First Thoughts Revived. In P. Kelly (ed.), *Multiculturalism Reconsidered*, Cambridge: Polity, 204–38.

Bauman, Z. 1996: The Concepts of Identity-Building and of Culture. In S. Hall and P. DuGay (eds), *Questions of Cultural Identity*, London: Sage 18–36.

Baumeister, A. 1999: Multicultural Citizenship, Identity and Conflict. In Horton and Mendus 1999: 87–102.

——2003a: Habermas, Discourse and Cultural Diversity. *Political Studies* 51: 740–58.

——2003b: Ways of Belonging: Ethnonational Minorities and Models of 'Differentiated Citizenship'. *Ethnicities* 3: 393–416.

Bell, D. 1993: *Communitarianism and its Critics*. Oxford: Clarendon Press.

Bellamy, R. 1999: *Liberalism and Pluralism: Towards a Politics of Compromise*. London: Routledge.

Benhabib, S. 1992: *Situating the Self*. Cambridge: Polity.

——(ed.) 1996a: *Democracy and Difference: Contesting the Boundaries of the Political*. Princeton: Princeton University Press.

——1996b: Toward a Deliberative Model of Democratic Legitimacy. In Benhabib 1996a: 67–94.

——2002: *The Claims of Culture: Equality and Diversity in a Global Era*. Princeton: Princeton University Press.

Berlin, I. 1969: *Four Essays on Liberty*. Oxford: Oxford University Press.

——1979: *Against the Current*. Oxford: Oxford University Press.

——1990: *The Crooked Timber of Humanity*. London: John Murray.

——and Williams, B. 1994: Pluralism and Liberalism: A Reply. *Political Studies* 42: 306–9.

Bickford, S. 1999: Reconfiguring Pluralism: Identity and Institutions in the Inegalitarian Polity. *American Journal of Political Science* 43: 86–108.

Billig, M. 1995: *Banal Nationalism*. London: Sage.

Bohman, J. 1996: *Public Deliberation: Pluralism, Complexity and Democracy*. Cambridge, Mass.: MIT Press.

——1998: The Coming of Age of Deliberative Democracy. *Journal of Political Philosophy* 6: 400–25.

——2003: Deliberative Toleration. *Political Theory* 31: 757–79.

——and Rehg, W. (eds) 1997: *Deliberative Democracy: Essays on Reason and Politics*. Cambridge, Mass.: MIT Press.

Braithwaite, V. and Levi, M. (eds) 1998: *Trust and Governance*. New York: Russell Sage Foundation.

Broome, J. 1991: *Weighing Goods*. Oxford: Blackwell.

Brubauer, R. 1996: *Nationalism Reframed: Nationhood and the National Question in the New Europe*. Cambridge: Cambridge University Press.

——1998: Myths and Misconceptions in the Study of Nationalism. In Hall 1998b: 272–306.

Buchanan, A. 1989: Assessing the Communitarian Critique of Liberalism. *Ethics* 99: 852–82.

——1991: *Secession: The Morality of Political Divorce from Fort Sumter to Lithuania and Quebec*. Boulder, Colo.: Westview Press.

Caney, S. 1992: Liberalism and Communitarianism: A Misconceived Debate. *Political Studies* 40: 273–90.

——2002: Equal Treatment, Exceptions and Cultural Diversity. In P. Kelly (ed.), *Multiculturalism Reconsidered*. Cambridge: Polity, 81–101.

Cannadine, D. 1992: The Context, Performance and Meaning of Ritual: The British Monarchy and the 'Invention of Tradition', c.1820–1977. In E. Hobsbawm and T. Ranger (eds), *The Invention of Tradition*, Cambridge: Cambridge University Press, 43–100.

Canovan, M. 1996: *Nationhood and Political Theory*. Cheltenham: Edward Elgar.

——2000: Patriotism is Not Enough. *British Journal of Political Science*. 30: 413–32.

——2002: Democracy and Nationalism. In A. Carter and G. Stokes (eds), *Democratic Theory Today: Challenges for the Twenty-First Century*, Cambridge: Polity, 149–70.

Carens, J. 2000: *Culture, Citizenship and Community*. Oxford: Oxford University Press.

——2004: Using Multicultural Practices to Challenge the Privileged Position of States in Multicultural Theory: A Reply to Andrea Baumeister. *Ethnicities* 4: 125–34.

Carrithers, M. 1992: *Why Humans Have Cultures*. Oxford: Oxford University Press.

Chambers, S. 1996: *Reasonable Democracy: Jürgen Habermas and the Poltics of Discourse*. Ithaca, NY: Cornell University Press.

——2001: A Critical Theory of Civil Society. In S. Chambers and W. Kymlicka (eds), *Alternative Conceptions of Civil Society*, Princeton: Princeton University Press, 90–110.

Chang, R. (ed.) 1997: *Incommensurability, Incomparability and Practical Reason*. Cambridge, Mass.: Harvard University Press.

Clarke, D. M. and Jones, C. (eds) 1999: *The Rights of Nations*. Cork: University of Cork Press.

Clifford, J. 1988: *The Predicament of Culture*. Cambridge, Mass.: Harvard University Press.

Cobban, A. 1944: *National Self-Determination*. London: Oxford University Press.

Cohen, J. 1997a: Deliberation and Democratic Legitimacy. In Bohman and Rehg 1997: pp. 67–92.

——1997b: Procedure and Substance in Deliberative Democracy. In Bohman and Rehg 1997: 407–37.

Coleman, J. S. 1990: *Foundations of Social Theory*. Cambridge, Mass: Belknap.

Connolly, W. 1991: *Identity/Difference: Democratic Negotiations of Political Paradox*. Ithaca, NY: Cornell University Press.

Cook, K. (ed.) 2001: *Trust in Society*. New York: Russell Sage Foundation.

Cooke, M. 1997: Authenticity and Autonomy: Taylor, Habermas and the Politics of Recognition. *Political Theory* 25: 258–88.

——2002: Five Arguments for Deliberation. In D'Entrèves (2002), pp. 53–87.

Costa, J. 2003: Catalan Linguistic Policy: Liberal or Illiberal? *Nations and Nationalism* 9: 413–32.

Cover, R. 1983: The Supreme Court 1982 Term, Forward: *Nomos* and Narrative. *Harvard Law Review* 97: 4–68.

Crowder, G. 1994: Pluralism and Liberalism. *Political Studies* 42: 293–305.

——1999: From Value Pluralism to Liberalism. In R. Bellamy and M. Hollis (eds.) *Pluralism and Liberal Neutrality*, London: Frank Cass, pp. 2–17.

——2002: *Liberalism and Value Pluralism*, London: Continuum.

Cunningham, F. 1997: Critical Notice: Russell Hardin, *One For All: The Logic of Group Conflict. Canadian Journal of Philosophy* 27: 571–94.

Dagger, R. 2000: Membership, Fair Play and Political Obligation. *Political Studies* 48: 104–17.

D'Agostino, F. 1996: *Free Public Reason*. Oxford: Oxford University Press.

——and Gaus, G. (eds) 1998: *Public Reason*. Aldershot: Ashgate Publishing.

Danley, J. R. 1991: Liberalism, Aboriginal Rights, and Cultural Minorities. *Philosophy and Public Affairs* 20: 168–86.

D'Entrèves, M. P. (ed.) 2002: *Democracy as Public Deliberation*. Manchester: Manchester University Press.

Deveaux, M. 2000a: Conflicting Equalities? Cultural Group Rights and Sex Equality. *Political Studies* 48: 522–39.

——2000b: *Cultural Pluralism and the Dilemmas of Justice*. Ithaca, NY: Cornell University Press.

——2003: A Deliberative Approach to Conflicts of Culture. *Political Theory* 31: 780–807.

Dryzek, J. 1990: *Discursive Democracy*. Cambridge: Cambridge University Press.

——2000: *Deliberative Democracy and Beyond: Liberals, Critics, Contestations*. Oxford: Oxford University Press.

——2005: Deliberative Democracy in Divided Societies: Alternatives to Agonism and Analgesia. *Political Theory* 33: 218–42.

Dunn, J. 1985: *Rethinking Modern Political Theory*. Cambridge: Cambridge University Press.

——1990: *Interpreting Political Responsibility*. Cambridge: Polity.

——1996: *The History of Political Theory, and Other Essays*. Cambridge: Cambridge University Press.

Dworkin, R. 1993: *Life's Dominion: An Argument about Abortion and Euthanasia*. London: HarperCollins.

——2000: *Sovereign Virtue: The Theory and Practice of Equality*. Cambridge, Mass.: Harvard University Press.

Eisenstadt, S. 1995: *Power, Trust and Meaning*. Chicago: University of Chicago Press.

Ellison, R. 1965: *Invisible Man*. Harmondsworth: Penguin.

Elster, J. (ed.) 1998: *Deliberative Democracy*. New York: Cambridge University Press.

Ely, J. H. 1980: *Democracy and Distrust*. Cambridge: Cambridge University Press.

Emcke, C. 2000: Between Choice and Coercion: Identities, Injuries, and Different Forms of Recognition. *Constellations* 7: 483–95.

Emerson, R. 1960: *From Empire to Nation*. Boston: Beacon Press.

Eusminger, J. and Knight, J. 1997: Changing Social Norms: Common Property, Bridewealth and Clan Exogamy. *Current Anthropology* 38: 1–24.

Favell, A. 1998: *Philosophies of Integration*. Basingstoke: MacMillan.

Festenstein, M. 1998: New Worlds for Old: Kymlicka, Cultural Identity and Liberal Nationalism. *Acta Politica* 33: 362–77.

——1999: Toleration and Deliberative Politics. In Horton and Mendus 1999: 146–62.

——2000: Cultural Diversity and the Limits of Liberalism. In N. O'Sullivan (ed.), *Political Theory in Transition*, London: Routledge, 70–90.

——2001: Pragmatism, Social Democracy and Political Argument. In M. Festenstein and S. Thompson (eds), *Richard Rorty: Critical Dialogues*, Cambridge: Polity 203–19.

——2002a: Deliberation, Citizenship and Identity. In D'Entrèves 2002: 88–111.

——2002b: Pragmatism's Boundaries. *Millennium: Journal of International Studies* 31: 549–71.

——2003: Politics and Acquiescence in Rorty's Pragmatism. *Theoria* 101: 1–24.

——2004: Pragmatism and Two Models of Deliberative Democracy. *European Journal of Social Theory* 7: 291–306.

Fishkin, J. S. 1991: *Democracy and Deliberation: New Directions for Democratic Reform*. New Haven: Yale University Press.

——1992: *The Dialogue of Justice: Toward a Self-Reflective Society*. New Haven: Yale University Press.

Flanagan, O. 1990: Identity and Strong and Weak Evaluation. In O. Flanagan and A. O. Rorty (eds), *Identity, Character and Morality: Essays in Moral Psychology*, Cambridge, Mass: MIT Press, 37–66.

Fraser, N. 1997: *Justice Interruptus: Critical Reflections on the 'Postsocialist' Condition*. New York: Routledge.

——2000: Rethinking Recognition. *New Left Review* 3 (May–June): 107–20.

——2001: Recognition without Ethics? *Theory, Culture and Society* 18 (2–3): 21–42.

——and Honneth, A. 2003: *Redistribution or Recognition? A Political-Philosophical Exchange*. London: Verso.

Frost, C. M. 2001: The Worth of Nations. *Journal of Political Philosophy* 9: 482–503.

Fukuyama, F. 1995: *Trust: The Social Virtues and the Creation of Prosperity*. New York: Free Press.

Galeotti, A. E. 1993: Citizenship and Equality: The Place for Toleration. *Political Theory* 21: 585–605.

——1999: Neutrality and Recognition. In R. Bellamy and M. Hollis (eds), *Pluralism and Liberal Neutrality*, London: Frank Cass, 37–53.

——2002: *Toleration as Recognition*. Cambridge: Cambridge University Press.

Gambetta, D. (ed.) 1988: *Trust: The Making and Unmaking of Cooperative Relations*. Oxford: Blackwell.

Gans, C. 2000: The Liberal Foundations of Cultural Nationalism. *Canadian Journal of Philosophy* 30: 441–66.

Gaspard, F. and Khosrokhavar, F. 1995: *Le Foulard et la République*. Paris: Decouverte.

Gaus, G. F. 1996: *Justificatory Liberalism*. Oxford: Oxford University Press.

——2003: *Contemporary Theories of Liberalism*. London: Sage.

Geertz, C. 1973: *The Interpretation of Cultures*. New York: Basic Books.

——1983: *Local Knowledge: Further Essays in Interpretive Anthropology*. New York: Basic Books.

——2000: *Available Light: Anthropological Reflections on Philosophical Topics*. Cambridge, Mass.: Harvard University Press.

Gellner, E. 1983: *Nations and Nationalism*. Oxford: Blackwell.

——1996: Reply to Critics. In J. A. Hall and I. C. Jarvie (eds), *The Social Philosophy of Ernest Gellner*, Amsterdam: Rodolpi, 625–87.

Geuss, R. 1996: 'Morality and Identity'. In Korsgaard 1996b: 189–99.

——1999: *Morality, Culture and History*. Cambridge: Cambridge University Press.

——2001: *History and Illusion in Politics*. Cambridge: Cambridge University Press.

Giddens, A. 1990: *The Consequences of Modernity*. Cambridge: Polity.

Gilbert, M. 1996: *Living Together: Rationality, Sociality and Obligation*. Lanham, Md.: Rowman and Littlefield.

Gilbert, P. 1998: *The Philosophy of Nationalism*. Boulder, Colo.: Westview Press.

——2000: *Peoples, Cultures and Nations in Political Philosophy*. Edinburgh: Edinburgh University Press.

Goodin, R. 2003: *Reflective Democracy*. Oxford: Oxford University Press.

Graham, K. 2002: *Practical Reasoning in a Social World: How We Act Together*. Cambridge: Cambridge University Press.

Gray, J. 1993: *Post-Liberalism: Studies in Political Thought*. London: Routledge.

——1995a: *Berlin*. London: HarperCollins.

——1995b: *Enlightenment's Wake: Politics and Culture at the Close of the Modern Age*. London: Routledge.

Green, L. 1995: Internal Minorities and their Rights. In Kymlicka 1995b: 256–72.

Grimm, D. 1995: Does Europe Need a Constitution? *European Law Journal* 1: 282–302.

Gutmann, A. 1993: The Challenge of Multiculturalism in Political Ethics. *Ethics* 102: 171–206.

——2003: *Identity in Democracy*. Princeton: Princeton University Press.

——and Thompson, D. 1996: *Democracy and Disagreement*. Princeton: Princeton University Press.

Gutting, G. 1999: *Pragmatic Liberalism and the Critique of Modernity*. Cambridge: Cambridge University Press.

Habermas, J. 1996: *Between Facts and Norms: Contributions to a Discourse Theory of Law and Democracy*, trans. William Rehg. Cambridge: Polity.

——1998: *The Inclusion of the Other: Studies in Political Theory*, trans. Ciaran Cronin and Pablo de Greiff. Cambridge: Polity.

Hall, J. A. (ed.) 1998a: Introduction in Hall 1998b: 1–20.

——1998b: *The State of the Nation: Ernest Gellner and the Theory of Nationalism*. Cambridge: Cambridge University Press.

Hampshire, S. (ed.) 1978: *Public and Private Morality*. Cambridge: Cambridge University Press.

——1983: *Morality and Conflict*. Oxford: Blackwell.

——1999: *Justice is Conflict*. London: Duckworth.

Hardimon, M. 1994a: *Hegel's Social Philosophy: The Project of Reconciliation*. Cambridge: Cambridge University Press.

——1994b: Role Obligations. *Journal of Philosophy* 91: 333–63.

Hardin, R. 1995: *One for All: The Logic of Group Conflict*. Princeton: Princeton University Press.

——1999a: Do We Want Trust in Government? In Warren 1999c: 22–41.

——1999b: *Liberalism, Constitutionalism, and Democracy*. Oxford: Oxford University Press.

——2002a: Liberal Distrust. *European Review* 10 (1): 73–89.

——2002b: *Trust and Trustworthiness*. New York: Russell Sage Foundation.

Hawthorn, G. 1988: Three Ironies in Trust. In Gambetta 1988: 111–26.

Heath, J. 1998: Culture: Choice or Circumstance? *Constellations* 5: 183–200.

Herder, J. G. [1784–91] 1969: *Ideas for a Philosophy of the History of Mankind*. In F. M. Barnard (ed. and trans.), *J. G. Herder on Social and Political Culture*, Cambridge: Cambridge University Press, 253–326.

Heugh, K. 2002: Recovering Multilingualism: Recent Language Policy Developments. In R. Mesthnie (ed.), *Language in South Africa*, Cambridge: Cambridge University Press, 449–75.

Hobsbawm, E. J. 1992: *Nations and Nationalism since 1780: Programme, Myth, Reality*, 2nd edn. Cambridge: Cambridge University Press.

Hollis, M. 1982: Dirty Hands. *British Journal of Political Science* 12: 385–98.

——1998: *Trust within Reason*. Cambridge: Cambridge University Press.

Holmes, S. 1995: *Passions and Constraints*. Chicago: University of Chicago Press.

Honig, B. 1992: Towards an Agonistic Feminism: Hannah Arendt and the Politics of Identity. In J. Butler and J. Scott (eds), *Feminists Theorise the Political*, New York: Routledge, 215–35.

——1993: *Political Theory and the Displacement of Politics*. Ithaca, NY: Cornell University Press.

——2001: *Democracy and the Foreigner*. Princeton: Princeton University Press.

Honneth, A. 1995: *The Struggle for Recognition: The Moral Grammar of Social Conflicts*, trans. J. Anderson. Cambridge: Polity.

——2001a: Invisibility: On the Epistemology of 'Recognition'. *Proceedings of the Aristotelian Society*, Supplementary Volume 75: 111–26.

——2001b: Recognition or Redistribution? Changing Perspectives on the Moral Order of Society. *Theory, Culture and Society* 18: 43–55.

Hont, I. 1987: The Language of Sociability and Commerce: Samuel Pufendorf and the Theoretical Foundations of the 'Four Stages Theory'. In A. Pagden (ed.), *The Languages of Early Modern Political Thought*, Cambridge: Cambridge University Press, 253–76.

Hoover, J. 2001: Do the Politics of Difference Need to Be Freed of a Liberalism? *Constellations* 8: 184–200.

Horowitz, D. L. 1991: *A Democratic South Africa? Constitutional Engineering in a Divided Society*. Berkeley: University of California Press.

Horton, J. 1992: *Political Obligation*. Basingstoke: Macmillan.

——2002: Rawls, Public Reason and the Limits of Liberal Justification. *Contemporary Political Theory* 2: 5–23.

——2003: Liberalism and Multiculturalism: Once More Unto the Breach. In B. Haddock and P. Sutch (eds), *Multiculturalism, Identity and Rights*, London: Routledge, 25–41.

——and Mendus, S. (eds) 1999: *Toleration, Identity and Difference*. Basingstoke: Macmillan.

Hurka, T. 1997: The Justification of National Partiality. In R. McKim and J. McMahan (eds), *The Morality of Nationalism*, New York: Oxford University Press, 139–57.

Hurley, S. 1989: *Natural Reasons: Personality and Polity*. Oxford: Oxford University Press.

Iliffe, J. 1979: *A Modern History of Tanganyika*. Cambridge: Cambridge University Press.

Ivison, D. 2002: *Postcolonial Liberalism*. Cambridge: Cambridge University Press.

Jaggar, A. M. 1999: Multicultural Democracy. *Journal of Political Philosophy* 7: 308–29.

James, M. R. 1999a: Critical Intercultural Dialogue. *Polity* 31: 587–607.

——1999b: Tribal Sovereignty and the Intercultural Public Sphere. *Philosophy and Social Criticism* 25: 57–86.

——2003: Communicative Action, Strategic Action, and Inter-Group Dialogue. *European Journal of Political Theory* 2: 157–82.

——2004: *Deliberative Democracy and the Plural Polity*. Lawrence, Kan.: University Press of Kansas.

Jennings, J. 2000: Citizenship, Republicanism and Multiculturalism in Contemporary France. *British Journal of Political Science* 30: 575–98.

Johnson, J. 2000: Why Respect Culture? *American Journal of Political Science* 44: 405–18.

——2002: Liberalism and the Politics of Cultural Authenticity. *Philosophy, Politics and Economics* 1: 213–36.

Johnson, P. 1993: *Frames of Deceit: A Study of the Loss and Recovery of Public and Private Trust*. Cambridge: Cambridge University Press.

Jones, P. 1994: Bearing the Consequences of Belief. *Journal of Political Philosophy* 2: 24–43.

——1998: Political Theory and Cultural Diversity. *Critical Review of International Social and Political Philosophy* 1: 28–62.

——1999: Beliefs and Identities. In Horton and Mendus 1999: 65–86.

Jusdanis, A. 2001: *The Necessary Nation*. Princeton: Princeton University Press.

Keating, M. 2001: *Nations Against the State: The New Politics of Nationalism in Quebec, Catalonia and Scotland*, 2nd edn. Basingstoke: Palgrave.

Keenan, A. 2003: *Democracy in Question: Democratic Openness in a Time of Political Closure*. Stanford: Stanford University Press.

Kekes, J. 1993: *The Morality of Pluralism*. Princeton: Princeton University Press.

Kelly, P. 2002a: Defending some Dodos: Equality and/or Liberty? In P. Kelly (ed.), *Multiculturalism Reconsidered*, Cambridge: Polity, 62–80.

——2002b: Introduction: Between Culture and Equality. In P. Kelly (ed.), *Multiculturalism Reconsidered*, Cambridge: Polity, 1–17.

Kenny, D. 1996: *Women's Business*. Potts Point: Duffy and Snellgrove.

Kernohan, A. 1998: *Liberalism, Equality, and Cultural Oppression*. Cambridge: Cambridge University Press.

Kingwell, M. 1995: *A Civil Tongue*. Toronto: University of Toronto Press.

Knight, J. and Johnson, J. 1994: Aggregation and Deliberation: On the Possibility of Democratic Legitimacy. *Political Theory* 22: 277–96.

——1997: What Sort of Equality Does Deliberative Democracy Require? In Bohman and Rehg 1997: 279–319.

Korsgaard, C. 1996a: *Creating the Kingdom of Ends*. Cambridge: Cambridge University Press.

——1996b: *The Sources of Normativity*. Cambridge: Cambridge University Press.

Kroeber, A. L. and Kluckhohn, C. 1952: *Culture: A Critical Review of Concepts and Definitions,* Papers of the Peabody Museum of American Archaeology and Ethnology, 47. Cambridge, Mass.: Harvard University Press, The Museum.

Kukathas, C. 1992: Are There Any Cultural Rights? *Political Theory* 20: 105–39.

——1997a: Cultural Toleration. In I. Shapiro and W. Kymlicka (eds), *Ethnicity and Group Rights*, Nomos 39, New York: New York University Press, 69–104.

——1997b: Liberalism, Multiculturalism and Oppression. In A. Vincent (ed.), *Political Theory: Tradition and Diversity*, Cambridge: Cambridge University Press, 132–53.

——1997c: Multiculturalism as Fairness: Will Kymlicka's *Multicultural Citizenship*. *Journal of Political Philosophy* 5: 406–27.

——1998: Liberalism and Multiculturalism: The Politics of Indifference. *Political Theory* 26: 686–99.

——2002: The Life of Brian, or Now for Something Completely Difference-Blind. In P. Kelly (ed.), *Multiculturalism Reconsidered*, Cambridge: Polity, 184–203.

——2003: *The Liberal Archipelago*. Oxford: Oxford University Press.

Kuper, A. 1999: *Culture: The Anthropologists' Account*. Cambridge, Mass.: Harvard University Press.

Kymlicka, W. 1989: *Liberalism, Community and Culture*. Oxford: Clarendon Press.

——1992: The Rights of Minority Cultures: Reply to Kukathas. *Political Theory* 20: 140–6.

——1995a: *Multicultural Citizenship*. Oxford: Clarendon Press.

——(ed.) 1995b: *The Rights of Minority Cultures*. Oxford: Oxford University Press.

——1996a: Social Unity in a Liberal State. *Social Philosophy and Politics* 13: 105–36.

——1996b: Three Forms of Group-Differentiated Citizenship in Canada. In Benhabib 1996a: 153–70.

——1997: The Sources of Nationalism: Commentary on Taylor. In R. McKim and J. McMahan (eds), *The Morality of Nationalism*, Oxford: Oxford University Press, 56–65.

——1998a: Ethnic Associations and Democratic Citizenship. In A. Gutmann (ed.), *Freedom of Association*, Princeton: Princeton University Press, 177–213.

——1998b: *Finding Our Way: Rethinking Ethnocultural Relations in Canada*. Don Mills, Ont.: Oxford University Press.

——2001a: *Politics in the Vernacular: Nationalism, Multiculturalism and Citizenship*. Oxford: Oxford University Press.

——2001b: Reply and Conclusion. In Kymlicka and Opalski 2001: 345–413.

——2001c: Western Political Theory and Ethnic Relations in Eastern Europe. In Kymlicka and Opalski 2001: 13–105.

——2002: *Contemporary Political Philosophy*, 2nd edn, Oxford: Oxford University Press.

——and Norman, W. (eds), 2000: *Citizenship in Diverse Societies*. Oxford: Oxford University Press.

——and Opalski, M. (eds) 2001: *Can Liberal Pluralism Be Exported? Western Political Theory and Ethnic Relations in Eastern Europe*. Oxford: Oxford University Press.

——and Patten, A. (eds) 2003: *Language Rights and Political Theory*. Oxford: Oxford University Press.

Laden, A. S. 2001: *Reasonably Radical: Deliberative Liberalism and the Politics of Identity*. Ithaca, NY: Cornell University Press.

——2003: Radical Liberals, Reasonable Feminists: Reason, Power and Objectivity in MacKinnon and Rawls. *Journal of Political Philosophy* 11: 133–52.

Lagenspetz, O. 1992: Legitimacy and Trust. *Philosophical Investigations* 15: 1–21.

Laitin, D. and Reich, R. 2003: A Liberal Democratic Approach to Language Rights. In Kymlicka and Patten 2003: 80–104.

Lamey, A. 1999: Francophonia for Ever: The Contradictions in Charles Taylor's 'Politics of Recognition'. *Times Literary Supplement*, 23 July: 12–15.

Larmore, C. 1987: *Patterns of Moral Complexity*. Cambridge: Cambridge University Press.

——1996: *The Morals of Modernity*. Cambridge: Cambridge University Press.

Levinson, M. 2003: Minority Participation and Civic Education in Deliberative Democracies. In D. Bell and A. de-Shalit (eds), *Forms of Justice: Critical Perspectives on David Miller's Political Philosophy*, Lanham, Md.: Rowman and Littlefield, 159–82.

Levy, A. 2004: *Small Island*. London: Headline Books.

Levy, J. 2000: *The Multiculturalism of Fear*. Oxford: Oxford University Press.

Lijphart, A. 1977: *Democracy in Plural Societies*. New Haven: Yale University Press.

Luhmann, N. 1979: *Trust and Power*. New York: John Wiley.

Lukes, S. 1991: *Moral Conflict and Politics*. Oxford: Clarendon Press.

——2003: *Liberals and Cannibals: The Implications of Diversity*. London: Verso.

Macedo, S. 2000: *Diversity and Distrust*. Cambridge, Mass.: Harvard University Press.

MacIntyre, A. 1981: *After Virtue: A Study in Moral Theory*. London: Duckworth.

——1988: *Whose Justice? Which Rationality?* London: Duckworth.

Manin, B. 1987: On Legitimacy and Political Deliberation. *Political Theory* 15: 338–68.

Mansbridge, J. 1999: Altruistic Trust. In Warren 1999c: 290–309.

——2000: What Does a Representative Do? Descriptive Representation in Communicative Settings of Distrust, Uncrystallized Interests, and Historically Denigrated Status. In Kymlicka and Norman 2000: 99–123.

Mara, G. 2001: Thucydides and Plato on Democracy and Trust. *Journal of Politics* 63: 820–45.

Margalit, A. and Halbertal, M. 1994: Liberalism and the Right to Culture. *Social Research* 61: 491–510.

——and Raz, J. 1990: National Self-Determination. *Journal of Philosophy* 87: 439–61.

Markell, P. 2000: The Recognition of Politics: Comment on Emcke and Tully. *Constellations* 7: 496–506.

——2003: *Bound by Recognition*. Princeton: Princeton University Press.

Marx, K. [1867] 1976: *Capital*, vol. 1, trans. by B. Fowkes. Harmondsworth: Penguin.

Mason, A. 2000: *Community, Solidarity and Belonging*. Cambridge: Cambridge University Press.

Matravers, M. 2002: Responsibility, Luck and the 'Equality of What?' Debate. *Political Studies* 50: 558–72.

May, L. 1987: *The Morality of Groups: Collective Responsibility, Group-Based Harm, and Corporate Rights*. Notre Dame, Ind.: University of Notre Dame Press.

May, S. 2001: *Language and Minority Rights: Ethnicity, Nationalism and the Politics of Language*. Harlow: Pearson.

McCrone, D. 1998: *The Sociology of Nationalism: Tomorrow's Ancestors*. London: Routledge.

McGarry, J. 2002: 'Democracy' in Northern Ireland: Experiments in Self-Rule from the Protestant Ascendancy to the Good Friday Agreement. *Nations and Nationalism* 8: 451–74.

Mendus, S. 2002: Choice, Chance and Multiculturalism. In P. Kelly (ed.), *Multiculturalism Reconsidered*, Cambridge: Polity, 31–44.

Mill, J. [1819] 1992: Government. In *James Mill: Political Writings*, ed. T. Ball, Cambridge: Cambridge University Press, 1–42.

Mill, J. S. [1861] 1991: *Considerations on Representative Government*. In *On Liberty and Other Essays*, ed. J. Gray, Oxford: Oxford University Press, 203–467.

Miller, D. 1989: *Market, State and Community*. Oxford: Oxford University Press.

——1995: *On Nationality*. Oxford: Oxford University Press.

——1998: The Left, the Nation-State, and European Citizenship. *Dissent* 45 (3): 47–51.

——2000: *Citizenship and National Identity*. Cambridge: Polity.

——2002: Group Rights, Human Rights and Citizenship. *European Journal of Philosophy* 10: 178–95.

——2003a: *Political Philosophy: A Very Short Introduction*. Oxford: Oxford University Press.

——2003b: A Response. In D. A. Bell and A. de-Shalit (eds), *Forms of Justice: Critical Perspectives on David Miller's Political Philosophy*, Lanham, Md.: Rowman and Littlefield, 349–72.

Misak, C. 2000: *Truth, Morality and Politics: Pragmatism and Deliberation*. London: Routledge.

Modood, T. 1998: Anti-Essentialism, Multiculturalism and the 'Recognition' of Religious Groups. *Journal of Political Philosophy* 6: 378–99.

Moody-Adams, M. 1997: *Fieldwork in Familiar Places: Morality, Culture, and Philosophy*. Cambridge, Mass.: Harvard University Press.

Moon, J. D. 1993: *Constructing Community: Moral Pluralism and Tragic Conflicts*. Princeton: Princeton University Press.

Moore, J. D. 1997: *Visions of Culture: An Introduction to Anthropological Theories and Theorists*. Walnut Creek, Calif.: Sage.

Moore, M. 2001: Normative Justifications for Liberal Nationalism: Justice, Democracy and National Identity. *Nations and Nationalism*, 7: 1–20.

——2002: *The Ethics of Nationalism*. Oxford: Oxford University Press.

Moruzzi, N. 1994: A Problem with Headscarves: Contemporary Complexities of Political and Social Identity. *Political Theory* 22: 653–72.

Mouffe, C. 2001: *The Democratic Paradox*. London: Verso.

Mulhall, S. and Swift, A. 1996: *Liberals and Communitarians*, 2nd edn. Oxford: Blackwell.

Mulhern, F. 2000: *Culture/Metaculture*. London: Routledge.

Musschenga, A. 1998: Intrinsic Value and the Preservation of Minority Cultures. *Ethical Theory and Moral Practice* 1: 201–25.

Nagel, T. 1979: *Mortal Questions*. Cambridge: Cambridge University Press.

Neuhouser, F. 2000: *The Foundations of Hegel's Social Theory: Actualizing Freedom*. Ithaca, NY: Cornell University Press.

Newey, G. 2002: Discourse Rights and the Drumcree Marches: A Reply to O'Neill. *British Journal of Politics and International Relations* 4: 75–97.

Nino, C. 1996: *The Constitution of Deliberative Democracy*. New Haven; Yale University Press.

Norman, W. 1998: The Ethics of Secession as the Regulation of Secessionist Politics. In M. Moore (ed.), *National Self-Determination and Secession*, Oxford: Oxford University Press, 34–61.

Offe, C. 2001: Political Liberalism, Group Rights, and the Politics of Fear and Trust. *Studies in East European Thought* 53: 167–82.

Okin, S. M. 1999: *Is Multiculturalism Bad for Women?* Princeton: Princeton University Press.

——2002: 'Mistresses of Their Own Destiny': Group Rights, Gender, and Realistic Rights of Exit. *Ethics* 112: 205–30.

O'Leary, B. 1998: 'Ernest Gellner's Diagnoses of Nationalism: A Critical Overview, or, What is Living and What is Dead in Ernest Gellner's Philosophy of Nationalism?', in Hall 1998b: 40–88.

O'Neill, J. 1992: The Varieties of Intrinsic Value. *Monist* 75: 138–61.

O'Neill, O. 1989: *Constructions of Reason*. Cambridge: Cambridge University Press.

O'Neill, S. 1997: *Impartiality in Context: Grounding Justice in a Pluralist World*. Albany, NY: SUNY Press.

——2000: Liberty, Equality and the Rights of Cultures: The Marching Controversy at Drumcree. *British Journal of Politics and International Relations* 2: 26–45.

——2001: Mutual Recognition and the Accommodation of National Diversity: Constitutional Justice in Northern Ireland. In Gagnon 2001: 222–41.

——2002: Democratic Theory with Critical Intent: Reply to Newey. *British Journal of Politics and International Relations* 4: 98–114.

——2003: Are National Conflicts Reconcilable? Discourse Theory and Political Accommodation in Northern Ireland. *Constellations* 10: 75–94.

Ortner, S. 1997: Introduction. *Representations* 59: 1–13.

Owen, D. 1999: Political Philosophy in a Post-Imperial Voice. *Economy and Society* 28: 520–49.

Pagden, A. 1982: *The Fall of Natural Man*. Cambridge: Cambridge University Press.

Parekh, B. 1993: A Misconceived Discourse on Political Obligation. *Political Studies* 41: 236–51.

——1994: Superior People: The Narrowness of Liberalism from Mill to Rawls. *Times Literary Supplement*, 25 February: 11–13.

——1997: Dilemmas of a Multicultural Theory of Citizenship. *Constellations* 4: 54–62.

——1999: The Logic of Intercultural Evaluation. In Horton and Mendus 1999: 146–62.

——2000: *Rethinking Multiculturalism*. Basingstoke: Macmillan.

Parry, G. 1976: Trust, Distrust and Consensus. *British Journal of Political Science* 6: 129–42.

Patten, A. 1999a: The Autonomy Argument for Liberal Nationalism. *Nations and Nationalism* 5: 1–17.

——1999b: Liberal Egalitarianism and the Case for Supporting National Cultures. *Monist* 82 (3): 387–410.

——2001a: Liberal Citizenship in Multinational Societies. In A.G. Gagnon and J. Tully 2001 (eds.), *Multinational Democracies*, Cambridge: Cambridge University Press, 279–98.

——2001b: Political Theory and Language Policy. *Political Theory* 29: 691–715.

Pettit, P. 1993: *The Common Mind*. Oxford: Oxford University Press.

——1998: Republican Theory and Political Trust. In Braithwaite and Levi 1998: 295–314.

Phillips, A. 1995: *The Politics of Presence*. Oxford: Oxford University Press.

——1996: Dealing with Difference: A Politics of Ideas or a Politics of Presence? In Benhabib 1996a: 139–52.

——1999: The Politicisation of Difference: Does This Make for a More Tolerant Society? In Horton and Mendus 1999: 126–45.

——and Dustin, M. 2004: UK Initiatives on Forced Marriage: Regulation, Dialogue and Exit. *Political Studies* 52: 531–51.

Poulter, S. 1986: *English Law and Ethnic Minority Customs*. London: Butterworth.

——1998: *Ethnicity, Law and Human Rights: The English Experience*. Oxford: Oxford University Press.

Putnam, H. 1995: *Pragmatism: An Open Question*. Oxford: Blackwell.

Putnam, R. D. 1993: *Making Democracy Work: Civic Traditions in Modern Italy*. Princeton: Princeton University Press.

Quong, J. 2004: Disputed Practices and Reasonable Pluralism. *Res Publica* 10: 43–67.

Ranger, T. 1992: The Invention of Tradition in Colonial Africa. In E. Hobsbawm and T. Ranger (eds), *The Invention of Tradition*, Cambridge: Cambridge University Press, 263–308.

Rawls, J. 1972: *A Theory of Justice*. Oxford: Oxford University Press.

——1993: *Political Liberalism*. New York: Columbia University Press.

——1999: *Collected Papers*, ed. Samuel Freeman. Cambridge, Mass.: Harvard University Press.

Raz, J. 1986: *The Morality of Freedom*. Oxford: Clarendon Press.

——1994: *Ethics in the Public Domain*. Oxford: Oxford University Press.

——1999: *Engaging Reason: On the Theory of Value and Action*. Oxford: Oxford University Press.

——2001: *Value, Respect and Attachment*. Cambridge: Cambridge University Press.

Réaume, D. G. 1988: Individuals, Groups and Rights to Public Goods. *University of Toronto Law Journal* 38: 1–27.

——1994: The Group Right to Linguistic Security: Whose Right, What Duties? In J. Baker (ed.), *Group Rights*, Toronto: University of Toronto Press, 118–41.

——2000: Official Language Rights: Intrinsic Value and the Protection of Difference. In Kymlicka and Norman 2000: 245–72.

——2003: Beyond *Person*ality: The Territorial and Personal Principles of Language Policy Reconsidered. In Kymlicka and Patten 2003: 271–95.

Rhees, R. (ed.) 1981: *Ludwig Wittgenstein: Personal Recollections*. Oxford: Blackwell.

Richardson, H. S. 1997: Democratic Intentions. In Bohman and Rehg 1997: 349–82.

——2002: *Democratic Autonomy: Public Reasoning about the Ends of Policy*. Oxford: Oxford University Press.

Ripstein, A. 1997a: Context, Continuity and Fairness. In R. McKim and J. McMahan (eds), *The Morality of Nationalism*, New York: Oxford University Press, 209–26.

——1997b: What Can Philosophy Teach Us about Multiculturalism? *Dialogue* 36: 607–14.

Rockefeller, S. 1994: Comment. In A. Gutmann (ed.), *Multiculturalism: Examining the Politics of Recognition*, Princeton: Princeton University Press, 87–98.

Rorty, A. O. 1994: The Hidden Politics of Group Identification. *Political Theory* 22: 152–66.

——and Wong, D. 1990: Aspects of Identity and Agency. In A. O. Rorty and O. Flanagan (eds), *Identity, Character and Morality: Essays in Moral Psychology*, Cambridge, Mass.: MIT Press), 19–36.

Rorty, R. 1989: *Contingency, Irony, and Solidarity*. Cambridge: Cambridge University Press.

——1991: *Objectivity, Relativism, and Truth: Philosophical Papers*, vol. 1. Cambridge: Cambridge University Press.

——1998: *Truth and Progress: Philosophical Papers*, vol. 3. Cambridge: Cambridge University Press.

Rousseau, J.-J. [1772] 1997: Considerations on the Government of Poland. In *The Social Contract and Other Later Political Writings*, ed. and trans. V. Gourevitch, Cambridge: Cambridge University Press, 177–260.

The Runnymede Trust 2000: *The Future of Multiethnic Britain: The Parekh Report*. London: Profile.

Sandel, M. 1982: *Liberalism and the Limits of Justice*. Cambridge: Cambridge University Press.

——1996: *Democracy's Discontent*. Cambridge, Mass.: Harvard University Press.

Sanders, L. 1997: Against Deliberation. *Political Theory* 25: 347–76.

Scott, D. 2003: Culture in Political Theory. *Political Theory* 31: 92–115.

Searle, J. 1995: *The Construction of Social Reality*. Harmondsworth: Penguin.

Seligman, A. 1997: *The Problem of Trust*. Princeton: Princeton University Press.

Shachar, A. 1999: The Paradox of Multicultural Vulnerability. In C. Joppke and S. Lukes (eds), *Multicultural Questions*, Oxford: Oxford University Press, 87–111.

——2000: Should Church and State be Joined at the Altar? Women's Rights and the Multicultural Dilemma. In Kymlicka and Norman 2000: 193–223.

——2001: *Multicultural Jurisdictions: Cultural Differences and Women's Rights*. Cambridge: Cambridge University Press.

Shapiro, I. 1996: *Democracy's Place*. Ithaca. NY: Cornell University Press.

——1999a: *Democratic Justice*. New Haven: Yale University Press.

——1999b: Group Aspirations and Democratic Politics. In I. Shapiro and C. Hacker-Cordón (eds), *Democracy's Edges*, Cambridge: Cambridge University Press, 210–21.

——2002: Democratic Justice and Multicultural Recognition. In P. Kelly (ed.), *Multiculturalism Reconsidered*, Cambridge: Polity, 174–83.

——2003: *The State of Democratic Theory*. Princeton: Princeton University Press.

Silverman, M. 1992: *Deconstructing the Nation: Immigration, Race, and Citizenship in Modern France*. London: Routledge.

Smith, G. and Wales, C. 2002: Citizens' Juries and Deliberative Democracy. In D'Entrèves 2002: 157–77.

Smith, N. H. 2002: *Charles Taylor: Meaning, Morals and Modernity*. Cambridge: Polity Press.

Spinner, J. 1994: *The Boundaries of Citizenship: Race, Ethnicity and Nationality in the Liberal State*. Baltimore: Johns Hopkins University Press.

Spinner-Halev, J. 1999: Cultural Pluralism and Partial Citizenship. In C. Joppke and S. Lukes (eds), *Multicultural Questions*, Oxford: Oxford University Press, 65–86.

——2000a: Land, Culture and Justice: A Framework for Group Rights and Recognition. *Journal of Political Philosophy* 8: 319–42.

——2000b: *Surviving Diversity: Religion and Democratic Citizenship*. Baltimore: Johns Hopkins University Press.

——2001: Feminism, Multiculturalism, Oppression, and the State. *Ethics* 112: 84–113.

Squires, J. 2002: Culture, Equality and Diversity. In P. Kelly (ed.), *Multiculturalism Reconsidered*, Cambridge: Polity, 114–32.

Sumner, C. 1994: *The Sociology of Deviance: An Obituary*. Milton Keynes: Open University Press.

Svensson, F. 1979: Liberal Democracy and Group Rights: The Legacy of

Individualism and its Impact on American Indian Tribes. *Political Studies* 27: 421–39.

Sztompka, P. 1999: *Trust: A Sociological Theory*. Cambridge: Cambridge University Press.

Tamir, Y. 1993: *Liberal Nationalism*. Princeton: Princeton University Press.

Taylor, C. 1985: Philosophy and the Human Sciences: Philosophical Papers 2. Cambridge: Cambridge University Press.

——1989: *Sources of the Self*. Cambridge, Mass.: Harvard University Press.

——1993: *Reconciling the Solitudes: Essays on Canadian Federation and Nationalism*. Montreal: McGill-Queen's University Press.

——1994: Reply and Re-Articulation. In J. Tully (ed.), *Philosophy in an Age of Pluralism: The Philosophy of Charles Taylor in Question*, Cambridge: Cambridge University Press, 213–57.

——1995: *Philosophical Arguments*. Cambridge, Mass.: Harvard University Press.

——1997: Nationalism and Modernity. In R. McKim and J. McMahan (eds), *The Morality of Nationalism*, New York: Oxford University Press, 31–55.

Thomas, W. I. 1928: *The Unadjusted Girl*. Boston: Little, Brown.

Thompson, J. B. 1990: *Ideology and Modern Culture: Critical Social Theory in the Era of Mass Communication*. Cambridge: Polity.

Tomasi, J. 1995: Kymlicka, Liberalism, and Respect for Cultural Minorities. *Ethics* 101: 580–603.

——2001: *Liberalism beyond Justice: Citizens, Society, and the Boundaries of Political Theory*. Princeton: Princeton University Press.

Tully, J. 1995: *Strange Multiplicity: Constitutionalism in an Age of Diversity*. Cambridge: Cambridge University Press.

——1999: The Agonic Freedom of Citizens. *Economy and Society* 28: 161–82.

——2000a: The Challenge of Reimagining Citizenship and Belonging in Multicultural and Multinational Societies. In C. McKinnon and I. Hampsher-Monk (eds), *The Demands of Citizenship*, London: Continuum, 212–34.

——2000b: Struggles over Recognition and Redistribution. *Constellations* 7: 469–82.

——2001: Introduction. In A.-G. Gagnon and J. Tully 2001 (eds.), *Multinational Democracies*, Cambridge: Cambridge University Press, pp. 1–34.

——2002a: The Illiberal Liberal: Brian Barry's Polemical Attack on Multiculturalism. In P. Kelly (ed.), *Multiculturalism Reconsidered*, Cambridge: Polity, 102–13.

——2002b: The Unfreedom of the Moderns in Comparison to their Ideals of Constitutional Democracy. *Modern Law Review* 65: 204–28.

——2004a: Approaches to Recognition, Power, and Dialogue. *Political Theory* 32: 855–62.

——2004b: Political Philosophy as a Critical Activity. In S. K. White and J. D. Moon (eds), *What is Political Theory?*, London and Thousand Oaks, Calif.: Sage, 80–102.

Turner, T. 1993: Anthropology and Multiculturalism: What is Anthropology that Multiculturalists should be Mindful of it? *Cultural Anthropology* 8: 411–29.

Uslaner, E. M. 2002: *The Moral Foundations of Trust*. Cambridge: Cambridge University Press.

Van Parijs, P. 2000: Must Europe be Belgian? On Democratic Citizenship in Multilingual Polities. In C. McKinnon and I. Hampsher-Monk (eds), *The Demands of Citizenship*, London: Continuum, 235–53.

Viroli, M. 1995: *For Love of Country: An Essay on Patriotism and Nationalism.* Oxford: Oxford University Press.

——2002: *Republicanism.* New York: Hill and Wang.

Waldron, J. 1993: *Liberal Rights: Collected Papers, 1981–1991.* Cambridge: Cambridge University Press.

——1995: Minority Cultures and the Cosmopolitan Alternative. In Kymlicka 1995b: 93–119.

——2000a: Cultural Identity and Civic Responsibility. In Kymlicka and Norman 2000: 155–74.

——2000b: *Law and Disagreement.* Oxford: Oxford University Press.

Walzer, M. 1973: Political Action: The Problem of Dirty Hands. *Philosophy and Public Affairs* 2: 160–80.

——1983: *Spheres of Justice: A Defence of Pluralism and Equality.* Oxford: Martin Robertson.

Warren, M. 1999a: Democratic Theory and Trust. In Warren 1999c: 310–45.

——1999b: Introduction. In Warren 1999c: 1–21.

——(ed.) 1999c: *Democracy and Trust.* Cambridge: Cambridge University Press.

Weale, A. 2003: Trust and Political Constitutions. In P. King (ed.), *Trusting in Reason: Martin Hollis and the Philosophy of Social Action*, London: Frank Cass, 69–83.

Wedeen, L. 2002: Conceptualizing Culture: Possibilities for Political Science. *American Political Science Review* 96: 713–28.

Weinstock, D. 1998: How Can Collective Rights and Liberalism be Reconciled? In R. Bauböck and J. Rundell (eds), *Blurred Boundaries: Migration, Ethnicity, Citizenship*, Aldershot: Ashgate, 281–304.

——1999: Building Trust in Divided Societies. *Journal of Political Philosophy* 7: 287–307.

——2003: The Antimony of Language Policy. In Kymlicka and Patten 2003: 250–70.

White, S. K. 1985: *Ethics and the Limits of Philosophy*, London: Fontana.

——2000: *Sustaining Affirmation: The Strengths of Weak Ontology in Political Theory.* Princeton: Princeton University Press.

Williams, B. 1981: *Moral Luck.* Cambridge: Cambridge University Press.

——1995: *Making Sense of Humanity, and Other Philosophical Papers.* Cambridge: Cambridge University Press.

Williams, M. 1995: Justice Toward Groups: Political not Juridical. *Political Theory* 23: 67–91.

——1998: *Voice, Trust and Memory: Marginalized Groups and the Failings of Liberal Political Representation.* Princeton: Princeton University Press.

——2000: The Uneasy Alliance of Group Representation and Deliberative Democracy. In Kymlicka and Norman 2000: 124–52.

Williams, R. 1961: *Culture and Society 1780–1950.* Harmondsworth: Penguin.

——1983: *Keywords: A Vocabulary of Culture and Society.* London: Fontana.

Wimmer, A. 2002: *Nationalist Exclusion and Ethnic Conflict: Shadows of Modernity.* Cambridge: Cambridge University Press.

Wittgenstein, L. 1958: *Philosophical Investigations*, 2nd edn, trans. and ed. G. E. M. Anscombe. Oxford: Basil Blackwell.

Wolin, S. 1961: *Politics and Vision.* London: Allen and Unwin.

Yack, B. 1996: The Myth of the Civic Nation. *Critical Review* 10: 193–211.

Young, I. M.

—— 1990: *Justice and the Politics of Difference*. Princeton: Princeton University Press.

—— 1996: Communication and the Other: Beyond Deliberative Democracy. In Benhabib, 1996a: 120–35.

—— 1997a: Difference as a Resource for Democratic Communication. In Bohman and Rehg 1997: 383–406.

—— 1997b: A Multicultural Continuum: A Critique of Will Kymlicka's Ethnic–Nation Dichotomy. *Constellations* 4: 48–53.

—— 2000: *Inclusion and Democracy*. Oxford: Oxford University Press.

Zurn, C. 2003: Identity or Status? Struggles over 'Recognition' in Fraser, Honneth, and Taylor. *Constellations* 10: 519–37.

# Index